DANCING ON THE EDGE

Dancing on the Edge

RICHARD HOLLOWAY

Fount
An Imprint of HarperCollins*Publishers*

Fount Paperbacks is an Imprint of
HarperCollins*Religious*
Part of HarperCollins*Publishers*
77–85 Fulham Palace Road, London W6 8JB

First published in 1997 by Fount Paperbacks

1 3 5 7 9 10 8 6 4 2

A catalogue record for this book is
available from the British Library

0 00 628041 2

Printed and bound in Great Britain by
Caledonian International Book Manufacturing Ltd, Glasgow

For Veda and Kevin Franz

Contents

Acknowledgements

The biblical quotations in this book are from the New Revised Standard Version.

I would also like to acknowledge my indebtedness to Kenneth E. Bailey, Chairman of the Biblical Department at the Near Eastern School of Theology, Beirut, for his exposition of the Lucan parables in *Poet And Peasant* and *Through Peasant Eyes*, both published by Eerdmans. Though I draw conclusions from his exegesis that he might disavow, I am grateful to him for the way he has opened my eyes to the truly radical nature of the parables of Jesus.

I would like to thank Caroline Dawnay, Sara Holloway and Murray White for their help and advice. As always I owe a special debt of thanks to my secretary, Christine Roy, for all her work.

Richard Holloway
Edinburgh

Introduction

The purpose of this book is to make a space for people who think of themselves as being on the edge of Christianity, for whatever reason. Many people have abandoned Christianity with no regret and a considerable feeling of relief. The relief they feel is not unlike the sense of freedom and possibility that some people discover when they remove themselves from a marriage that has oppressed and damaged them. They are not necessarily opposed to marriage as such, but they know that their experience of it was life-denying and imprisoning. Many people feel like that about the Church. They do not necessarily want to claim universal validity for their own experience, but they know that their life in the Church imposed upon them burdens of guilt and hypocrisy that lifted when they left. Sometimes they come back to the Church, years later, with a completely different attitude. The heaviness, the sense of oppression and guilt that marked their previous association with Christianity have gone, and they return to it with a greater sense of their own autonomy and freedom. To some extent they are able to say that, having left and come back again, they see the Church with fresh eyes. The spiritual life is important to them, the meaning and example of Jesus Christ still attracts them, but they now sit more lightly to many of the claims and pretensions that Christianity, as an authoritarian institution, has made about itself. They have matured into adult human beings and their increased self-confidence makes it easier for them to handle the kind of false or arrogant claims that institutions, including spiritual institutions, make about themselves. They have learned the important lesson that movements and institutions that convey meaning and value through history do not have to be offered absolute allegiance. They can be valued for the beauty and wisdom they convey and not necessarily for the claims they make about their own role. Being human constructs, however effectively they point to spiritual realities beyond themselves, churches must be understood and forgiven, while not necessarily being taken at their own self-valuation.

However, there are many people who may lack the confidence to achieve the kind of dialectical relationship with the Church that enables them to benefit from the memories and traditions it carries through time, without abdicating their own moral and intellectual autonomy. It may be that some of these people have been severely hurt by the Church in one of its guises and cannot return to it without anxiety or fear. It may be that the Church has been too successful at enforcing its own claims in their minds, so that they feel they can only be associated with Christianity on its own terms. Since they have rejected these terms, they may feel they cannot, with integrity, any longer be members of the Church. This does not necessarily mean that they have lost the sense of themselves as spiritual creatures or that they have ceased to ask questions about the meaning of life. In Paul Tillich's phrase, they may be people who still wrestle with questions of ultimate concern, questions about the depth of meaning and value that come with the human experience, questions about how best to live. They may still feel in themselves the need to pray, though they may not define the term with great precision. They open themselves to mystery and transcendence, and at times they encounter a strange sense of homesickness and loss.

These are the ones who need to be encouraged to come home, who need to be told that Christianity is big enough to hold them and is poorer without them. Jesus told us that in his father's house were many rooms. He gathered round himself people from the edges, the kind of people who feel uncomfortable in the Church that claims his name today. It is important for them to be made to feel that they are an accepted and welcomed part of Christianity, not kept in some sort of concessionary role, as honorary members or supporters of the real thing at the centre. There may be an institutional or organizational centre, there may even be something called an Establishment or Magisterium, but that is only the human reality, the kind of appropriation of value that is always taking place in human affairs. It ceases to impress once we have seen through the claims and official clothes to the very ordinary people underneath. Even if the people in charge go on making their claims and striking their attitudes, there is no reason why we should allow ourselves to be impressed or over-awed by them. Truth and the presence of the divine are not necessarily or exclusively found there and cannot, anyway, be controlled and marketed by God's official guardians. 'The wind blows where it chooses, and you hear the sound of it, but you do not know where it comes from or where it goes. So it is with everyone who is born of the Spirit' (John 3:8).

There are various ways of feeling that we belong on the edge of Christianity. Sometimes the feeling is induced by our own intel-lectual struggle with the doctrinal elements of the Church; some-times it is imposed upon us by the moral disapproval of prominent Christians, because of the way we live or the kind of people we are.

The sense of theological marginalization is usually induced by other Christians who tell us that we can only come in if we agree to eat everything that is on the menu. In Chapter 3 I shall look at this accusation that is levelled against so-called 'cafeteria Christians'. The irony of this kind of casual excommunication is that it is usually levelled against people for whom truth has a very high value. Simone Weil reminds us that whenever we have to choose between truth and Christ, we must choose truth, because Christ is truth before he is anything else, and if we choose truth we cannot go far without falling again into his arms. Truth is an absolute value for Christians. It can never be right to expect anyone to submit to a form of words or a propositional encapsulation of the truth which they cannot accept without dishonesty and the violation of their own intel-lectual integrity. It is true, of course, that we can be wrong, that our conscience can be ill informed, that we might one day change our minds or be persuaded that we were mistaken. The fact remains that, while remembering all these things as we wrestle with truth, and being modest about our own claims, we have no alternative but to follow our conscience on these mat-ters, because it is the place where (as we now are) we encounter truth and its claim on our integrity. It is one thing to examine the claims of Christianity and reject them all as false; it is quite another thing to be rejected by Christianity or made to feel unwelcome within it, because we want to remain members of the Church, while accepting the integrity of modern knowl-edge and scientific truth. It is inconceivable that a place cannot be found in Christianity for this kind of painful honesty.

Behind the disputes in Christian truth-seeking there often lies a mistaken understanding of theology. The mystery and power behind the Christian movement is the experience of God mediated through Jesus Christ. The paradox of all spirituality and revelation is the role of the speech we use to convey or interpret them. We cannot do without words, but we must constantly remember their provisional and revisable character. Words are symbols that put us in touch with the realities they point to. In religious discourse, their function is to refer to the divine mystery, to help us describe our experience of God. They are not provided to be experienced for their own sake. The vehicle that conveys the revelation is not itself the mystery that is revealed, though it is a means to its apprehension. The sign that points to something is a symbol, not the thing itself. Religious symbols are unavoidable but dangerous realities. The constant human temptation, as we shall see throughout this book, is to make them significant in their own right. This danger is endemic to human experience. We turn the symbols that convey the meaning we are searching for, however obliquely, into substitutes for the meaning itself. This is what makes theology both precarious and fascinating. We are constantly tempted to find substitutes for the Grace that redeems us in our weakness, by submitting to absolute systems that offer us the strength of personal certainty. The danger of these offers is that they can become demonic. Since they are essentially projections of our own fear and insecurity, not real experiences of God, they are not genuinely healing or sanctifying. We often sense this in our own hearts, but dare not face it. Our uncertain certainties make us angry at those who challenge us, either by the way they express their own doubts or by the quality of their own freedom, and this can easily turn us into condemners or persecutors.

Theology does not have to be as intense and emotional as this. If we understand its real status, it will guide us more deeply into the silence of the divine mystery that lies behind our words. We will recognize that theology is the record of what Christian thinkers have made of the human experience of the divine. The important thing is the experience that lies behind the words we have used to describe it. Theological symbols are to God what spiritual aids are to prayer: aids dispose us to prayer, which starts when they have done their work and fall away. People who want to pray, to open themselves to the divine, use various devices, such as beads, mantras and methods of meditation. Their function is to concentrate the attention, to focus the mind, to help to empty the consciousness of distraction, so that the true prayer of divine infilling can start. We use the aids with confidence, but we know they are means to prayer, not the end or purpose of prayer itself.

People on the edge of the Church, therefore, who are searching for God or mourning their sense that God may be dead, should be confident enough to translate theology and its symbols into usable spiritual meaning, without being over-impressed by the interpretations offered by official preachers. Good preachers and teachers can be found who create the kind of theological living-space we need in our search for meaning. They are worth looking for. It is worth searching for the kind of preachers who preach with intrinsic authority, from their own pain and passion for truth. These are the kind of guides who make the journey with their listeners rather than insisting that they have already arrived at the destination. Some churches and ministers have abandoned theological defensiveness. They allow people to bring their questions into the sanctuary without insisting on the acceptance of pre-packed answers. They recognize that the processes of doubt and anger are part of the mystery of the spiritual life and have to be included in God. Christians on the theological edge, if they are wise, will not be in a hurry to find answers, anyway. They are usually people who have learned that it is all right to ask questions. Indeed, they have come to understand that faith is a way of living with questions, without being afraid.

Christianity has never been at its best when it has turned its back on uncomfortable truths and new knowledge. It has nothing to fear from the truth, no matter how challenging, and in its most creative periods it has adapted its central message to the ideas of the day and has sought to express itself through the best intellectual or scientific models for understanding reality. This confident openness to new truth has always been in tension, not only with a valid desire to be true to its own tradition, but with static and authoritarian versions of Christianity. Today this kind of Christian openness is threatened by a number of pressures.

At the heart of the mystery of faith there is an inescapable act of trust in the possibility of God; but the secondary aspects of faith – its language, its organizational and ethical systems – are provisional and revisable. This creates a fruitful though painful tension in the Christian life between trust in God and detachment from the structures we create to express and define that trust. Christianity invites us to a generous and open-hearted commitment to God, though not necessarily to the words we use to talk about God or the systems we develop to respond to God. However, there is a tendency in Christianity to load everything with theological significance, thereby making reappraisals of traditional attitudes unusually difficult. To take a trivial example from the field of human sexuality, in Christianity the act of masturbation has been given a significance that is out of all proportion to its nature as a universally practised way of dealing with sexual pressure. More seriously, at the organizational end of Christianity, the way we arrange the ordained ministry of the Church is sometimes seen, not as the best way of getting things done, but as divinely decreed and intrinsically significant. This tendency to load everything with meaning accounts for the distressing feuds between different expressions of Christianity, usually focused on their organizational systems, all of which compete for exclusive divine approval. It is this tendency towards spiritual and theological inflation in Christianity that has made it one of the most contentious religions in history and one of the most intrusive in the lives of its followers. An instructive example is provided by the status of contraception in the Roman Catholic Church. Official Catholic teaching prohibits the use of artificial means of contraception, though it is obvious that many Roman Catholics ignore the prohibition as inappropriate and unacceptably intrusive. Such Roman Catholics could be viewed either as 'cafeteria Catholics', taking from the menu only what they like, or as mature Christians who refuse to be treated as spiritual and moral children and, with clear consciences, make moral choices appropriate to their situation. The Roman Catholic Church, being the largest and most authoritarian of the Christian bodies, reflects the kind of pressures we have been discussing more vividly than other churches, but it is by no means unique in the way it gives expression to these inherent contradictions.

All the authoritarian versions of Christianity have created refugees who have been wounded and excluded by their oppressive certainties, in both the theological and the moral spheres. These are the people who find themselves on the edge of the

Church and wonder if there is any longer a place for them in official Christianity. Some of them are people who have intellectual difficulties with the way the Christian faith is officially expounded; some of them, because of their sexual orientation or way of life, feel uncomfortable in a Church that seems to discount or denigrate their humanity. This book is an attempt to reach out to those who find themselves on the edge of Christianity, to assure them that they are not alone, and to invite them to continue the journey with us. It is addressed to people who find themselves on the difficult frontier between belief and unbelief, the kind of people who would like to enter the Church, if only they did not have to park their minds and consciences outside before entering. This book invites them to come in and look round and to make sure they bring their minds in with them. The tone of the book will be polemical at times, but its purpose is positive, even evangelical: it wants to reach out to the many good people who have given up the Church and to offer them not a way back, but a way forward to a future that contains the promise of God.

PART I

Making Sense of God

CHAPTER ONE

Making Sense of God

I

Some years ago I presented a television series for the BBC called *When I Get To Heaven*. I interviewed celebrities about their lives, their attitude to death, and whether they believed in an afterlife. It turned out to be a useful formula for exploring the values and convictions of some very interesting people. One of the interviews I remember most vividly was with Jonathan Miller, the famous polymath, doctor, comedian, theatrical producer and culture critic. He was a charming man, whose atheism was unyielding and implacable. I am most comfortable with borderline thinkers – people who easily or uneasily straddle a frontier, such as believers with doubts, or sceptics troubled by the insistent whispers of belief. I feel most comfortable with people like this because I myself straddle this mysterious boundary, so that I can share both faith and doubt. Indeed, my definition of faith sees it as intrinsically associated with doubt. The opposite of faith is not doubt but certainty. Where we have certainty we need no faith. Faith comes in where we take something largely on trust, whatever the grounds of our trust may be. It will be obvious, therefore, that utterly convinced believers with no shred of doubt in their make-up, and utterly convinced unbelievers can be equally uncomfortable company for the man or woman who inhabits this strange borderline of faith.

Jonathan Miller made no concessions whatsoever to faith. With dismissive eloquence he repelled any suggestion that there might be anything in the religious hypothesis. His certainties had a mesmerizing and paralysing effect on me. While it was true that I was there to elicit the views and opinions of my interviewee, it was obviously expected that I would offer some counter-arguments to

Miller's passionate and sometimes angry dismissal of religion as dangerous nonsense. In a review, one critic, himself a sardonic mocker of religion, said that I had the face of someone who was haunted and made anxious by doubt. Looking back on the Miller interview, I can see that he was finding my weakest spots; with brutal certainty he was beaming back to me my own scepticism.

This is part of the paradox of being a Christian believer, or the kind of believer I am. The response of faith operates on a number of different levels in human experience, but debate about it tends to operate only on the rational or intellectual level. Yet the experience of faith is more like the decathlon than a boxing match. A decathlete may lose or do badly in a particular contest, yet still win the prize by an accumulation of points in other areas. Faith certainly has to include the mind. There is an inescapably rational component to it, but it is a way of responding to the mystery of the universe that is wider and more comprehensive than the mind alone. This is part of what Pascal meant when he said, 'The heart has its reasons which reason knows nothing of.'

The Counter Culture of the sixties, later to be metamorphosed into the New Age movement, was a response to the rationality of a scientific, technological culture that had led the United States into an enormous social and political crisis. The logic of the theory of nuclear deterrence and the cool and analytical way in which thinkers calculated the effects of various levels of nuclear strike, all carefully disguised in a euphemistic vocabulary, led a generation of young Americans to revolt against a type of consciousness that had lost touch with human emotion and seemed to be controlled exclusively by clinical rationality. We are more than our rationality. We have depths to our nature – emotional, aesthetic and spiritual – and if we lose touch with them we diminish and distort our humanity. The thinkers of the movement, such as Theodore Roszak, reminded people that there were different kinds of consciousness, and that poets like Wordsworth and Blake had apprehended ranges of meaning and experience that were unavailable to the narrow rationalist. He repudiated what he called 'the myth of objective consciousness' – the idea that the mind, gazing out on the universe from the confines of the self, could truly apprehend reality. Science itself now reminds us that the observer affects what is observed; that we see, not necessarily what is there, but what we observe;

and what we observe is always affected by who we are and by the width of the lens through which we gaze.

The trouble with purely intellectual debate about faith is that it engages the subject on too narrow a front. This is why arguments about religion are usually inconclusive and unsatisfying and can sometimes be demoralizing for the intelligent believer. I watched Richard Dawkins, the brilliant, charismatic scientist and crusader against religion, demolish John Habgood, then Arch-bishop of York, in a debate on science and religion. Habgood went to the debate expecting a mutual exploration of the mystery of the universe. He came up against a mind utterly convinced of its own rightness and brilliantly contemptuous of the perspective of faith. It fell to some believing scientists in the audience to point out to him that, contrary to his own claims, his dismissal of religion, which was certainly cogent and persuasive, was philosophically, and not scientifically based. We saw in Dawkins a good example of how easy it is to counter Christianity on the intellectual level alone because, as the philosopher Ian Crombie pointed out during a celebrated debate with J. B. S. Haldane, 'Atheism may encounter fewer intellectual difficulties, but that is because it is not a hypothesis but a refusal to look for explanations of a certain type.'[1] Obviously, if we rule out what Crombie calls 'explanations of a certain type', or the idea that the human person has a number of ways of apprehending reality, then it will be very easy to dismiss the credibility of religion.

Most debate about religion is conducted at this level, and it has had some significant effects. The first effect is that it has severely damaged the plausibility of faith. A plausibility structure is a system of value and meaning that we partly create for ourselves and partly inherit. We tend to interiorize the prevailing view, so that dissenting minorities feel increasingly beleaguered and often end by absorbing it. In the language of the sociologist Peter Berger, they 'go native'. If we were to move from late twentieth-century Western scientific culture to a remote country with its own plausibility structures, with no one to support the intellectual system that we brought with us, it would become increasingly difficult to sustain as plausible those Western attitudes, which would be incomprehensible to those amongst whom we lived. The important thing to note here is that a plausibility structure need not be true to be powerful. A prevailing world-view has enormous power and exerts a sort of totalitarian control over the minds and hearts of people.

If we read the biographies of African Americans, especially from the earlier part of this century, we become aware that it took an enormous effort of will for many of them to challenge, even in their own hearts, the assumption in the prevailing White culture that Black people were morally and intellectually inferior. The prevailing plausibility structure, however unspoken (and it was, in fact, spoken very loudly), was that Africans were inferior. This accounts for the various movements in the fifties and sixties designed to persuade Blacks that they *were* beautiful, that Black *was* good, that they were not inferior adjuncts to White culture. The moral and intellectual revolution in Black consciousness had to force its way against all the plausibility structures of centuries of oppression and neglect. We have witnessed a similar pilgrimage in the women's movement. According to received opinion (much of it derived from the Bible), women were essentially subordinate to men; they were created as permanent helpmates for their masters. Since this was the prevailing view, the dominant plausibility structure, it is not surprising that it was interiorized by women themselves, many of whom were the strongest opponents of the development of women's rights and women's consciousness.

We find similar contrasts in the encounter between European colonizers and the aboriginal peoples they met in the countries they invaded. In his book *Blackfoot Physics*, F. David Peat writes:

> All of us see the world through the spectacles of our world-views, through our particular ways of seeing and thinking about reality and society. Moreover, we hold these world-views in a largely unconscious way. We are not normally aware that we experience the world through their transforming, or distorting, power. Since much of our world-view is culturally shared, we simply talk about 'the way the world is', or 'the very nature of reality'.[2]

His book explores the world-view of Native Americans, a community traditionally dismissed by Western consciousness as superstitious and primitive, and shows how subtle, complex and compelling a world-view it is. The grim history of genocide and exploitation that characterized the relationship between Europeans and the Native peoples they encountered in the Americas does little to commend the Western world-view, with its contemptuous dismissal of a way of life which it made no attempt to understand. Peat succeeds in demonstrating how difficult it is for any of us to enter a different kind of consciousness and how prone we are to dismiss what we do not understand because we have no experience of it. He refers to Thomas Kühn's book, *The Structure of Scientific Revolutions*, and reminds us that every scientist serves an apprenticeship during which she or he picks up, in a largely unconscious way, certain ways of thinking. Scientists operate within the limits defined by a paradigm that is rarely questioned:

> It is only when a world-view has been stretched to its limits that it breaks down in what Kühn calls a scientific revolution. In the aftermath a new paradigm rapidly evolves and then, for the generation of scientists that follow, it becomes the inevitable way of seeing things and doing research.[3]

Peat believes that when a particular paradigm or world-view is held by a society that wields considerable power, then its way of seeing begins to dominate other cultures and forces on them a single perspective where before there had been diversity and mutual respect. This is one of the most tragic effects of Western colonization of so-called primitive societies whose spiritualities, usually based on a deep reverence for nature, have been all but destroyed by Western arrogance. Only now is Western consciousness beginning to explore the depths of these cultures and to realize how impoverished our world-view is in comparison.

Peat's book applies to a particularly grim episode in the history of Western arrogance, and Christianity must bear a large part of the blame. Now it is being hoisted on its own petard, especially in Northern Europe. It is a cognitive minority in a sceptical culture that denies any reality that is not available to the instruments of objective consciousness.

These reversals are what makes the history of ideas so fascinating. They should make us slow to reject a point of view simply because it goes against the prevailing trend. Today's minority view may become tomorrow's plausibility structure. There is little doubt that the plausibility of faith has been eroded in the intellectual milieu of Western Europe. Faith has become an implausible minority option, indulged for historical reasons, at best tolerated, sometimes treated with amused disdain, sometimes with dismissive contempt. Various things have eroded the plausibility of faith, but there are two that are particularly worth noting, both of which apply mainly to the Christian Faith.

The ideas that eroded the plausibility of faith are themselves valid, as far as they go, but they succeed only against a type of faith that is no longer possible today, in any case. The most damaging of all the attacks upon faith was against what Bonhoeffer called 'the God of the gaps'. This phrase refers to the kind of religious approach that used God to plug holes in human knowledge systems. In a non-scientific culture the use of religious myth to explain the physical mysteries of the universe is understandable and appropriate. Difficulty arises when new discoveries are made about the universe that deny or run counter to the non-scientific explanatory myth. A classic example is the discovery by Copernicus that the sun was the centre of the solar system. He prepared the way for the work of Kepler, Galileo and Isaac Newton, but his discoveries were repudiated by the Church of the day because they contradicted the explanatory myth that had been followed for centuries, which was a literal reading of the creation narratives in the Book of Genesis. Down the centuries religious systems have usually supported the prevailing plausibility structures. The current moral and cognitive systems, though not essential parts of the faith, become so important to the religious authority that a challenge to them is interpreted as a challenge to the faith itself. Believers are just as resistant as any other human group to the discomforts of new knowledge.

However, the particular danger in which religious conservatism of this sort places itself is not that it resists change and intellectual evolution, but that it welds the reality of God onto transitory systems, so that when they are defeated God seems to be killed. The ironic thing about this whole process is that at the heart of biblical religion there is a constant warning against identifying God with human systems. This false identification is called idolatry. It makes the relative into something absolute, the time-bound into something eternal. But if we use God as a mystical substance to fill up gaps in our knowledge we can end by placing God in opposition to truth itself.

John Polkinghorne addresses this issue in his book *Reason and Reality: The Relationship Between Science and Theology.* Over the centuries the God of the gaps has been pushed out of the created universe and now clings precariously to the edges as the mysterious reality that pushed the button that fired the Big Bang. Polkinghorne writes:

> Perhaps no subject has given rise to more confusion than the inter-relationship of science and theology and the question of how things began. It has often erroneously been supposed that the Christian doctrine of creation is principally concerned with initiation, with the primary instant. To think that is to confuse Christianity with Deism. The doctrine of creation is concerned, not just with what God did, but with what he is doing; its subject is ontological origin, not temporal beginning. Its central assertion is that the physical world, at every instant of its existence, is held in being by the will of God.

He goes on to argue that if physical cosmology were to abandon a datable beginning for the world, then no great theological upheaval would follow. He writes:

> Stephen Hawking has proposed a highly speculative, but just conceivably correct, quantum cosmology in which the universe is a kind of fuzzy space-time egg with no sharp beginning. He says, 'If the universe is really completely self-contained, having no boundary or edge, it would have neither beginning nor end; it would simply be. What place then for a creator?' It is theologically naïve to give any other answer than 'every place' – as the ordainer and sustainer of the space-time egg. God is not a god of the edges, with a vested interest in boundaries.[4]

God ought not to be understood in mechanical terms, though we have to confess that for centuries Christianity committed itself to a mechanical understanding of the biblical creation myth.

The use of the word 'myth' is not a subtle way of hinting that we are dealing with ungrounded constructions of the imagination – with untruths. Myth is a way of expressing truth so profound that only narrative or story is an appropriate vehicle for it. The story of Adam and Eve and what Milton called 'man's first disobedience' is a description of human alienation, it is not a historical account of a primeval disaster. We will see later on that myth is a very important device that is not exclusively tied to a fictitious or poetic way of conveying truth. Historical events can achieve the status of myth and be released into time as a way of conveying truth. Too narrow an understanding of myth has often forced Christians to deny reality itself. If God is, God is not a God of the gaps, there to fill holes, but an all-encompassing and all-accompanying reality. By its own neurotic objectification of God and by its frightened opposition to genuine scientific discovery, the Christian faith has helped to erode its own plausibility throughout this century.

The second and, in many ways, the more damaging element in this process of erosion has been the moral one – the record of Christianity as a human agency in history. A case can easily be made against religion as a destructive element in human relationships. Engage in a religious discussion in the local school or in the neighbourhood pub, and we will soon hear the claim that religion is largely responsible for human misery. Both systemically and individually it has divided humanity. It has tormented individuals with guilt by laying upon them burdens impossible to be borne, so that many, 'created sick, commanded to be sound',⁵ have been reduced to suicidal despair. There is something that the Christian can say about these accusations, but our first word ought to be a word of penitence, because we are guilty of these things and many more than we could find time to express.

The case for faith, therefore, has to be made against the background of actions that have damaged the plausibility of Christianity in our century. We have, too often, been a cause of evil and a source of human misery; and for too long we have opposed the discovery of new truth, because it contradicted our false and idolatrous abuse of God.

To summarize the argument so far: there has been a powerful, two-pronged attack against the plausibility of Christian faith, and, by its defensiveness, Christianity has assisted in its own demolition. It has allowed itself to be used as a kind of false alternative science, a different way of explaining how the universe works. As our knowledge of the universe increased, God was pushed further and further to the edges. Christians do not need to be trapped in this way of understanding God. Christianity, if it is honest, has to be congruent with the best of human knowledge, with truth as we have discovered it, however uncomfortable. The Church has often allowed itself to be too closely associated with transient systems, so that when they were challenged and overthrown the Church's plausibility went with them. This has happened repeatedly in political and intellectual history. The most embarrassing example is the way the nineteenth-century Church opposed Darwinism, not on scientific but on theological grounds, and made itself a laughing stock in the process. The problem lies in the false association of Christianity with transient intellectual fashions, not with Christianity in its essence.

The second powerful challenge to Christianity is the moral one, and a more considered response to it will be given in the next chapter, when we come to look at the Christian doctrine of humanity. Nevertheless, we have to admit that frightful things have been done in the name of Christianity, and they count against the actual record of the Church. However, that is not to admit that Christianity is intrinsically evil. All human systems are flawed. Immanuel Kant reminded us that from the crooked timber of humanity nothing entirely straight can be built. Even the best of our institutions, our noblest aspirations, are compromised by our own faults. If we are determined to oppose something, we ought, at least, to challenge its best account of itself and try to understand its best statement of its own nature.

The difficulty with the debate between belief and unbelief is its intractability and the impossibility of any of the protagonists ever being able to deliver a final and conclusive proof. Had that been possible, the debate would have ended long ago in the triumph of one side or the other. The fascination and frustration of the subject lies precisely in its uncertainty, though there is no lack of champions on each side of the debate who claim absolute certainty for their point of view. We can, if we choose, dismiss the persistence of belief as another depressing manifestation of the irrationality and credulity of *homo sapiens*. It is certainly true that religion has been disfigured by these characteristics, and this is one reason why those who go on believing should welcome the continued criticism of atheists and agnostics. Without their challenges religion can too easily slip into superstition and idolatry.

Nevertheless, the persistence of belief is capable of another interpretation: it could be a valid response to reality. That is why it is important to offer faith the compliment of a respectful hearing and to afford it the status of a reasonable response to the mystery of life, even if we ourselves find it personally elusive or unpersuasive; and the tone and temper of the discussion is as important as the conclusions we reach. We are dealing with the question of the ultimate meaning of existence itself or whether it has any meaning, apart from the private purposes we discover in our own experience. This is a truth issue, something that we dare not engage in fraudulently, because it concerns a fundamental human value – that of honesty before the facts. We might even say that, in a sense, truth is God and has absolute authority over us, so that what we decide to be the truth for us must be obeyed, no matter where it leads us. That primary commitment to the truth should rescue us from the defensiveness that often characterizes discussion about matters of faith and ultimate concern. We should rejoice when people commit themselves to truth as they understand it, even when it is in contradiction to our own commitment. This is what Tillich meant when he said there was no true atheism, because the atheist's passionate pursuit of the truth, no matter where it leads, has something absolute about it and should evoke our admiration.

The fact remains, however, that faith also persists in the human experience as an honest response to the facts of existence. In the nature of the case, it is no more able to deliver the knockout blow against atheism than atheism has been able, in spite of its many brilliant and persuasive protagonists, to persuade humanity to decide against the possibility of faith. What faith must not do is doctor the facts or ignore uncongenial truths in its defence of God, because dishonest belief is a greater danger to faith than honest disbelief. Let us now look at the three elements of religious experience that give it its cumulative power. Even if we admit that they are not absolutely and logically persuasive, we may agree that they do add up to a considerable level of probability, and leave us with a challenge; the choice to believe or not to believe, to trust them or not to trust them.

2

The sense of the holy

In a telling phrase Maggie Ross said that God cannot be posited, God can only be encountered. We could put that in a slightly different way by saying that we experience God before we are able to talk about God. This is why even the most philosophically cogent argument for the existence of God repels believers themselves. It suggests that the experience of the divine is something that we ourselves can control by our cleverness or rationality. This is perhaps what Paul was hinting at in 1 Corinthians when he wrote:

> Where is the one who is wise? Where is the scribe? Where is the debater of this age? Has not God made foolish the wisdom of the world? For since, in the wisdom of God, the world did not know God through wisdom, God decided, through the foolishness of our proclamation, to save those who believe.

> (1 Corinthians 1:20–21)

God is encountered before language comes along to interpret the experience. If we wish to make a serious attempt to understand Christian faith, then we have to pay attention to the record of human experience of the divine. We have already noted how difficult it is to transcend our own world-view and pay attention to the wisdom and insights of an alien paradigm. But we do not have to enter a strange culture to encounter this phenomenon. Most of us have had painful experiences either of our own inability to understand and interpret the messages others were sending us or of their inability to understand us. The first line of Stevie Smith's poem 'Not waving but drowning' captures the experience perfectly. We find it difficult to pay attention to one another, so it should not surprise us that we find it difficult to attend to something as elusive and problematic as the voice of the divine. In every generation there are many who do listen, some by gradual increments of attention, some by a dramatic summons that splits their life in two. Evelyn Underhill captures it well:

> For the most part, of course, the presence and action of the great spiritual universe surrounding us is no more noticed by us than the pressure of air on our bodies, or the action of light. Our field of attention is not wide enough for that; our spiritual senses are not sufficiently alert. Most people work so hard developing their correspondence with the visible world, that their power of corresponding with the invisible is left in a rudimentary state.
>
> There are many different ways in which the step can be taken. It may be, from the ordinary human point of view, almost imperceptible: because, though it really involves the very essence of man's being, his free and living will, it is not linked with a special or vivid experience. Bit by bit the inexorable pressure is applied, and bit by bit the soul responds; until a moment comes when it realizes that the landscape has been transformed, and is seen in a new proportion and lit by a new light. But sometimes the step is a distinct and vivid experience. Then we get the strange facts of conversion: when through some object or event, in the external world, another world and its overwhelming attraction and demand is realized. An old and limited state of consciousness is suddenly, even violently broken up and another takes its place. It was the voice of a child saying, 'Take, read!' which at last made St Augustine cross the frontier on which he had been lingering, and turned a brilliant and selfish young professor into one of the giants of the Christian Church; and a voice which seemed to him to come from the Crucifix, which literally made the young St Francis, unsettled and unsatisfied, another man than he was before. It was while St Ignatius sat by a stream and watched the running water, and while the strange old cobbler Jacob Boehme was looking at a pewter dish, that there was shown to each of them the mystery of the Nature of God. A spring is touched, a Reality always there discloses itself in its awe-

inspiring majesty and intimate nearness, and becomes the ruling fact of existence; continually presenting its standards, and demanding a costly response. And so we get such an astonishing scene, when we reflect upon it, as that of the young Francis of Assisi, little more than a boy, asking all night long the one question which so many apparently mature persons have never asked at all: 'My God and All, what art Thou and what am I?' and we realize with amazement what a human creature really is – a finite centre of consciousness, which is able to apprehend, and long for, Infinity.[6]

We do not offer an appropriate response to these experiences, whether dramatic and life-changing or gentle and reassuring, when we try to explain them away by a method of external interpretation rather than by an attempt to understand them from within their own integrity. It is easy to offer an account that reduces them to a set of neural actions in the brain; but we find ourselves in an unavoidable circularity here, wherever we go for an explanation. Experiences of God are self-evidencing to the participant. They operate within their own integrity, follow the logic of their own experience and require no external authority to validate them; they validate themselves. But the same logic applies to the kind of discourse that repudiates them. Reductionist interpretations of mystical or spiritual experience also beg the question and take for granted the logic that denies them any reality beyond the materialist explanation. There is no way out of this circularity that offers us a test for infallibly judging between the claims. We have to make a choice: is there a reality beyond the experience to which it refers? Or is the experience self-referential, an entirely subjective adventure of the human psyche? In a sense it could be both, of course. Every experience of transcendence, whether in art or religion, is mediated through our senses and through material realities. The experience that comes to us as we listen to Elgar's *Cello Concerto* is communicated through quite precise physical objects, but it is also something beyond them, something that transcends them. This extra dimension is what George Steiner calls 'real presence', using a religious category to capture something of the elusive experience of art. In Christian theology the bread and wine of the eucharist are, and obviously remain, just bread and wine, but for the

Christian believer they also convey a spiritual reality which we call the real presence of Christ. Steiner borrows this paradox to oppose all theories of art that reduce it to the mechanisms used to convey it. Every experience of transcendence is obviously mediated through our senses, through some material form. The question we have to ask is whether something *beyond* is communicated to us in and through the experience. This is where the element of trust or faith comes in, and it is always based on assumptions about the matter. There are mysteries in human experience about which we can never reach a conclusion, because it always seems to recede in front of us. We have to make a decision that cuts through the endless regress and provides us with a base for action. This assumption is a kind of faith, even if it chooses to interpret human experience in non-transcendental terms. There is the faith that chooses to believe and the faith that chooses not to, but faith itself – the decision to act in a certain way towards the mystery that confronts us – is inescapable. The faith that believes, however, does not lack evidence to support its decision, even though we may have to admit that the evidence confirms itself. These self-evidencing experiences of the transcendent mystery which we call God in shorthand cannot be reduced to anything beyond themselves, though they always leave us with a question. Living with and through that question is the life of faith. The difficulty that faces people who believe they have experienced God or have been captured by the possibility of God is that their experience is incommunicable to others. They might be able to write about it, attempt to describe it even, but they are never able to find a formula that actually conveys the self-evidencing power of what happened to them. It is only because others have also encountered these mysteries that some kind of mutual understanding is possible between people when they try to discuss spiritual experience. Poetry is about the only form of expression that comes close to capturing the immediacy of transcendence in a way that communicates its intensity. The final three stanzas in a poem written by Edward Hirsch about Simone Weil in Assisi capture something of the power as well as the elusiveness of the experience of the holy:

She disliked the Miracles in the Gospels.
She never believed in the mystery of contact,
here below, between a human being and God.
She despised popular tales of apparitions.

But that afternoon in Assisi she wandered
through the abominable Santa Maria degli Angeli
and happened upon a little marvel of Romanesque
purity where St Francis liked to pray.

She was there a short time when something
  absolute
and omnivorous, something she neither believed
nor disbelieved, something she understood –
but what was it? – forced her to her knees.[7]

The sense of requiredness

One of the most common criticisms of the life of faith is that it is an escape into wishful thinking, a system of false consolation, a warm blanket to shelter us from the icy winds of nothingness that circle the universe. While it is undoubtedly true that religious faith can be consoling, one of its primary characteristics is the sense of demand that comes with it. Abraham Heschel calls this aspect of religious faith 'requiredness'.

With the experience of the divine mystery comes a sense that something is required of us. This has been one of the main characteristics of the great religious heroes and liberators. It can, of course, turn into a harsh and unlovely moralism, and we shall have occasion to look at this too frequent distortion in Christian history. The history of faith is filled with men and women who were called by their encounter with the divine to a life of struggle, testing and persecution. This is the story of Moses and Jeremiah and Jesus Christ. It is also the story of Martin Luther King and Desmond Tutu in our own day. Their political witness, their passion for human liberation, springs from their experience of God. God is known to them as righteousness as well as beauty. God is experienced by them as anguish for the oppressed, and their obedience to the divine vision places them on a collision course with all worldly oppression and injustice. Their claim is Peter's claim: they must obey God rather than man, even if they pay with their own lives.

I am not a heroic Christian. My life has been one of comfort, punctuated by half-hearted attempts at discipline and commitment, but I have been immensely heartened as well as challenged by my own encounters with Christian heroism. When I visited El Salvador in 1990, during the Civil War, I was taken to a dormitory at the university where a group of Jesuits, their housekeeper and her daughter had been machine-gunned by a military death squad. The corridors were still smeared with their blood. The atrocity did not silence the Jesuit witness against the corrupt and oppressive regime. It is worth noting an irony here. In my brief encounter with the situation in El Salvador, it became obvious that the Christian community was in collusion with tyranny as well as in valiant opposition to it. This illustrates one of the points which this chapter has been trying to establish. Religious systems too easily ally themselves with intellectual and political structures that take them over and transform their values into those of the world. It is the task of moral leadership to challenge these conformities, though the prophets who issue these challenges usually suffer for their courage. Moral and political systems are like all other human realities. They are transient, influenced by context and subject to change. They can become oppressive. It is the prophet, the one who has been with God, who challenges every moral status quo, however thickly anointed by religious institutions. Religious people sanctified slavery; but it was religious people who overthrew it in the name of the God who had been falsely co-opted by the oppressors. Religious systems institutionalized racism, but it was religious champions, such as Martin Luther King and Desmond Tutu, who, in the name of the God who had been falsely co-opted by the tyrants, opposed these evils and gave their lives or risked their safety in the process.

It must be acknowledged, therefore, that to fall into the hands of God, to experience the holiness and righteousness of the divine, is not an escape. It is a call to acute moral challenge, to disturbance, development and endless change. In Abraham Heschel's words, 'To the biblical mind man is above all a commanded being; a being of whom demands may be made. The central problem is not: What is being? but rather: What is required of me?'[8]

For atheists this moral imperative, this sense we have that we are commanded creatures, is simply a way of talking about our own best values. That is an arguable point of view, but there is equal if not greater force in something John Polkinghorne wrote:

> If God is just a manner of speaking about the individual moral quest it is difficult to see what is the ground of the imperative we feel urging us to that quest. On the other hand, if God is the creator of the world and through it is achieving his purposes of love, then our perceptions of the moral imperative will be intuitions of his will and find their authority in that fact.[9]

The religious consciousness at its highest feels that it is responding to a moral purpose that is not of our own making and that frequently goes against our own selfish interests. The passion as well as the anguish of the moral life lies in the sense that we are responding to a personal, not an abstract claim.

The strangeness of the universe

The third element in the religious claim is the boldest and most controversial of its aspects. It attempts to explain the mystery of the universe and the way we experience it. This explanatory function of religion is not, as we have already noted, a way of filling gaps in our knowledge systems with supernatural cement. God is not there to fill gaps, but is the ground and stay of the universe in its wholeness. The whole universe has to be congruent with the divine reality, not just spiritual experiences. Religion in its explanatory mode does not have the compulsive power of unassailable, unarguable fact. We still have to make a choice, run a risk, lay a wager, but we do not commit blindly; we do it after studying the form and making our best guess and acting upon it boldly. As we have seen, there is no escape from this choice. To live is to bet, to take sides, to decide. One choice, and a heroic one, is to believe that the universe came out of nothing and will return to nothing, and ultimately means nothing. The human tragedy is to have become sentient beings who understand their own nature and know that their end is destruction.

But this kind of absurdism is not the only horse in the race. There is another way of interpreting the universe. There is the strange fact, so familiar that we take it for granted, that the universe is intelligible to us. There is an extraordinary relationship between the workings of our minds and the workings of the physical world. The need to survive in the evolutionary struggle provides some explanation for this congruence, but that can only apply to the relation of ordinary experience to everyday thinking. Polkinghorne says that it is hard to believe that the ability to conceive of quantum field theory is just a spin-off from evolutionary competition:

> In its most articulate form science involves the use of mathematics as the basic expression of our understanding of the physical world. Something very odd is going on when this happens. Mathematics is the free invention of the human mind. Our mathematical friends sit in their studies and think their abstract thoughts. Yet some of the most intricate patterns they evolve prove to be just those realised in the physical structure of the world. Mathematics is the abstract key which turns the lock of the physical universe.[10]

It is worth pausing for a few seconds to meditate on the extraordinary relationship between mathematical techniques and the intricate structure of the universe. The truths of mathematics, far from being only the action of the human mind that first thinks them, seem just as likely to be ever-existing realities that are discovered but not constructed by the explorations of the mind. The great mathematician and logician Kurt Gödel wrote of the concepts of set theory: 'Despite their remoteness from sense experience, we do have something like a perception of the objects of set theory, as seen from the fact that the axioms forced themselves upon us as being true.'[11] In *Reason and Reality* Polkinghorne explains the implications of this fact:

> The meta-question of the unreasonable effectiveness of mathematics insists on being answered. A coherent and elegant explanation would lie in the theological claim that the reason within and the reason without are linked together by their common origin in the rationality of the creator. The physical universe seems shot through with signs of mind. That is indeed so, says the theist, for it is God's mind that lies behind its rational beauty. I do not offer this as a knock down argument for theism but

as a satisfying insight which finds a consisten: place in a theistic view of the world.[12]

If the fact that the human mind, through the discovery of mathematical axioms, puts us in touch with the structure of the universe is not intriguing enough, the emergence of humanity itself is another tantalizing coincidence. The fact that a ball of energy becomes, after 15 billion years, a home for self-conscious beings, is also worth meditating on. In scientific terms this is not any old world, but one that is very specific in the finely tuned balance of its nature and circumstances. Scientists call these elements anthropic balances. We know that if the earth were a little closer to the sun it would be too hot for life and if it were a little further away it would be too cold. David Wilkinson points out that 'the orbit of the earth is very finely tuned to the existence of life. It is an example of an anthropic balance – if it were different then life on earth would not exist.'[13] He explains the emergence of life in a cartoon of a machine called 'The Acme Universe Making Machine'. The machine has two dials: one dial controls the expansion force of the Big Bang, the force that spreads the universe out; the other dial controls gravity, the force that pulls everything back together. We set the dials to what we want and out would come the universe. After a few billion attempts we would begin to realize that in order to get a universe that would produce carbon-based life, these two dials would need to be set quite precisely. If we get the gravitational force too high, then the universe would appear, but in a microsecond gravity would pull everything back together into the opposite of the Big Bang, which is a Big Crunch. If we get the expansion rate too high, then the universe would expand at such a rate that gravity would be unable to form stars and galaxies from whose dust carbon-based life would evolve. In order to get structure within the universe, these dials would need to be balanced to within 1 part in 10 to the power of 60 – that is, 1 followed by 60 zeros.[14]

Paul Davies, another writer on science, says that this is the same accuracy as shooting at a target one centimetre square on the other side of the universe and hitting it. Davies sees these anthropic balances as the most compelling evidence for an element of cosmic design. These delicate adjustments do not only refer to the earliest instance but to the continuing history of the world and its detailed process. This extraordinary fine tuning, or coincidence, appears to be necessary at every stage of world development.

There are various ways of accounting for these mysterious balances, but the theistic account is as persuasive as any of them, though it is no more logically coercive. The extraordinary congruence between our minds and the universe, and our ability to receive by means of mathematical revelation the knowledge of its intricate structure; the remarkable coincidences of the anthropic balances, the fact that the emergence of sentient life can be accounted for as a result of the detailed fine tuning of the universe, lends support to the theistic hypothesis, the claim that our mind is congruent with the universe because the universe itself is the result of mind. This is why the Princeton physicist Freeman Dyson said in a BBC broadcast on 12 December 1979: 'I do not feel like an alien in this universe. The more I study the details of its architecture the more evidence I find that the universe in some sense must have known we were coming.'

This approach to the religious hypothesis does not add up to an absolute proof, but it has evidentiary value and a cumulative effect. If we are looking for absolute proof of God's existence we will never find it. Something that C. S. Lewis wrote to a friend is worth pondering:

> As to why God does not make his existence demonstrably clear: are we sure that he is even interested in the kind of Theism that would be a compelled logical assent to a conclusive argument? Are we interested in it in personal matters? I demand from my friends a trust in my good faith which is certain without demonstrative proof. It wouldn't be confidence at all if he waited for rigorous proof. The magnanimity, the generosity which will trust on a reasonable probability is required of us. But supposing one believed and was wrong after all? Why then you would have paid the universe a compliment it doesn't deserve. Your error would even so be more interesting and important than the reality. And yet how could that be? How could an idiotic universe have produced creatures whose mere dreams are so much stronger, better, subtler than itself?[15]

Jesus taught his followers to do no violence, either physical or intellectual. We do not seek to compel people to an act of faith, or at our best we try not to: rather, we give reasons for the hope

DANCING ON THE EDGE

that is in us. We set forth our own experience and convictions for others to weigh and ponder. We believe that they are consistent with our own complex nature as rational, intuitive, beauty-loving creatures. We believe that we have encountered something of the mystery that lies behind the universe; it has spoken to the deep places of our hearts. With its call has come a sense of demand, a commitment to struggle for righteousness, a care for the oppressed and a bias towards the despised. The mystery of God that captures our hearts and commands our wills also secures the assent of our reason. The intelligibility of the mystery corresponds to our own need and ability to understand the universe. The cumulative effect of these experiences is to call us, however tentatively, to an act of commitment which we call faith.

However, there are many people whose attitude to faith has not yet been described in this chapter. They are not confident unbelievers. They are troubled by the possibility of faith, and often feel themselves to be on the very edge of it, yet their very honesty keeps them from moving more confidently into the community of believers. Far from being an act of courage, such a gesture would, for them, be a surrender of personal integrity. They may admit the cogency of the so-called case for the existence of God, but they feel towards this kind of reasoning what they feel towards those who argue, from the opposite pole, for a demonstrable atheism: a sense, though they cannot quite define it, that the point is being missed. The most such arguments can achieve, for and against, is the outlining of a hypothetical possibility or probability, depending on how strongly one esteems them. Any of the conclusions from such a process remain human constructs. They do not warm the heart or create that sense of inner trust that should characterize faith, no matter how co-active it is with doubt.

Even the romantic defiance of C. S. Lewis does not work for them. Its passion may appeal to them, but it is essentially a decision to choose to believe almost as an act of protest. It echoes Unamuno's famous definition of faith as resistance to the nothingness that awaits us, because it would be 'an unjust fate'. This courageous will to believe is not quite the last ditch of faith. There is another ditch, over to the side of these impressive, but self-dramatizing existentialists. This is where we find those who love truth so much that they are afraid of submitting, through emotional exhaustion, to an authority that will relieve them of the pain of indecision, but at the terrible price of intellectual suicide. In spite of themselves, they continue to feel drawn not so much to the community of faith, as to the mystery that may lie at its heart. Paradoxically, these may be the ones who are closest to God, just as it was the outsiders of his day who felt closest to Jesus. They come very close to the confession of unworthiness, usually as a result of rejection by the religious community, that Jesus commended in his story of the Pharisee and the Publican, where he said that it was the sinful Publican rather than the righteous Pharisee who was justified in God's eyes. The community of faith is a community of longing, not possession. It is for those who have glimpsed something of the divine, as well as for those who have not, but long to. It is for those who have achieved some level of discipline and control in their lives and for those who have not, but long to. Saint Augustine once described the Church as a school for sinners, not a museum for saints. It should be as wide as humanity; it should include all who wish to be attached to it; it should welcome their desire to explore the mystery that besets us. In the chapters ahead we shall try to explore what Christianity believes that mystery to be like. Our investigation will be in what Buddhist teachers call 'inner science'. The external universe is not the only one that is available to our senses. There is an inner universe of meaning and spirit open to our exploration.

CHAPTER TWO

Can God Have a Son?

I

*I*n the previous chapter we explored something of the human encounter with God. Without denying that there were alternative explanations for them, we attempted to outline a series of experiences that believers point to as grounds for faith in a divine reality, a reality that is related to us and to the universe as the sustaining ground of our existence. If such a reality does exist, what is its nature and in what way does it relate to us? Before exploring the Christian answer to that series of questions, it would be helpful to stop and ask questions about ourselves. We have already seen that human intelligence puts us in touch with the mysterious structure of the universe. In many ways we are frail creatures, easily broken by the great forces of nature, yet we transcend nature by our consciousness, by our ability to observe, remember and draw conclusions from what we discover. Pascal captured this paradox of weakness and strength when he said:

> Man is only a reed, the weakest thing in nature – but a thinking reed. It does not take the universe in arms to crush him; a vapour, a drop of water, is enough to kill him. But, though the universe should crush him, man would still be nobler than his destroyer, because he knows that he is dying, that the universe has the advantage of him; the universe knows nothing of this.[1]

We are thinking, remembering, imagining creatures. Many of our joys and most of our miseries are related to this complex ability to range backward in regret and forward in fear in our thoughts and dreams. We are also, in some sense, moral creatures. We have a capacity for goodness. We feel that something is required of us. We have a sense of duty towards at least some of our fellow creatures. The moral adventure calls us to expand that sense of requiredness, of duty towards the other, from the purely local or tribal to the universal. In order to talk about these mysterious realities at all we have to use words. Words, the greatest invention of humanity, are both blessing and bane. We use words to refer to non-verbal realities, to encounters with other people, to abstract states. The words refer to them, point to them, in some sense express their nature, but they are decidedly not the things to which they refer, though we are constantly tempted to treat them as though they were. We fight over words. Christians, for instance, have spilled blood and wasted time on whether a particular phrase, or even a particular vowel, adequately expressed the nature of the divine.

That is why at this point we ought to register a warning about the whole religious enterprise. We have already noticed the first danger in language, which is to treat the words that refer to something as though they were the thing itself. This danger comes in two forms. The first is to give the words too much significance – to treat, for example, a particular way of talking about God as though it were itself divine or sacrosanct. The opposite but related danger is to refuse the language any meaning at all, unless the things to which it refers are ascertainable by our physical senses. We either claim too much or too little for our words. We treat them as though they were divine, or we refuse to recognize that they can put us in touch with the transcendent, with things we did not know we knew, realities we had only dimly perceived.

The second danger in using them is that, in order to talk about something in particular and not about everything in general, we have to compartmentalize, we have to divide a whole reality into bits. We do this when we talk about ourselves. We have already talked about our rationality, our ability to think, our consciousness, as though this were a specific faculty, as though we were not thinking beings, but beings part of whose system did the thinking. An old version of this approach to humanity takes our moral nature, our capacity for virtue, and locates it in the will. We will use this compartmentalizing approach in this chapter, with the modification we have already registered about the inadequacy, yet inescapable necessity of language.

Our anxiety about the ability of language to connect us to reality may only be a current neurosis, an aspect of our bondage to a world-view that is cutting us off from other universes of experience.

DANCING ON THE EDGE

There is a modern view of language that sees it as an arbitrary human construct, something that comes only from within our own heads, and this is particularly true of religious language. Since, it is claimed, there is nothing beyond the words themselves that our senses can obviously verify, they can only refer back to ourselves. Peat believes this is a good example of imprisonment within the Western rationalist paradigm. He tells us that in so-called primitive traditions words themselves were held to have power because of their connection to other energies in nature. He recalls the fact that in many traditions, including the Hebrew tradition, the name of God is considered to be so sacred that it is never pronounced and only referred to obliquely. He goes on:

> Within indigenous science, to say something is to create an objective event and release a process of energetic vibrations that enter into relationships with the other powers and energies of nature. Thus, since every sound is an event of significance, a person must take responsibility for whatever he or she says.
>
> Language was created by the Ancestors as a direct connection to nature… In Mic Maq the names of trees are the sound that the wind makes as it moves through their leaves in the fall. The name of a tree is therefore far from arbitrary. It is based upon the direct experience of listening to a specific sound that refers to a particular tree – for each of the different species of trees makes a different sound.[2]

Language, in this view, offers us the possibility of communion with realities outside ourselves; it has a sacramental function, it connects us to things beyond us, including the mystery of God. The so-called objective use of language may, in fact, be a trap for us, imprisoning us within our own heads and causing us to doubt the reality of anything beyond our own self-limited nature. The paradox is that this failure to connect with spiritual reality 'out there' may be blinding us to the nearness of God in our own lives. As Eckhart wrote: 'God is near us, but we are without, God is at home, we are in the far country.' We need not despair, therefore. As long as we do not overrate or underrate the role of language, it can serve as a means of encounter with realities beyond ourselves, including the reality of spirit. We must trust, we must have faith in language itself. There is no other device for exploring and expressing the mystery of our own nature.

Let us now return to an exploration of our own nature and its mysteries, recognizing that, though it is inadequate to the purpose, language is the only tool we have. If, then, we perceive our nature to be under some sense of requirement, capable of seeking the good and possessing a predisposition towards righteousness, we have immediately to enter an opposite truth. The Christian religion has produced several psychological geniuses who have wrestled with the strange paradoxes of humanity. The Christian doctrine of human nature has been misunderstood and used in evil ways, but it does set forth a view that is both realistic and comprehensive; it captures both aspects of our human experience – its glory and its ugliness, its capacity for heroic goodness and its tendency towards cruelty and indifference. The Christian shorthand for the latter is the doctrine of original sin. The phrase is misleading, especially the word 'sin', because it suggests a particular act, whereas we are referring to a characteristic, a tendency in our nature that complicates the pursuit of our best ideals. It is best, when thinking about this topic, to see it in the concrete and not in the abstract. Peter the Apostle provides us with an instructive example.

Peter's story is well known. Even people who know little about the Bible recognize elements in Peter's story because they have entered the folk-memory of the race. Most people respond to the heart-breaking story of his three denials of Jesus. They remember the words of Jesus, 'Before the cock crows twice thou shalt deny me thrice.' One of my favourite paintings is *Peter the Penitent* by Giovanni Francesco Barbieri, painted for Cardinal Rocci in 1639. It hangs in the Royal Scottish Gallery in Edinburgh. It shows Peter crying bitterly, ravaged by anguish and guilt, just after his third denial, when Jesus had turned and looked at him. Peter's life is essentially the story of the human desire for commitment, the longing for heroic goodness, or even ordinary goodness, held back by its own moral impotence and incapacity. Saint Augustine put the paradox in a characteristic way: 'I was swept up to thee by thy beauty and torn away from thee by my own weight.' We pose ideals for ourselves, ideals of purity, discipline and goodness. They are genuine ideals, true aspirations that reflect our best sense of ourselves, our most honourable ambitions, but the weight of our own nature drags us from the fulfilment of these aspirations. Peter loved Jesus and swore to follow him. He misunderstood him, but it wasn't a failure of intellect that led to his betrayal, so much as a failure of will. He wanted to do the good thing but was unable to. His experience is perfectly summed up by St Paul in the Letter to the Romans: 'I do not understand my own actions. For I do not do what I want, but I do the very thing I hate' (Romans 7:15).

When we talk about these mysterious realities we try to capture them in figures of speech, we try to transpose the experience into language, and it is important to remember the limitations of language in this particular context. The story of Adam and Eve is an example of this complexity. If a child were to ask, 'Why are human beings sinful?' an ancient way of answering the question would be to say, 'Because Adam disobeyed God and ate the forbidden fruit at the bidding of his wife Eve. As punishment, God sent them out of the Garden of Eden, the garden of contentment, into the world of pain and struggle.' On deeper examination that is not really an explanation at all. It is not a persuasive way of accounting for the way we are, but it is a vivid way of describing the way we are. Nevertheless, the story itself is important. Stories convey abstract information more immediately than theories, and this story provides us with a number of shorthand symbols that enable us to say complicated things in simple ways. Myth is a way of conveying complex, possibly abstract truth in vivid narrative form. C. S. Lewis said that Christianity was a *true* myth. It uses great symbolic events rooted in, yet transcending history, to convey enduring truths in the form of narrative or story. The great myth of the Fall of Adam and Eve and the fruit of the forbidden tree captures the paradox of human nature: our sense of responsibility and our experience of helplessness, our idealism and our selfishness, our longing for peace and our proclivity for war. These paradoxes are particularly true of humanity in its collective sense, because in our group relationships, in the great systems we create – such as the tribe or nation, even the institutional Church – a new dimension, a sort of multiple personality is added, making it even more difficult to make moral appeals. This is why political scientists in their dispassionate observations claim that all nations seek only their own interests. Our own experience of being part of a heedless crowd underlines this flight from personal responsibility.

Years ago, when Hugh Gaitskell was leader of the Labour Party in Britain, he came to Glasgow to address a May Day rally. I was a member of a radical fringe of the Campaign for Nuclear Disarmament at the time, and we planned to disrupt the meeting and make it impossible for him to speak. We managed to infiltrate the enclosure, and when Gaitskell stood to argue the case for a multilateral approach to disarmament, we started shouting him down and parading round the enclosure. There were too many of us shouting for him to be heard, though I can distinctly remember him telling us to go and demonstrate in Red Square in Moscow and see how we would get on there. We would not let him make the speech he came to deliver. We had been taken over by a kind of group violence that grew on its own indignation. Being part of such a mob was an intoxicating and frightening experience, however righteous we thought we were. In a group we are capable of a cruelty that few of us would be capable of in our more intimate relationships. Reinhold Niebuhr, one of the greatest political thinkers in twentieth-century America, called one of his books *Moral Man and Immoral Society*, to underline this point, this heightening of sinfulness in our collective dimensions. Towards the end of his life he said that he probably ought to have entitled it *Immoral Man and Even More Immoral Society*.

Modern evolutionary science has given us new insights into this ancient complexity in our nature. The old myths of decline from a previous golden age or of falling from a previous state of perfection, while they retain enormous dramatic resonance, are not consistent with what we now know about the history of the universe and the evolution of our own species. There is no need to discard the basic human insight that we are imperfect creatures, prone to error, cruelty and selfishness; but there are more suggestive and appropriate images to account for this enduring reality. If Christianity is to follow its ancient practice of making itself consistent with the best human knowledge available, then we must make this profound insight congruent with what we now know of our history. The evolutionary paradigm seems more appropriate and suggestive today than the myth of decline or fall. We are immature creatures, struggling towards perfection, experimenting with right and wrong and not always sure which is which. Dr Arthur Peacocke of the Society of Ordained Scientists is quite explicit in his treatment of this theme. He says:

There is no sense in which we can talk of a past perfection. There was no golden age, no perfect past, no original perfect, individual Adam from whom all human beings have now declined. What is true is that humanity manifests aspirations to a perfection not yet attained, a potentiality not yet actualised, but no original righteousness. Sin, which is real, is about us falling short of what God intends us to be and is concomitant with our possession of self-consciousness, freedom, and intellectual curiosity. Classical conceptions of the fall and of sin that dominate Christian theologies of redemption urgently need reinterpretation if they are to make any sense to our contemporaries.[3]

The important thing to grasp here is not that Christianity is contending for a particular explanatory myth of origins, but has within its tradition a sophisticated, psychologically acute and empirically persuasive account of human nature that sees it as incomplete. Part of the tragedy of our condition is that we feel ourselves to be both responsible and helpless, capable of knowing the good, yet strangely incapable of achieving it, able to pose ideals and respond to them with passion and commitment, yet prone to self-delusion and failure. Peter is representative of our human state in his passionate protestations of loyalty and in his vehement betrayal of it. Paul, Peter's opponent in the dispute in early Christianity about whether it was a universal or a sectional faith, captured the human predicament perfectly: 'For I do not do the good I want, but the evil I do not want is what I do' (Romans 7:19).

The Christian religion at its best responds to the human predicament in an extraordinarily fitting way. Its approach is focused on the teaching and example of Jesus of Nazareth, a first-century preacher and prophet, the mystery of whose nature still dominates and fascinates a Western consciousness that has taken official leave of him. His response to the human predicament exactly fits our need. We find in Jesus of Nazareth a profound level of understanding and mercy combined with an equally profound level of challenge and demand. His character responds to both poles of our nature: our capacity for righteousness and our failure to achieve it. In Jesus of Nazareth we encounter absolute mercy and absolute demand. He responds to our moral impotence and helplessness with forgiveness, yet at the same time he heightens the sense of what is required of us to an almost unbearable level. In his encounters with suffering and sinful humanity he provoked a powerful response. Sinners, especially publicly notorious sinners, flocked to him and found acceptance, understanding and mercy. We also know that the cruel (and very often they were the professionally religious) were stung to murderous anger by his challenges to their cynicism and hypocrisy. He knew the human condition and responded to it with acute psychological insight. This is why the New Testament and Christian history are full of outcasts who were marginalized by the officially righteous elements in society, such as prostitutes, the sexually frail, addicts and traitors. These are the kind of people who define themselves as outcasts, yet they found acceptance in Jesus and became part of his company.

A photograph in a newspaper some years ago represented this whole category of humanity. It showed a mob in Somalia beating up a young woman for fraternizing with UN troops. We don't know what need led her to fraternize with the occupying enemy, but history is full of people like her, often helpless women, who have been cast in the role of professional outcasts, adulterers, the kind of women whose heads were shaved by the Resistance in France during the German occupation. This attractive young woman was a symbol of this human experience. She was the kind of person whom Jesus championed and protected, like the woman caught in adultery by a religious lynch mob who wanted Jesus to order her stoning. His response to this kind of human helplessness was enormously compassionate. He clearly understood the way we exile ourselves from our own peace. One of his most famous parables, the story of the Prodigal Son, is about a character like this, the kind of person most likely to provoke the disapproval of respectable, law-abiding citizens:

There was a man who had two sons. The younger of them said to his father, 'Father, give me the share of the property that will belong to me.' So he divided his property between them. A few days later the younger son gathered all he had and traveled to a distant country, and there he squandered his property in dissolute living. When he had spent everything, a severe famine took place throughout that country, and he began to be in need. So he went and hired himself out to one of the citizens of that country, who sent him to his fields to feed the pigs. He would gladly have filled himself with the pods that the pigs were eating; and no one gave him anything. But when he came to himself he said, 'How many of my father's hired hands have bread enough and to spare, but here I am dying of hunger! I will get up and

DANCING ON THE EDGE

go to my father, and I will say to him, "Father, I have sinned against heaven and before you; I am no longer worthy to be called your son; treat me like one of your hired hands." ' So he set off and went to his father. But while he was still far off, his father saw him and was filled with compassion; he ran and put his arms around him and kissed him. Then the son said to him, 'Father, I have sinned against heaven and before you; I am no longer worthy to be called your son.' But the father said to his slaves, 'Quickly, bring out a robe – the best one – and put it on him; put a ring on his finger and sandals on his feet. And get the fatted calf and kill it, and let us eat and celebrate; for this son of mine was dead and is alive again; he was lost and is found!' And they began to celebrate.

Now his elder son was in the field; and when he came and approached the house, he heard music and dancing. He called one of the slaves and asked what was going on. He replied, 'Your brother has come, and your father has killed the fatted calf, because he has got him back safe and sound.' Then he became angry and refused to go in. His father came out and began to plead with him. But he answered his father, 'Listen! For all these years I have been working like a slave for you, and I have never disobeyed your command; yet you have never given me even a young goat so that I might celebrate with my friends. But when this son of yours came back, who has devoured your property with prostitutes, you killed the fatted calf for him!' Then the father said to him, 'Son, you are always with me, and all that is mine is yours. But we had to celebrate and rejoice, because this brother of yours was dead and has come to life; he was lost and has been found.'

(Luke 15:11–32)

The parable of the loving father and the two sons is absolutely central to the teaching of Jesus about the nature of God. If we lost the New Testament and retained these 22 verses we would have everything we needed to understand why we call the Christian message 'the gospel' or 'the good news'. In this brief exposition we will draw out only the central elements in a story that contains layers of meaning that repay detailed study.

The first and most obvious thing to note is that the younger son's request was insulting as well as deeply wounding. He told his father, in effect, that he could not wait till he was dead, so that he might get his part of the estate. At any time and in any culture this kind of conduct would be viewed as reprehensible; in the patriarchal society of the Middle-Eastern village it was unforgivable. The listeners would expect the young son to be banished, penniless, from his father's home. Instead, the father, with a broken heart, divided the inheritance between his two sons, and the young one departed. The thing to observe is that, though the father had given in to the son's monstrous request, the village, too, had been insulted and the prodigal was now a marked man.

The next thing to register is the thinking of the young man at the point of destitution, after wasting his inheritance. The conventional way to understand his inner monologue is as a moment of repentance. The text suggests that it was a calculated act of self-preservation. He reminded himself that on his father's estate there was need for many workers. Maybe his father would employ him if he were suitably ingratiating, so he made up a little speech: 'Father, I have sinned against heaven and before you; I am no longer worthy to be called your son; treat me as one of your hired hands – please, give me a job.' First, however, he had to get through the village to his father. By insulting his father, he had brought shame on the village. If the village got to him before he reached his father he would be in deep trouble. He would be shunned as an outcast, no help would be given to him and he would be sent back into exile. He was already on the point of starvation, so the moment of return to the village would be the point of greatest danger.

Here we come to the heart of the parable. We are told that the father, seeing him at a distance, *ran* to meet him. The meaning of any story is in the detail and this is a profoundly important detail. The higher a man's status was in this culture, the *slower* he moved. Running or rushing was undignified; it might expose a man's legs to common view – a profoundly shaming possibility. The father's action was an abandonment of patriarchal dignity. To save his son from the wrath of the village he humiliated himself and rushed to welcome the prodigal home. It was this action, this act of self-emptying, that finally changed the attitude of the son. His prepared speech, the self-preserving pieties he had strung together in his mind, now became a genuine act of repentance. He owned and confessed his bad behaviour *and did not ask for a job.* This brings us to the scandalous heart of the message of Jesus: the Father's forgiveness *precedes* our repentance and is its cause. It was his recognition of the father's broken-hearted love for him that changed the prodigal from selfish calculation to genuine repentance. We love, we become able to love, when we know we are first loved. It is the security of unconditional love that burns through all our destructiveness and defensive anger and changes our hearts. God's acceptance of us, in spite of all we know against ourselves, is the cause, not the result of our repentance. This word 'repentance' is interesting in this context. It means a real change of mind, not a calculated pretence of change, nor the adoption of a form of words that might suggest change, but an actual event in the mind and heart that turns our view of reality around.

This is the principle that lies at the centre of the Christian message. It is why we call that message good news. Though its proclamation is primarily about God's act in re-establishing a saving relationship with us, it is a principle that can be applied to all our relationships, especially those that have been broken by human sin. We can punish people for behaving badly; by all the mechanisms of shame and fear we may even prevent them from behaving badly; but they will only ever become good by a change of heart; and changes of heart are the result of a new way of seeing that is always, in some sense, a gift to the self from the other. This new way of seeing, this change of heart, may be enormously painful – a burning with shame, a piercing recognition of harm done. Even this is part of the gift, part of the new reality; it is the necessary prelude to the deeper changes in the personality that follow from the initial recognition. It seems, sadly, to be the case that the sinners of passion and excess, the ones who lack self-control and whose sins are all too obvious to themselves and everyone else, are more likely to recognize the gift of unconditional love when it is offered to them than those whose sins are at the more spiritual or intellectual end of the scale. This is why the kind of people whom the Prayer Book describes as 'open and notorious sinners' flocked round Jesus, while the people who led apparently ordered lives despised him. The other brother in the parable is a good example of this phenomenon.

His disorders were less visible than those of his scapegrace brother; spiritual arrogance usually is. If the young brother did the wrong thing for the wrong reason, the elder seems to have done the right thing for the wrong reason. We can safely guess that his filial obedience was not based on spontaneous love. No more than the prodigal did he really understand the gift of the father's love. He, too, ended by insulting his father and publicly humiliating him. To refuse to enter his father's house during a public banquet and greet him respectfully was insolently insulting. Again, it was the father who took the initiative. His love for this son was also unconditional. He ignored the insult and abandoned his own patriarchal dignity in the face of his friends by *going out* to plead with his son. We do not know how the elder brother responded. We do not know if the father's loving forgiveness caused him to repent of his hard-heartedness. We are not told because the parable is not ended. It is still addressed to us.

In Jesus' relationship with Peter we see the parable of the prodigal son in action. The response of Jesus to Peter's betrayal was consistent with the compassion of the father for human weakness. There is no word of reproach for Peter in scripture, but at the end of John's Gospel there is a moving scene where Jesus sought not the withdrawal of Peter's denials but the reaffirmation of his abiding love for the man he had deserted:

> When they had finished breakfast, Jesus said to Simon Peter, 'Simon son of John, do you love me more than these?' He said to him, 'Yes, Lord; you know that I love you.' Jesus said to him, 'Feed my lambs.' A second time he said to him, 'Simon son of John, do you love me?' He said to him, 'Yes, Lord; you know that I love you.' Jesus said to him, 'Tend my sheep.' He said to him the third time, 'Simon son of John, do you love me?' Peter felt hurt because he said to him the third time, 'Do you love me?' And he said to him, 'Lord, you know everything; you know that I love you.' Jesus said to him, 'Feed my sheep.'

> (John 21:15–17)

This side of Jesus' teaching and person responds to one side of our condition. We want to be understood in our failures, not denounced, because we spend so much time denouncing ourselves to ourselves,

drowning in our own guilt, wallowing in self-abasement. In our insecurity what we need, if we are to make any progress, is unconditional
acceptance, not judgement. We dimly perceive that we won't make
any moral progress until we are accepted absolutely as we are, and are
led lovingly from where we are to where we long to be. The unconditional love and acceptance that Jesus exemplified is the insight that
lies behind the best of modern therapeutic methods, especially in
dealing with the terrible dependencies in which human beings trap
themselves. This is the grace that lies behind Alcoholics Anonymous
and many of the approaches that have been based upon its insights. A
rigorous honesty is required, of course, but there is no moralizing, no
preaching. Instead, there is acceptance of people in their actual state.
This is also the attitude that characterizes modern counselling methods,
where the counsellor does not impose a value system on the persons
counselled, but creates an atmosphere of trust and acceptance that
allows them to grow in self-acceptance and human maturity.

The mechanism that Christians call grace or unconditional love
is an extraordinary discovery in a universe that could easily be interpreted as a jungle, in which the race goes to the fleetest, the decision
to the strongest. Here we have an extraordinary leap, a moral and
spiritual evolution that recognizes and sympathizes with the unfit and
the weak and accompanies them in their condition. Another way in
which the New Testament proclaims this is by its assertion that Jesus
died for us not in our goodness, but in our sinfulness:

> For while we were still weak, at the right time Christ died
> for the ungodly. Indeed, rarely will anyone die for a right-
> eous person – though perhaps for a good person someone
> might actually dare to die. But God proves his love for us
> in that while we still were sinners Christ died for us.

> (Romans 5:6–8)

That, of course, deals with only one side of the paradox of the
human character. It responds to one side of our nature and speaks
of one side of the message and example of Jesus. Though it is the
foundational principle of Christianity, it is incomplete. We want to
be understood, forgiven, accepted utterly as we are. We also want
to be transformed. We want to grow. It is here that Jesus of
Nazareth, who consoles us in our weakness, sets before us and

exemplifies in his person a level of goodness that challenges us and haunts us with its sublimity and perfection. It calls upon us to love our enemies; to do good to those who would do evil to us; to give more than we are asked for; to go the second mile; to be merciful, gentle, pure, unself-regarding; to be bold in our pursuit of righteousness, valiant for truth. The heart of this message is found in a body of teaching that is called the Sermon on the Mount:

> When Jesus saw the crowds, he went up the mountain; and after he sat down, his disciples came to him. Then he began to speak, and taught them, saying:
>
> 'Blessed are the poor in spirit, for theirs is the kingdom of heaven.
>
> 'Blessed are those who mourn, for they will be comforted.
>
> 'Blessed are the meek, for they will inherit the earth.
>
> 'Blessed are those who hunger and thirst for righteousness, for they will be filled.
>
> 'Blessed are the merciful, for they will receive mercy.
>
> 'Blessed are the pure in heart, for they will see God.
>
> 'Blessed are the peacemakers, for they will be called children of God.
>
> 'Blessed are those who are persecuted for righteousness' sake, for theirs is the kingdom of heaven.
>
> 'Blessed are you when people revile you and persecute you and utter all kinds of evil against you falsely on my account. Rejoice and be glad, for your reward is great in heaven, for in the same way they persecuted the prophets who were before you.
>
> 'You are the salt of the earth; but if salt has lost its taste, how can its saltiness be restored? It is no longer good for anything, but is thrown out and trampled under foot.
>
> 'You are the light of the world. A city built on a hill cannot be hid. No one after lighting a lamp puts it under the bushel basket, but on the lampstand, and it gives light to all in the house. In the same way, let your light shine before others, so that they may see your good works and give glory to your Father in heaven.'

(Matthew 5:1–16)

DANCING ON THE EDGE

A version of the same material (this time delivered in a field) is found in Luke 6. It is a systematic reversal of competitive values. It turns selfish aspirations and ambitions upside down and calls the resulting condition 'blessed' or 'happy'. It is a haunting standard of perfection that goes far beyond mere respectability or moderate goodness and calls us to a level of spiritual and moral heroism that has haunted some of the noblest souls in history. It places before us an ideal of a sanctified human community, the society of the Beatitudes, that reverses the trend of human history. In this new society, called by Jesus the Kingdom of Heaven, there would be no outcasts, no enemies, no exploiters or exploited, but a society of mutual love. Knowing that people who try to live like this usually end up on crosses only increases its appeal, its power to cut us to the heart with longing as well as shame. Those of us who try to follow this way find it a tormenting comfort, a consoling torture. We feel ourselves accepted utterly as we are, yet called to a different way of being that requires a level of self-giving which we know is humanly achievable, though rarely, alas, by us.

2

Many people claim to be attracted to the teaching and example of Jesus of Nazareth. They respond affectionately to his compassion; they admire his courage and passion for justice. They do not like hypocrisy, and in the words of Jesus they find the most biting challenge to human hypocrisy ever made. They see it in his cartoon of the ostentatiously religious who, before going up to the temple to give alms, hire the local brass band to accompany them. They cannot forget his image of human self-deception in the picture of the man with a large wooden beam sticking out of his eye, who is warning his brother that a speck of sawdust has just entered his. There was anger in Jesus, but it was not the neurotic anger that characterizes many of us, in our defensiveness and insecurity. This is the anger of the hurt child, the anger of the person ignored or damaged. In Jesus, anger was objective; it was anger for others, at the way the mighty manipulated, ignored or oppressed them. His approach to human values was the opposite of the modern materialist approach, with its appeal to cupidity and competitiveness that generate extraordinary successes and dramatic failures, dividing society into winners and losers in the process.

If we want to take Jesus of Nazareth seriously we have to explore the claims he made about the origin of his insights, the source of his anger and the heart of his compassion. Jesus was compelled by his relationship with the divine mystery to do and say what he did. He claimed to be expressing the anger and compassion of God. This is why the author of the Gospel of John, in thinking upon the meaning of Jesus, begins his account with a metaphysical meditation. In his amazement at the insights and power behind the words of Jesus he comes up with an image of Jesus as the Word of God, as the expression in a human life of the mind, the thinking, the values of God. What God was the Word was, he tells us. Christians call this identity between Jesus and God the Incarnation, from the phrase in John 1 where the author tells us that the Word of God, the Creative Mind of God, which existed 'from the beginning', came into history, 'and was made flesh' in Jesus. Christians understand the doctrine of the Incarnation in a quite specific way, but the principle characterizes most religious systems of any subtlety. In most of them there is a tradition of particularly gifted souls who are the bearers of divine insight, of news from the mystery that tantalizes us, and who offer us glimpses of the divine reality revealed in human form. The writers of the Gospels are not metaphysicians; they are not given to speculative philosophical thought, and they struggle to account for the fact that they experienced an identity between the fact of God and the fact of Jesus of Nazareth. His words and example had for them the power of divine command and example. They heard through the words of the man of Nazareth a divinely compelling demand. This is the experience that lies behind the attempts by Christianity to define the nature of Jesus of Nazareth in his relationship with God.

We need not contend for any particular theory of the bond between Jesus and God. Theological theorizing is rarely spiritually productive. What we ought to realize is that whatever theory we adopt, whatever propositions we use, it will be sterile and damaging, unless we can get back to that original sense of astonishment. What Jesus stood for had enormous intrinsic power. It compelled people, it converted them, it turned them around; or it angered them so powerfully that they worked murderously against him. Those who followed him – often in spite of themselves, and rarely with complete success or conviction, and sometimes just doggedly, like Peter – felt they were responding to the very nature of things, the very mystery behind the universe, to what Dante called 'the love that moved the sun and the other stars'. They felt that the God they had sought to understand had been expressed with disturbing clarity in this human life. This astonishing recognition led them to elaborate and mythify many aspects of the life of Jesus of Nazareth. It is important not to be too obsessed by the detail of the embroidery, but to hold to the central astonishment.

John V. Taylor boldly inverts the usual way of talking about Jesus. Rather than following the traditional line that Jesus reflected or expressed the image of God, he prefers to talk about the Christlikeness of God. It is through Jesus called Christ that we know what God is like. God is compassionate and merciful, utterly forgiving, unconditionally loving, just like Christ; and God is overpowering in his anger at injustice and oppression, at the grinding of the faces of his little ones, just like Christ. God, like Christ, is scathing about the hypocrisies of the religiously deluded, the judgers and condemners, the ones who heap great burdens upon God's children, because they do not understand the source of their own hatred and fear. This Christlike God accepts us utterly in our frailty and impotence; yet those who penetrate most deeply to the heart of the divine mercy feel most acutely the torment of the divine demand and know themselves called to the way of obedience, as well as to the way of consolation.

In Christian experience, the mystery intensifies and our encounter with God becomes threefold. There is the sense of the originating reality, the great mystery that sustains the universe. This ground of being, this mystery behind all mysteries, is expressed in the life of Jesus of Nazareth. So powerful is this life, so compelling in its urgent demand upon those who follow it, that they identify it with the divine mystery. By a leap of intuitive genius, they identify the nature that has so baffled them with this nature. The mystery that fascinates them, according to the Christian claim, is Christlike in its nature: what the Word is God is. Even that leap of identification is not the end. Those who commit themselves to this way of knowing God feel themselves accompanied in their own struggles by the God made known in Jesus of Nazareth. They use the language of spirit to describe the experience of being companioned on the way, empowered and strengthened by the divine love they have found in Jesus.

It is this complex human experience that lies behind the Christian symbol of God as Trinity. The mathematical conundrum of a reality that is one in three or three in one is baffling, if taken literally, so it is important to understand that when we use this kind of language we are using it allusively, not arithmetically. We are describing our experience of the divine mystery; we are trying to talk honestly about how we have known God; we are not trying to create a metaphysic for its own sake. The Christian experience of God as Trinity, as divine community, is of profound practical importance. It is the basis of the claims we make about human community.

Christians use the word 'revelation' to describe these insights. They are not made up; they are discovered, in the same way that mathematicians of genius discover the structure of reality and allow it to invade their minds and be expressed through them with pencil on paper. The claim that is made by Christians is that behind the immensity of the universe, this great explosion of being, is a divine reality whose life is one of eternal mutuality and self-giving, one of communion.

This apparently abstract metaphysic has solid political and social implications. We see something of the mystery of sharing, of going forth from the self towards others, that is the answer to the ancient philosophical question: Why is there something and not just nothing? Faith finds the answer in the nature of God as self-giving love. Trinity calls us to communion, to community, to giving for the sake of the other. At the heart of the mystery of the cosmos there seems to be a law of sacrifice. We know that we are made from the dust of carbon deposits of burned-out stars. Their destruction created the conditions that allowed life forms to emerge in our planet. This same principle might account for much that troubles us in the history of the world. Life on our planet could be described as a giant food chain: we live off one another, we are dependent on one another and we need to die that others might live. The pain and anguish of the process seem to be the price we pay for life itself, and they ought to prompt us to sympathy with all that lives.

This is a tragic insight we seem to have lost in the technological societies of the West, where we are distant from nature and have little sense of reverencing it, of belonging to it. It is the so-called primitive societies that understood the sacrificial relationship between themselves and nature. The Aboriginal religion of

Australia and the religion of Native Americans have more sensitivity to this mutuality, this reverence for the creation. We see it in the natural compassion of the hunter, who seeks the forgiveness of the deer as he sends the arrow into its heart. There is a poem by Conway Powers that captures this tragic yet beautiful symbiosis:

> We are all bowmen in this place.
> The pattern of the birds against the sky
> Our arrows over print, and then they die.
> But it is also common to our race
> That when the birds fall down we weep.
> Reason's a thing we dimly see in sleep.[4]

If there is meaning in the universe could it not be seen, however tragically, along this line: the divine mystery pours itself into a universe that, however distortedly, reflects the divine pattern of self-sacrifice and mutuality. This planet of ours, a mote of dust in the vastness of interstellar space, becomes a laboratory for the emergence of human community after billions of years of evolutionary struggle and sacrifice, so that as we look at the extraordinary story we are filled with a sort of exhilarated humility.

I often think of the sacrifices my mother made so that I could be educated. She took two jobs – one scrubbing office floors at the crack of dawn, and the other in a fruit shop from nine till five – in order to help me study for the ministry. Parents make these sacrifices with love. Sometimes love and duty call us to make the supreme sacrifice. As we weep at all the loss and dying, we should also recognize that it is the law of life itself, the law that gave us being. It should purge us of arrogance and contempt for others, especially those weaker or less intelligent than ourselves. It should fill us with a passionate gentleness, especially towards those who are thrown to the furthest edges by the selfish energies of society. It is the Christlike pattern that asserts itself, the pattern of absolute understanding and acceptance, conjoined to absolute demand. The Christian terms for this potent combination are 'forgiveness' and 'sanctification'. We are constantly, endlessly, unfailingly, unconditionally forgiven; but we are relentlessly drawn to the life of holiness, sacrifice and self-surrender. Others gave their lives for us; should we not give our lives for others? We have been forgiven, should not we also forgive? The mystery of being has shared its being with us;

should we not also share the substance of our being with others? The Christian understanding of God is not abstract mathematics; it is a revolutionary insight that provokes extraordinary responses from men and women; and it is the revolutionary insight that matters, not the status of the language we use to express it.

There is an ancient Christian vocabulary that has tried to capture these inexpressible realities. As we have already noticed, the technical term for this use of language is 'metaphor'. We convey the truth we can't quite express by using one that is available to us. Jesus did it constantly in his use of parable and simile. Theological metaphor is the poetry of God. Much of it has lost its surprise and has been used wrongly by insecure believers as code and password to test the authenticity of others. Theology, talk about God, has been used as a way of dividing rather than uniting and illuminating people, yet most believers who examine their own history of faith will recognize the many ways in which the uses have changed and the metaphors have gone in and out of fashion. The Scottish theologian John McQuarrie defines God as the mystery that lets us be. God lets the universe be. Maybe the phrase is too passive. Maybe something more passionate was the spur, some eternal instinct of generosity that went forth from itself. That may explain the longings we feel, as well as the sense of loss; it may account for the recognitions, the regrets and the prayers that thrust themselves upon us. Some great self-giving love seems to haunt the universe.

CHAPTER THREE

Is God a Fundamentalist?

I

I was a student in the United States in 1968. It was an apocalyptic year in Western politics, especially in the USA. Just
before I was due to graduate, universities throughout the
country erupted in protest and violence. There was a combination of
factors involved, but the main one was the Vietnam war. It was a war
that polarized American public opinion, divided families and alienated
the young, especially the students. I watched with appalled fascination
as riots erupted in city after city. Martin Luther King was assassinated;
President Johnson announced his resignation; and Robert
Kennedy sought the Democratic nomination. Most people can
remember where they were on 22 November 1963 when President
John F. Kennedy was assassinated. I can remember where I was when
his brother Robert was shot. At 6.30 a.m. on 5 June 1968 I turned on
the radio in the Barth Hotel, Denver, Colorado, where I had spent
the night, and heard that Robert Kennedy had been shot in Los
Angeles the day before. I spent the next night on the train to San
Francisco and discovered at breakfast that he had died. When I
reached San Francisco I went into Grace Cathedral on Nob Hill to
pray. In front of the altar they had placed the Stars and Stripes, draped
in black, between two candles. Like many people that weekend, I
found myself crying – not only for Kennedy, but for all of us and for
everything. Something about Robert Kennedy had attracted me as
his campaign had developed. Like all the Kennedys, he was a complex
and opportunistic figure, but I think he became increasingly gripped
by a vision of what America could be like, or what it ought to be like.
It was a society divided by race, by class and by its attitude to this terrible war in Vietnam that seemed endless and beyond resolution.
American commentators, with their capacity for illuminating

metaphor, were now calling the war 'the big muddy'. Kennedy became increasingly visionary as he sped around the country calling on people to embark on a great crusade to build a just and perfect society. He would cry out, 'Some men see things as they are and say, "Why?" I dream of things that never were and say, "Why not?"'

I do not know if Robert Kennedy would have delivered his dream, but I do know that he had become captured by it. He became a type: the visionary, the man of the future, who strives to build a better world. Human history throws up different types of men and women, and classifying the types is a diverting and instructive exercise. For instance, there are writers who set down what they see with enormous compassion towards the blind actors in the human drama, and there are others who raise a great cry against the evils and injustices of history. In a strange way this dichotomy corresponds to the paradox of the divine response we noted in the last chapter: the understanding and forgiveness of God for our frailties, and the anger of God at our folly and cruelty.

There is another categorization or typology that is worth noting, though it is probably more political than theological or literary. This is the distinction between conservatives, especially romantic conservatives, and progressives; between people who look back with almost unbearable nostalgia to a vanished golden age, and people who look forward with almost unbearable longing to a perfected society. There is a parallel between this distinction and the theological paradox of original sin and original righteousness, the defining of humanity by its potentiality for good or its proclivity towards evil. If we emphasize original sin, our capacity to get things wrong, then we are likely to be conservatives who hark back to an imagined time of stability, a previous golden age. If we tend to affirm the good possibilities of human nature, then we are more likely to be progressives, looking forward to a reformed society, one in which justice will prevail.

Each tendency has its own peculiar temptations and pathologies, but I want to concentrate on the pathology of conservatism, the danger inherent in our nostalgia for an imagined golden age. One British writer who exemplified this tendency to a fascinating degree is Evelyn Waugh. All his life he sought permanence. Stannard called the second volume of his biography *No Abiding City*, because Waugh was haunted by the desire for stability, for unchanging perfection, for 'the glimpsed good place permanent', as R. S. Thomas put it. It gives to his best writing its unbearable sense of loss, as well as its occasionally crushing nostalgia. It also accounts for his cruelty and anger, which seemed to be aimed at time itself. It was time he mourned, time he sought somehow to arrest. We find the same mood in Shakespeare, more tenderly expressed. It is worth leafing through the *Sonnets* to see how he spoke of his great obsession, 'Devouring time; swift footed time; old time; unswept stone besmirched with sluttish time; time's fell hand; time's thievish progress.'[1]

Waugh sought his elusive permanence in a highly idealized fantasy of the English aristocracy, powerfully and movingly portrayed in *Brideshead Revisited*. He sought it in the great Roman Catholic Church, to which he converted as a young man, and found, to his subsequent dismay that it, too, was subject to change and entered a period of rapid transition after the Second Vatican Council. He even sought permanence in the English language, and bitterly regretted any understanding of it as dynamic, which was one reason why he had a snobbish contempt for American English, with its creativity and irreverence. Waugh never found his 'good place permanent' in this life, or in any of the institutions of history that are so obviously creatures of time and subject to its laws. He might well have meditated on the words of another conservative romantic, C. S. Lewis. He, too, resisted change and refused to call it progress, but he was better than Evelyn Waugh at seeing that the previous imagined perfect place was itself transient and fleeting. Lewis saw behind this longing for permanence and beauty our longing for God. In a famous sermon in Oxford called 'The Weight of Glory' he said this:

> The books or the music in which we thought the beauty was located will betray us if we trust to them; it was not *in* them, it only came *through* them, and what came through them was longing ... They are not the thing itself; they are only the scent of a flower we have not found, the echo of a tune we have not heard, news from a country we have never yet visited.[2]

This important quotation from Lewis points to the fundamental truth we have already noted, which is the provisionality of all systems, religious or secular, as well as their symbols and instruments. The glory may come through them but is not to be identified with them. All sorts of things can mediate meaning, mediate the divine, but they are not themselves the meaning, not themselves divine. Our difficulty is that what we long for, whether it is beauty or God or any other kind of perfection, seems beyond our understanding, beyond our grasp, as it is in itself, though it clothes itself in form so that we can apprehend something of its meaning. Whatever it is comes through the music or the book or the flash of significance, but they are not the thing itself. Since we cannot live without these mediating signs, these mechanisms of glory, our temptation is to sacralize the vehicle, make holy the thing that conveyed the holy, make absolute the transient object that carried the glimpse of the unchanging reality that haunts us.

This dangerous but almost unavoidable absolutizing of created realities is what the Bible calls idolatry. Anything can become an idol. Idolatry is to make the relative absolute, to make the contingent final. It is to take something that is created and offer it a loyalty that nothing created can bear. It is to give divine authority to things that are not divine, even though they may on occasion have been instruments of the divine. The motive for idolatry is understandable. It is bred of our deep longing for permanence and security, our inability to live with the whispers and signals we receive and our longing for something loud and positive and overwhelming. Idolatry comes from our anxiety and insecurity, our inability to live by the uncertainties of faith, our loneliness before the elusiveness of God. An idol is the objectification of these needs and anxieties.

The classic text on idolatry is Exodus 32, in which we read of the Israelites' impatience with Moses and the demanding, elusive God he represents. During one of his absences on the Holy Mount the people come to Aaron and say to him: 'Come, make gods for us, who shall go before us; as for this Moses, the man who brought us up out of the land of Egypt, we do not know what has become of him.' In the famous story, Aaron takes earrings from their wives, their sons and their daughters and fashions them into a golden calf and says, 'These are your gods, O Israel, who brought you up out of the land of Egypt!' The idol consoled the children of Israel because it was a controllable object, something they could possess, something they could relate to. They exchanged the loneliness and freedom of the real God for an idol that consoled even as it enslaved.

Another name for this process of dangerous objectification, of giving to created realities, however sacred and important, an absolute

DANCING ON THE EDGE

authority and power, is fundamentalism. The fundamentalist is made anxious by the impermanence of things, the elusiveness and uncontrollability of the life of the spirit in human history. Like magicians, fundamentalists want to control the divine, have power over it, so that they can create an absolute system of knowledge and certainty, the very thing we long for in our anxiety and insecurity. The tragic thing about fundamentalism is that it takes genuinely important, even sacred, things – things that have conveyed meaning and mediated the divine – and turns them into ends; it absolutizes and objectifies them; it converts them into idols.

Many of the things we rely on in our rational and spiritual lives have an unavoidable circularity about them. For instance, the claim that reason puts us in touch with reality is one of our major operating assumptions, and it has turned out to be a very creative assumption. It is a kind of faith or trust. The paradox is, of course, that the only way we can check the claims of reason is by means of reason, so there is an inevitable circularity to the whole process. It is conceivable that reality is other than our minds conceive it to be and that we are deluding ourselves. There is a philosophical position that holds that our perceptions create external reality and that we cannot get in touch with what is out there as it is in itself, but only as we perceive it to be. Whatever line we take on any of these disputed questions, there is a certain irreducibility about our rationality. There is also a sense that we are always begging the question. There should be, in any of our human endeavours, a certain reserve, a certain caution, because we can be so terrifically mistaken. This is very definitely the case in the religious sphere. Religions make assumptions that work for them; but sometimes the assumptions are pushed too far and we get the fundamentalism we have just been talking about. The status of sacred writings is a very good example of this phenomenon.

Most of the great religions have writings, sacred scriptures of one sort or another, and they are variously interpreted and handled. At the most obvious level, we would expect sacred scriptures, writings that have particular spiritual power, to have achieved that status because of their own intrinsic authority. They work because they work: they actually challenge people, compel their assent, illuminate their thinking, humble them, inspire them, move them, comfort them. Sacred writings do all of these things. The test is pragmatic. We reverence them because they are reverenceable. They have *intrinsic* authority and need no external authority to compel us to reverence them. They themselves draw reverence from us. This is the secret of their power. We don't need to be told, for instance, that we should pay attention to the parables of Jesus. When we hear them they compel our attention. They have no need of an extrinsic authority, ordering us to listen to them. They have authority in their own right. We know a lot about the history of the scriptures of the different religions and particularly about the Bible. Whatever spiritual authority we think it has, or however clearly it speaks to us of God, the Bible actually had a human history and we know something about it. The Old and New Testaments were put together at different times by different people, and most of the authors are unknown to us. In the case of the New Testament, it took several hundred years for the Church to decide what to leave in and what to take out. The New Testament is the creation of the Church.

H. M. Kuitert, a professor in the Free University of Amsterdam, says a number of helpful and provocative things about the Bible. He makes the obvious point that it is not one book but a collection of books, covering a period of more than twelve centuries:

> Now as surely as the people who told their stories or wrote them down didn't have the ideas we do now, there is variation and even development within the books of the Bible. The Bible isn't a statue hewn out of one stone but rather a mosaic, a composition. That makes reading it extraordinarily exciting.[3]

He goes on to reflect on one of the most common views of the Bible, which is that the Holy Spirit of God inspired holy men to put into writing what God gave them. There are various versions of this approach, from the theory of automatic writing to a more organic theory, whereby the authors are in control of what they write but are inspired by God to express the divine mind. This theory of the inspiration of the Bible has been criticized in a number of ways recently and it has provoked a crisis for some groups of Protestant Christians, for whom the Bible plays something of the same role that the Pope plays in the Roman Catholic Church, as a source of absolute authority. Abandoning this view leaves us in the air with no certainty. Professor Kuitert says some interesting things about this approach:

This view of the Bible denatures belief, because it makes the certainty of faith rest on a theory about the Bible, namely its inspired character. If people can't cope with an aspect of Christian tradition, then they have to accept it nevertheless 'because it's in the Bible'. That's really to stand things on their heads: we don't believe because something is in the Bible but because it affects us, makes us think or whatever. Certainty isn't rooted in a theory but in the Word that is addressed to us.[4]

He goes on to point out that this hard theory of scriptural inspiration cannot bear the burden that is placed upon it, because it is itself a statement of faith. He writes:

The statement 'the Bible is the word of God inspired by the spirit' is of precisely the same order as 'Jesus is God's son' or 'God is gracious and merciful'. It can't both be a statement of faith and at the same time a foundation for one. The Bible isn't the firm ground on which faith is anchored: the firm ground is God.[5]

He goes on to inform us that the Bible contains what Israel thought of God and what the evangelists thought about Jesus. He asks:

Why do we attach belief to what Israel and the apostles say about God? Because it makes an impression on us, because we can make something of it, because it does something to us, makes us clear about ourselves or however you care to put it. Those who believe, believe in what they find in the Bible and what is in it. The content of the Bible makes the book important and not vice versa; it isn't as if what is in it is important because it's in the Bible.[6]

The Church had a whole period without a book, with oral tradition before it became a text, so the Christian Church comes before the Bible and itself established its extent and composition. The Bible and the creative Word of God are not the same thing, though people of faith claim that the Bible contains the Word of God, or is one of the places where we encounter God. It is important to remember that the Church was there before the Bible, because this makes it clear that the

Bible is not definitive for Christians in the way that the Koran is definitive for Muslims. The Bible is part of the tradition of the Church, it is one of the ways in which the Christian experience of God has been provisionally expressed. This is why Christians claim that their faith is based upon a living word, the man Jesus, not upon a written word, though the written word does bear important witness to him.

The power of the Bible lies in its intrinsic authority and because, in Kuitert's language, it is the oldest and most widespread form of the Christian puzzle-picture of God. Then he offers an interesting analogy. He compares it with the maps that Vasco da Gama had at his disposal when he tried to sail round South America to the Pacific Ocean. The maps had authority for him because they actually showed him the way, they corresponded to the conditions he encountered. The maps were authoritative not because they had been pronounced so by king or emperor, but because they actually worked.

Like the maps used by Vasco da Gama, the Bible is still a useful guide, but we have to recognize that it is a creature of its time. It is a bit like maps of road systems that are not completely up to date: they are still useful on the old roads, but they are little or no help in dealing with motorways or brand-new ring-roads round our cities. If we try to negotiate a new system of roads round a city with an old map we will get seriously confused. The same thing is true of the Bible, particularly in its moral systems. The morality of the Bible is time conditioned, male centred and patriarchal. For instance, polygamy is a sign of wealth and the person who can count lots of wives is blessed by God. Slaves are allowed as long as they are treated reasonably. Most people, even those who claim to believe in the literal inerrancy of the Bible, make choices in their use of it. They rarely subscribe to the stringent dietary provisions of the Book of Leviticus, though they may claim that the Ten Commandments are timeless in their authority. Even here things are not as straightforward as they might appear. The beauty of the Bible is that it shows us a serious people seriously evolving appropriate moral structures for their day. That gives us confidence to do the same; but to claim to be able to read out from the Old Testament a timeless moral code is problematic. Let us look at the commandment which most people would claim has abiding authority, commandment number seven − 'Thou shalt not commit adultery.' The force of this commandment is very different in our culture to what it was at the time of its promulgation. First of all, in the Old Testament, it is addressed only to the male, and the male was allowed to do much in

the sexual sphere in that culture: he could have several wives and con-
cubines; he could even throw out his wife. What he was *not* allowed to
do – and this is the precise focus of the commandment – was to use
another man's sexual property. Adultery was stealing, making use of
another male's possession, because that was what a wife was. By contrast,
the woman was allowed little or nothing. She was a bit of property in a
male-dominated society. Today the Church would base its opposition
to adultery on different, more consequentialist grounds: it destroys
trust, is productive of enormous human pain and applies to both men
and women. We are forced, as rational creatures seeking human well-
being, to find appropriate moral rules for our own culture that reflect
our own needs, knowledge and understanding. The fact that the tenth
commandment implies that a woman is simply another possession, like
a house or an ox or an ass that is not to be coveted, would suggest that
biblical morality, while it can provide us with useful axioms or general
principles, will not yield a universally compelling moral code. Jesus
himself challenged many of the moral and social structures that were
inherited from Old Testament times, most notably on Sabbath observance. His saying on this subject illustrates the main point, that moralities are made for human flourishing and not the other way round. In
his dispute with the Pharisees about the Sabbath, Jesus famously said
that 'the Sabbath was made for man and not man for the Sabbath.'
With these words he underlined the provisional status of all human
systems, including moral systems. This should not unnerve us.

The fact that moralities change from era to era, if not from generation to generation, is difficult for many people to accept. We have
already seen that one of the ways in which world-views work is by
becoming interiorized, so that individuals accept them, without question, as the way things *are*, not simply as the way things are *done*. We
have already seen that some people are always looking back to an
imagined golden age. This itself is strong evidence that changes in
moral systems and values have always characterized human history.
Calls to return to so-called biblical morality are themselves strongly
ideological and usually emanate from a particular political attitude that
is just another arguable point of view. There is no single moral system
in scripture that we can easily appropriate and apply straightforwardly.
The exciting thing in engaging with the Bible is to discover the timeless truths and separate them from the time-bound elements.

If we look at one or two examples from the time-bound moral
themes in scripture we will recognize that we have already moved far

from them. The most blatant example is the existence of slavery. This was an institution known all over the ancient world. Scripture modified it but made no attempt to eradicate it as a system. Both the Old and the New Testaments encourage slave owners to be kind and considerate to their slaves, but they take the system for granted:

> Let all who are under the yoke of slavery regard their masters as worthy of all honor, so that the name of God and the teaching may not be blasphemed. Those who have believing masters must not be disrespectful to them on the ground that they are members of the church; rather they must serve them all the more, since those who benefit by their service are believers and beloved. Teach and urge these duties.

> (1 Timothy 6:1–2)

In the Letter to Philemon we read that Paul sent a runaway slave back to his master, hoping that his conversion to Christianity would improve the relationship. The interesting thing to note is that Paul does not feel that the Christian gospel itself challenges slavery as an institution, as a moral system. This tolerance of an obvious evil continued for centuries. The African slave trade, in particular, had the support of the Church. A bull of Pope Nicholas V instructed his followers to 'attack, subject, and reduce to perpetual slavery the Saracens, Pagans and other enemies of Christ, southward from Cape Bojador and including all the coast of Guinea.'

A more modern example of moral evolution is provided by the status of women. We have already alluded to the fact that women had few rights in Old Testament culture. They were the property of their fathers until they were contracted to become the property of their husbands. This is why it is difficult for us, living in a very different social system, with very diverse values and aspirations, to agree with the Bible's regulations for managing relations between men and women. They were written for a culture that is totally alien to ours. The thing to note here is that the community of faith in any age seems to accept most of the going moral structures of the day, and operates within them. When we study Church history we discover that this has been the case. Every society needs an accepted set of moral norms and systems. They act to bind society together and maintain some kind of order in its life. But these systems are themselves arbitrary and provisional. It is no accident that the word that lies behind our word 'moral' also means 'custom'. Moral customs and moral systems have varied from culture to culture. We need a moral system in the same way as we need a highway code; but in some countries they drive on the right and in some countries they drive on the left. What matters is that the particular country accepts the system and operates within it. Moral systems are obviously provisional and they do change. The way they change is usually by the pressure of new knowledge upon previously unquestioned moral assumptions and by the pressure of prophetic individuals who see to the flawed heart of human systems and challenge their fairness and justice. This is what happened in the case of slavery. It is what happened in the case of the institutionalized subordination of women. It is what happened in the industrialization of child labour and child prostitution, and many of the other aspects of the allegedly highly moral Victorian culture.

We face moral challenges in our day that were unthinkable to previous generations. The most obvious and revolutionary one in our own era has been the invention of reliable methods of contraception. This has totally altered human attitudes to sex, a subject we shall return to in later chapters. Sex that is free from the consequences of conception will be thought of very differently from sex that almost invariably leads to it. More immediately current, and extremely painful to deal with, are the ethical challenges that modern medicine places before us, such as genetic engineering and the new reproductive technologies. The evolution of human knowledge, for better or for worse, presents us with new moral challenges, and we have to work out systems so that we can live with them and make sense of them.

It is usually very difficult for people from conservative religious groups to see how dynamic and revolutionary moral systems are. It is particularly hard for them to acknowledge that the faith communities to which they belong absorb many of the conventional and accepted standards of the day from the surrounding culture, but this is certainly the case. The Christian Church, for instance, has offered support to political systems that we would now see as unjust, and to social institutions that we would now see as evil. This is where Christianity, when radically understood, overturns many of our conventional ideas. Moral systems reflect and influence the different stages of human development. They are what Paul called Law. We need Law but we must not treat it as absolute and objective; we must be prepared to alter it, to judge it inadequate, sometimes even unjust. It is important to make a fundamental distinction here. Moral systems are invented and applied for the sake of humanity. We must not make the mistake of thinking that God commands our systems for his sake. They may order and organize our relationships with each other and with society; it is quite a different matter to claim that they also serve to govern our relationship with God. We have already looked at a revolutionary doctrine embedded in the New Testament that is so explosive that it has never been fully accepted. It is Paul's doctrine of justification by faith. Paul himself was a moralist and strongly favoured right conduct of the sort he held to be important, but he was also a religious visionary and theological genius, and he penetrated to the revolutionary heart of Christ's work. He recognized that God's gift of grace is freely offered to us while we are yet sinners, while we are making a mess of things, as we invariably and inevitably do, and that we must not use human systems as analogies for our relationship with God. But that is precisely what we do. That is why people were horrified by Jesus' parable of the labourers in the vineyard; to give all the workers the same wage was obviously contrary to any sane, legal system of industrial relations. Yet Jesus said it indicated God's absolute favouritism to us all, that we are all given the same unmerited love and grace. God certainly has ambitions for us, but they are better defined by the word 'holiness' than by the term 'morality'. Morality, however appropriately and carefully practised, usually conveys a sense of conformity to an abstract law or principle, and it is always possible to put the principle before the person – to take an example from the story of Jesus, to put Sabbath observance before human need. Holiness, which is another word for 'God-likeness', operates intuitively, not formally, and penetrates instinctively and fearlessly to the heart of human need. It recognizes that all human moral systems should be contingent upon human well-being and may have to be revised accordingly. It is hard for people who claim to get their moral systems through religious revelation to recognize that even these are revisable, and that the Bible itself confronts us with situations where God's word corrects itself. The moral radicalism of Jesus is the most powerful example of this, but we find the same thing going on in the life of the earliest Christian community. An interesting example of divine revisionism is found in Acts 10. Peter is wrestling in his mind with the issue of the admission of Gentiles to the young Church, the first of many controversies in Christian theological history. The matter is theologically resolved for him by a dream he has at Joppa, in which he hears God telling him to kill and eat certain creatures that were condemned as unclean by Old Testament dietary laws. Peter's refusal is countered by the divine voice: 'It is not for you to call profane what God counts clean' (Acts 10:15, *Revised English Bible*). The important thing to grasp here is that moral systems are important, and wise communities struggle to inculcate them for the sake of social cohesion and stability. The paradox is that the more successful they are, the greater are the dangers they run, because tradition elevates them above criticism and moral changes induce anxiety in people. This is why the role of the prophet is always dangerous and frequently leads to persecution and death. Achieving the moral versatility to operate a value-system without being enslaved by it is extremely difficult and can only be achieved if we place the category of the personal above that of abstract principle. Human needs vary throughout history, whereas the principles we develop to assist those needs tend to be less mobile and versatile and can end by being the enemy rather than the friend of human flourishing. Unfortunately, traditional Christianity has over-played its moral hand and has given people the impression that getting their morality right is what qualifies them for God's favour. This catches morality in a double-bind: on the one hand, it makes it too important, literally a matter of the difference between Heaven and Hell, so that we follow it to keep out of trouble and not because our heart consents to it; yet on the other hand it trivializes morality by reducing it to something like superstition, a conformity to traditional practices and customs long after they have lost their meaning or usefulness. It is because morality is so important that we must not exaggerate its importance, and we do this when we elevate it above debate by claiming divine authorization for it. If we place it above argument and the test of usefulness, we become its servant and not the other way round. If we treat it as important, but not as of final importance, we can struggle to discover the best morality for our own time. In the introduction to this book we noted the tendency of Christianity to treat too many things as of final moment, rather than as usefully provisional and not, therefore, to be taken too seriously. The paradox is that the essence of the

Christian message is liberatingly simple and should free us from this anxiety.

The central claim of Christianity is that we are accepted in our sinfulness, forgiven and understood as we are, with all our moral confusions, both of intellect and of will; understood when we know the right thing and do not do it, and understood when we do not know what the right thing to do is. God knows, understands, forgives and offers us the divine love, the divine mercy. That is the single most important element in the Christian gospel. It is why we call it good news and not good advice. It is the dramatic claim that, as we know ourselves to be now, we are already loved by God. And yet, as we have already seen, there is also God's great longing to draw us into the divine life, the life of self-giving mutuality and love; to sanctify us, make us Godlike. This is a totally different thing from making us respectable, law-abiding members of the Church. It is important, therefore, to remember that the moral life, which is fundamental to a healthy society and an ordered community, has more to do with our relationships with each other than with our relationship with God, though there is an inevitable tendency to want to claim divine warrant for our moral systems. That is why we constantly need to engage in debate about the best moral systems and to identify where changes can be made, where things can be abandoned, where we should move to overturn old ways and experiment with new ones. This is what human beings have been doing for millennia. We should not lose our nerve or fall into paralysing anxiety, because we are currently in a particularly fast phase of moral transition. It is significant that when Jesus was asked to describe the most important moral commandments he answered with a generality so sweeping that it gives us little precise advice in specific situations, but if we lived by it our behaviour would be radically altered. He told us we are to love God, and love our neighbours as ourselves.

One of the things that characterizes moral debate in history is that people inevitably and appropriately take sides, have their own angles on things, their own point of view. Very few of us are disinterested in this. We support systems that confirm our virtues and ignore our vices, and we tend to identify the vices of our enemies and ignore their virtues. There are two great values in human moral discourse: the value of order and the value of freedom. They frequently conflict, and people tend to characterize themselves by leaning towards one or the other. There are people who prize order highly. They are usually disciplined, sometimes emotionally repressed and not infrequently authoritarian in outlook. These characteristics produce results that are good as well as bad. Stability and regularity are the great virtues of the ordered society. Those who prize the values of freedom, on the other hand, may be less disciplined and more relaxed about things which authoritarians think are fundamental; there may even be a certain laziness in their make-up, but they allow people the space to breathe and the opportunity to develop their individuality. An ideal society would achieve a wise balance between order and freedom, stability and creativity. Unfortunately, we tend to divide ourselves into opposing groups, and rather than co-operate to discover a healthy society that balances the complementary virtues, we tend to opt for one side of the dualism. So the religious right campaigns for a return to a type of moral conformity that is anathema to liberals, who believe that people should be left to behave according to their own desires, as long as they are not engaged in activities that exploit the weak and damage society. There is no doubt that each side of this debate has its strengths and weaknesses. It is being mentioned for one reason only, and that is that the religious right, who support the morality of order in preference to the morality of freedom, claim to be more biblical and Christian than the liberals whom they love to vilify. In fact, there are many liberal values in scripture. Christ himself overturned the accepted moral order of his day. We have already seen that his attitude to moral traditions was radically revisionist: they were made for humanity, not the other way round. It was no accident that he was constantly surrounded by the sort of people whom the defenders of order and discipline repudiated. 'This man receives sinners and eats with them', was the charge against him that prompted his greatest parables in Luke's Gospel. Many of the charges that are levelled against liberals, who are trying to respond to the complexities of human need in today's world, sound very like the attacks made against Jesus by the moral guardians of his culture, for whom the letter of the law was a weapon that killed rather than an aid that assisted suffering humanity. Authoritarian ethical systems invariably fall into this trap, and they seem to attract people in whom the urge to punish is strong, an invariably suspect emotion. In moral debate it is better to offer our programme not because we believe it has been decreed from on high, but because we think it works best and produces the healthiest society. These are claims that can be tested, measured and debated. Once we start invoking God for our point of view, rational argument becomes impossible. History is disfigured with the claims of haters of humankind who have persecuted their brothers and sisters in the name of the man of Nazareth, who told us not to judge, to turn the other cheek, not to throw the first stone and to let the weeds grow alongside the corn. The reason behind Jesus' suggestion that we should not judge others, or that we should leave such judgement to God, is that we can never truly comprehend the full scope of any moral act, including our own. Berdaev, the Russian philosopher, warned us that it is impossible to judge any matter ethically unless it is taken as a unique case, and every human act is a unique case. *We* only see the act and judge it, usually harshly; God sees all the surrounding, attendant and determining circumstances and forgives it. That is why we say that to know all is to forgive all, and only God knows all.

The religious right is particularly obsessed with human sexuality, in contrast to Jesus, who hardly spoke about the subject. There is considerable irony in the fact that those on the religious right are usually great champions of capitalism and the riches it heaps up for them, while they are apparently able to ignore or interpret away the trenchant and damning things Jesus said about the wealthy and the danger of riches. They ignore or reverse the challenge of Jesus on a subject about which he was clearly passionate, while greatly exaggerating the importance of a subject about which he seemed to be hardly exercised. We can be quite certain that were Jesus alive today he would be more interested in what goes on in our boardrooms than in our bedrooms. The current preoccupation with sexuality to the exclusion of weightier moral concerns is itself an interesting psychological phenomenon, which is why a whole section of this book will be dedicated to it. There is no doubt that we have witnessed a disconcertingly rapid re-evaluation of the ethics of sexuality in the last three decades, but the fact is that we have often changed our minds over the years and survived. Every generation is morally selective. There are vices in our current social systems, but there are as many virtues. The Victorians had their virtues; we know now how grim their vices were. We should struggle with confidence to find the best systems for ourselves and our children and apply them with modesty, trusting that if they are good they will commend themselves to healthy-minded people, most of whom, like most of us, are partially deluded and partially committed to the moral life, the good life, the life that helps us all to flourish. We will be restrained in identifying God too closely with our moral traditions, though we will always bear in mind the great imperative to love our neighbours, to seek their good and to take care not to despise God's little ones.

The Bible is full of stories we can use to stimulate our thinking, without expecting them to dictate precisely how we should live or what we should do in our highly complex scientific culture at the end of the second millennium. The important thing to remember is that God accompanies us today, as God accompanied the children of Israel from the morality of being a slave people to the very different morality of being a free people tempted to enslave others. God accompanies us, as God accompanied the Church when it excommunicated emperors and kings, blessed crusades, exterminated peasants and burned witches. We will not, in fact, be over-impressed by the moral record of Christianity, but we *will* acknowledge that, in all generations, God has had his witnesses who have called the Church, and society through the Church, to concentrate on the things that really count. Moralizing is one of the least attractive of human characteristics. The best antidote to it is to measure the gulf between ordinary human respectability and the sanctity of that handful of saints who truly reflect the utter self-giving of God. In the holy we rarely encounter judgement or moralizing. Instead, we feel ourselves to be in the presence of an absolute compassion that accepts us as we are. The paradox is that this level of acceptance and sympathy is so overwhelming that it shows us, more clearly than any moralizer could, our own distance from sanctity and our own longing to be given utterly to some great and good thing. An ounce of sanctity does more good for humanity than a ton of morality. Augustine told us to love God and do what we liked; Hugh Walpole warned us against the fanatics who hate the devil more than they love God; because love, not hatred, is the fulfilling of the law.

CHAPTER FOUR

Why Does God Allow Suffering?

I

The names of certain places enter our language as a result of particularly hideous experiences and become the shorthand of evil: the Black Hole of Calcutta; Devil's Island; Auschwitz. Treblinka was arguably worse than any of these. It was an extermination camp in Poland where hundreds of thousands of Jews were gassed by the Nazis – 18,000 a day when production was at its highest. They came by train from Warsaw. As soon as they arrived at the station they were told to undress and take a shower, and then the gas was turned on. Train load after train load filled the pits at Treblinka with bodies. The Nazis kept a squad of Jewish slaves to clear out the gas chambers and bury the bodies, until they went mad or killed themselves. Few survived Treblinka. One who did has captured the horror of Hitler's Final Solution in a single image. He describes how the Jewish prisoners had to open the doors of the gas chambers and drag the bodies to the grave. He says that sometimes they found living children among the warm bodies – little children, still alive, clinging to their mothers. They strangled them before throwing them into the grave. People who visit Auschwitz say that the thing that most shatters them is the pile of children's shoes. The twentieth century has been one of the bloodiest in human history, and historians disagree with each other as to the most horrific episode. Was it Stalin's policies of extermination and imprisonment? Was it the genocide of the Khmer Rouge in Cambodia? Or was it the Holocaust, the extermination of six million Jews by the Nazis in Europe?

Every two or three years I force myself to read a new book about the Jewish Holocaust. I do it for two reasons. First, as an act of remembrance and solidarity. The second reason is more complicated. As the full scale of the suffering of Jews during the Third Reich became known after the War, it began to alter the way in which thinkers, including theologians, saw the world. The most truthful tore up their systems and said that from now on theology could only be done in the light of the Holocaust. God had to be brought to account. I go on reading about it so that I will not forget. One of the books I read recently was by Primo Levi.

He was an Italian Jew, a chemist and mountaineer. On 22 February 1944 he was sent to Auschwitz with 649 others. Only he and two others survived. He dedicated the rest of his life to meditating upon and writing about his experience. His first book was an account of his time in the camp before it was liberated by the Russian army. He called it *If This Is A Man*, because the whole purpose of the Nazi programme of extermination was to deny the humanity of the prisoners. One of his companions was called Iss Clausner. Levi writes: 'Clausner shows me the bottom of his bowl. Where others have carved their numbers, and Alberto and I our names, Clausner has written: *Ne pas chercher a comprendre.*'[1]

Though we cannot compare it to the Holocaust, for many of us today theology can only be written in the light of the slaughter of the children of Dunblane. Six weeks later in Tasmania an even more horrifying atrocity took place, so theology now has to be done after Dunblane, after Tasmania, though they are minor tragedies compared to the stories of genocide that come from the African continent. Wherever the scene of the horror is, God has to be brought to account.

There are many good intellectual reasons for refusing to believe in the existence of God, but the fact of suffering and the mystery of human evil are probably the most powerful factors in undermining belief. People who are converted from belief, clearly, sometimes heroically, changing their mind about it, as opposed to people who simply drift lazily away from it, are usually forced to it by their inability to maintain belief in God in the face of evil and suffering. According to Richard Dawkins this is what happened to Charles Darwin. 'I cannot persuade myself,' Darwin wrote, 'that a beneficent and omnipotent God would have designedly created the Ichneumonidae with the express intention of their feeding within the living body of caterpillars.' Dawkins goes on:

A female digger wasp not only lays her eggs on a cater-pillar so that her larva can feed on it but she carefully guides her sting into each ganglion of the prey's central nervous system so as to paralyse *but not to kill it*. This way, the meat keeps fresh. It is not known whether the paralysis acts as a general anaesthetic, or if it is like curare in just freezing the victim's ability to move. If the latter, the prey might be aware of being eaten alive from inside but unable to move a muscle to do anything about it. This sounds savagely cruel but nature is not cruel, only pitilessly indifferent. This is one of the hard-est lessons for humans to learn. We cannot admit that things might be neither good nor evil, neither cruel nor kind, but simply callous – indifferent to all suffering, lacking all purpose.[2]

The existence of suffering is a major problem for the believer; indeed, it is really a problem only for the believer, because it raises a difficulty for belief; whereas, for the unbeliever suffering is not a problem, it is simply an unhappy fact, as Dawkins observed. The unbeliever who thinks that the universe is a fact without final meaning sees the horrors of history as a mere detail on a tiny speck in a distant corner of an exploding universe with no one to notice it but us. Our tragedy is that we do notice it. In us the universe has achieved consciousness and watches itself and mourns. This does not mean that the unbeliever is without values or principles and does not engage in efforts to modify the horrors; but the fact of suf-fering is a challenge to the unbeliever's compassion, not to her system of belief; whereas, for believers suffering raises enormous difficul-ties for faith itself. The dilemma has been put in this way: Given the awful facts of history, if God is good, God cannot be almighty; if God is almighty, God cannot be good.

There are sophisticated ways out of this dilemma that may be intellectually satisfying, but they never seem to touch the heart of the difficulty. The oldest religious answer to the problem of suffering is that it is a straightforward punishment for wrongdo-ing. One of the most powerful and puzzling books of the Old Testament wrestles with this answer. It tells the story of a right-eous and prosperous man who loses everything: his family, his possessions, his health. His friends gather round to find out what he has done to provoke such divine anger. Job is convinced he has done nothing to deserve his pain. Since he is righteous and yet suffers, the current theory must be wrong. His friends are outraged at this blasphemous rejection of official theology, and Job is left to debate with God himself. It is an unsatisfactory book from a philosophical point of view, because it ends not with an answer to the problem, but with the realization that we have to learn to live with the mystery of suffering, and bring it to God in trust. Living with unexplained suffering itself becomes part of faith.

No moral justification for suffering can be offered that does not run into difficulties. Some see this life as a vale of soul-making, a spiritual survival course, in which difficulties are sent to test, purify and perfect us. The Hindu doctrine of the transmigration of souls is a version of this approach, and it seems to have a calming effect on Eastern attitudes to suffering. If there are many incarnations in front of us, then we can afford to take the long view and be more relaxed in our attitude towards the tragedies of time. Another ancient answer, which is not inconsistent with the previous view, is the positing of an evil force that is opposed to the reality of God. There are traces of this theory in scripture, though we sometimes read back into scripture notions we pick up from other sources, such as Milton's *Paradise Lost*, where the poet tells the story of Lucifer's rebellion against God in heaven and his descent to earth, over which he roams, tempting the children of God. There is enormous dramatic beauty in this view, and part of its power lies in the fact that it seems to correspond to human experience. Life does often feel like a battle. We seem to be battling against powers of evil within our own hearts, in society and in the spiritual realm. The trouble with dualistic theories of this sort is that everything ends up as God's responsibility, anyway, unless we posit an eternal system of evil that is co-equal with the good God. Christians have resisted that solution, because they prefer to believe that evil is an aspect of created reality, not something that exists in its own right. That is why Augustine defined evil as the absence or deprivation of good. It is certainly the case that really bad people seem to lack a moral sense, a conscience, and the ability to empathize with others.

No matter which approach we adopt, we are always brought back to the same question: Why does God allow it? Here we have to do what we are learning to do with all religious symbols and metaphors. We acknowledge that they are essentially ways of talking about our experience of reality; they have validity if they capture the truth of the way we live, but they are not themselves to be given final status. There is a sense in which all the attitudes to suffering say something useful. Suffering can reduce us to bitterness and misery; but it can refine and purify us, and some people respond to adversity with heroic courage. Though we may not be comfortable with the idea that suffering is divine punishment or discipline, it is undoubtedly true that actions have consequences, and much suffering can be traced back to human choices. The decisions we make, however helplessly, make us into something, good, bad or indifferent. This does not explain the mystery of exactly why we make wrong choices, but it accords with certain aspects of human experience. These echoes from old theories still touch a chord in us. Even the ancient dualistic answer that in the universe death and life are contending, light and darkness are in conflict, evil is arraying itself against good, has about it a certain dramatic appropriateness that we can respond to and make use of.

All of these approaches to the problem of evil come under Dr Arthur Peacocke's model of revisability. He says:

> It is the aim of science to depict reality as best it may. Since this can be only an aim, the critical realist has to accept that it may well meet with varying degrees of success. Models and metaphors are widely used in science but this does not detract from the aim of such language to refer to realities while it does entail that models and metaphors are always in principle revisable.[3]

He goes on to suggest that theology, which is the intellectual formulation of religious beliefs, also employs models which are revisable. This is an important point, and it may be best to use a scientific example to grasp it. Science deals with external reality, but it talks about it symbolically and metaphorically. It is unavoidably engaged in something not unlike theology. It finds ways of describing realities that are too subtle, enormous or mysterious to grasp in their entirety. Professor R. C. Lewontin gives many fascinating examples in his book *The Doctrine of DNA: Biology as Ideology*. In talking about evolutionary theory, he reminds us that for Darwin there was a universal struggle for existence because more organisms were born than could survive and reproduce, and in the course of that struggle the more efficient, better designed, cleverer and stronger organisms survived and left offspring. As a consequence of this victory in the struggle for existence evolutionary change occurred. Lewontin goes on:

> Yet Darwin himself was conscious of the source of his ideas about the struggle for existence. He claimed that the idea for evolution by natural selection occurred to him after reading the famous *Essay on Population* by Thomas Malthus, a late eighteenth-century parson and economist. The essay was an argument against the old English poor law, which Malthus thought too liberal, and in favour of a much stricter control of the poor so that they would not breed and create social unrest. In fact, Darwin's whole theory of evolution by natural selection bears an uncanny resemblance to the political economic theory of early capitalism as developed by the Scottish economists. What Darwin did was take early nineteenth-century *political* economy and expand it to include all of *natural* economy.[4]

The recognition that Darwin used a political metaphor to convey his scientific discoveries does not undermine the value of the discoveries, but it does alert us to the provisional element in anything we say about science and religion. We should not be too committed to our models and metaphors, either scientific or religious, and we should look gratefully on the possibility of employing new, though equally revisable, models if they help us in the task of understanding reality and conveying meaning. This is where some modern scientific work is helpful for believers. We no longer operate with a picture of a static three-decker universe, the model found in the book of Genesis – a universe of fixed natures and defined roles. The picture presented to us by modern physics is of natural processes that are continuously and inherently creative. Life, as we know it, is the result of an unbelievably long process that originated in the Big Bang 15 billion years ago. At that stage everything in the universe, all the matter that now composes billions of stars and billions of galaxies, was a dense mass, so small it could pass through the eye of a needle. From that point it expanded very rapidly. The expansion was so rapid and violent that astronomers coined the phrase 'the Big Bang' to help us think about it. David Wilkinson thinks that the term Big Bang, while suggestive, can make us think of something that creates destruction and disorder. He thinks a better picture might be the blooming of a flower, something that gives rise to order and beauty. We are told that the universe is still expanding. Everything is in dynamic process and new realities go on appearing. This is why Arthur Peacocke believes that we need new models to help us deal with old questions. He says:

> If we are to think of God as creator of such a universe, we are bound to re-emphasise that God is still creating in, with, and under the processes of the natural world. God as creator not only, in this perspective, sustains and pre-serves the world but must now be regarded as continu-ously creating. God is now to be understood as exploring and actualising the potentialities of creation, achieving ends flexibly without laying down determinate lines in advance. God is improvising rather as did J. S. Bach before the King of Prussia, or perhaps like an extemporis-ing New Orleans jazz player in Preservation Hall. Creation is the action of God the composer at work.[5]

He goes on to suggest that science affords us some new perspec-tives on the perennial mysteries of death, pain and suffering:

> We now know that the death of the individual is the precondition of the evolving by natural selection of new life and new forms of life. Furthermore, consciousness, and so awareness, cannot evolve without the develop-ment of nervous systems and sensitive recording organs which inevitably have to be able to react negatively to their environment with what we call pain. It appears that pain and suffering are the preconditions of sensitivity and consciousness, and that the death of the individual organism is the precondition for new life to appear. What religious thinkers used to call natural evil now appears in a new light as a necessary part of a universe

capable of generating new forms of life and consciousness. This is the corollary that for our notion of God to be at all acceptable morally, we have to regard God as himself suffering in, with, and under the creative processes of the world. God is, then, to be conceived as enduring what we call natural evil for achieving the ultimate good and fruition of what is being created: free willing, self-conscious persons.[6]

That is not an unanswerable argument, and it only deals with 'natural evil' – the blind sufferings of nature – not the intentional wickedness of humanity, but it does provide us with a model that has both biblical and cosmological echoes: that is, the model of sacrifice. We see this most clearly in the ecological model of the animal creation. The nature films of David Attenborough impress us by the picture they give us of the extraordinary balances of nature, and particularly by the way animals live off one another and thereby maintain the stability of their own species. The red deer that are now a nuisance in the Scottish Highlands, because their natural predators are extinct, are a very good example of this strange mystery of sacrificial mutuality. If wolves still roamed the Highlands they would prevent the deer from over-running, over-grazing and overcoming other species. John Stewart Collis wrote a book called *The Worm Forgives The Plough* that makes the same point. We have already referred to the symbiotic relationship between so-called primitive peoples and the animals they hunt, so that 'when the birds fall down they weep.' Developed societies have lost that mysticism, although something of it may be coming back as a result of modern scientific models and discoveries, as well as our renewed appreciation of Native American and Aboriginal spirituality. For instance, the claim that we are the result of burnt-out stars is moving as well as provoking. Angela Tilby in her book *Soul* writes:

The very elements of which our bodies are made were not present in the universe at the beginning. They could not have been created until the universe had reached a particular point in its expansion at which the clouds of hydrogen and helium were cool enough to condense into the galaxies which formed the first stars. Stars are the great nuclear furnaces in which all the complex elements are made. Their metals and minerals and gasses are released into space in giant supernovae explosions. These can only happen when the balance between the internal pressure of a star and its own force of gravity breaks down and the star explodes. All these processes, the forming of stars, the slow cooking of the elements, the explosive release into space, take over ten billion years to complete.[7]

We come from these burnt-out stars. The whole process is prodigal and costly and sacrifice seems to be one of its governing principles, the giving up of life for others. From the point of view of faith, the paradox of natural evil is that the world has to be the way it is for us to be here at all. That may not morally justify suffering but it does show that, things being what they are, it is an inescapable aspect of a universe that creates life as we know it, so to question it is to question our own existence and the conditions that made it possible. There are mysterious echoes here of Paul's famous words about the pot and the potter: 'Will what is molded say to the one who molds it, "Why have you made me like this?"' (Romans 9:20). This kind of thinking has some of the problems associated with the argument for the existence of God we looked at in Chapter 1, because it seems unconvincingly cerebral and logical. It may work on the level of argument, but it does not touch the heart, and it is the heart that is bruised by the existence of suffering and sorrow. This is why theologians after the Holocaust found the traditional picture of God as transcendentally above the battle no longer morally convincing.

In one of the great texts of the Holocaust, Elie Wiesel describes the execution by hanging of a young boy in one of the concentration camps. He tells us that as the boy twitched in his death throes on the end of the rope, a voice was heard crying out: 'Where is God now?' To which came back the answer: 'God is there; hanging on the gallows.' For many of us there will be a deliberate ambiguity in the reply, and it is the anguish of faith to live with the ambiguity. To believe that God was killed with the little Jewish boy or with the little children of Dunblane can mean that from now on the conventional idea of God is dead, since it was unable to survive the meaninglessness of these great outrages. Or it can mean that God is so identified with us in our sorrows that God dies our deaths and goes with us to all our calvaries.

Which is it? That is the question that gives faith its anguish.

The theologians who responded to the Holocaust had to abandon many of the ideas about God they had previously held. Like Darwin, they were unable to believe in an omnipotent God who was also beneficent, all loving. If God existed, God could no longer be both loving and omnipotent: if God was omnipotent, then God clearly was not loving; if God was loving, then God could not be omnipotent. The only God who could retain our allegiance was a suffering God. It is, of course, easier to abandon God than to go on making excuses for him. Yet many of us cannot quite do that. There is something about life itself that calls us to believe, even though our faith co-exists with pain and doubt. We believe that life is more than sorrow and horror. There is also beauty and meaning; there is love and compassion; there are great saints and great souls. All of these pose as much of a problem as evil: how did they arise in a meaningless universe? The answer of faith is that some purpose of love lies behind it all. We cannot prove its existence; indeed there are times when we hold on to the belief in spite of what appears to be overwhelming evidence against it. Yet it continues to assert itself against all meaninglessness, against the view of the universe as a pitiless accident. At our most beleaguered we choose to go on believing as an act of defiance against the great emptiness that threatens to engulf us. If the universe is ultimately pitiless and without meaning, then we are better than all of it, because we are also capable of compassion; we are able to cry at the sorrow of it and be moved with love for the beauty of it; and these are greater things than emptiness, they are more powerful than the great void. So we go on saying *yes*, trusting that our confidence, however frail, is responding to some great love beyond ourselves that haunts the universe.

2

Church leaders frequently meet people who are committed to the Christian life but are worried because they cannot assent to every phrase in the Christian creed. Some parts are just unavailable to them; other parts, when they are honest with themselves, they find repellent; and they are troubled by their desire to be selective. Tougher-minded Christians, who claim to consume everything on the menu, can be highly effective at inducing guilt in such people. They make two points, and the first is of undoubted importance. They say that Christianity is a revealed religion that claims to have received true knowledge of God, and we must either take it or leave it. The honest thing to do is either to submit to its authority and eat the whole menu or get out. What is dishonest is to be a 'cafeteria Christian', one who selects from the menu the bits that please, help or taste good, while rejecting the others. The second claim is that Christian doctrine is a precisely articulated whole, and if we pull out one thread the whole thing will unravel.

It is here I confront a personal difficulty. Human nature is an eccentric thing that expresses itself in strange ways, and I do not want to deny human beings an approach to spiritual reality that will comfort, strengthen or maybe even perfect them. For instance, I am not myself a Sabbatarian and certainly think that today's secular Sunday is greatly to be preferred to the dull Sabbaths I knew in my boyhood in the Vale of Leven; I am not a Muslim and enjoy eating pork; but I do not want to impose my view of the Sabbath on a member of the Free Church from the Isle of Harris or my fondness for pork on a member of Glasgow's Pakistani community. I do not have to believe in the historical existence of Adam and Eve in order to recognize that human nature is seriously flawed, is both righteous and sinful, capable of espousing ideals and just as capable of terrible evil. I find the story of the Fall in the Book of Genesis a fine way to express these complex realities, but I do not believe it describes an actual historical event. Nevertheless, I do not want to impose my attitude to the status of these texts upon someone who handles them in a different way. The fact is that believers have used scripture in many different ways down the centuries. There is something valuable in scripture that has persisted throughout different interpretative schemes, some of which look outlandish to us today. Liberals have a double difficulty, therefore. We want to maximize religious freedom, and especially the freedom to interpret scripture, even in ways that we find uncongenial and unpersuasive. The problem is that our *laisser-faire* attitude provokes the wrath of the person who believes in the literal inerrancy of scripture.

People who believe in this way are not grateful for our proffered latitude towards them, because they see us as being in dangerous error. There is a divide here that is difficult to bridge.

The dilemma goes deeper, and it confronts a fundamental element not in some scheme of interpretation, not in the external side of religion, but at the very heart and conscience of it. There are obviously areas where a multiplicity of approaches enriches and adds colour and variety to the human scene, but there are places where we confront a fundamental contradiction. Let us look at the role of women in religion, since it is one of the sore points in contemporary Christianity. According to the point of view taken in this book, revealed religion comes through human instruments. God communicates to us through the instruments, but it is wrong to identify God with them. Inevitably, however, the mediating symbols become important, become sacred to us, so we have to learn to make a fundamental distinction. We have to separate the enduring from the time-bound, and we have to acknowledge that there is a developmental side to Christianity, so that things that were hidden from our forebears become piercingly clear to us. One of the great debates in Christianity today concerns the role of women. There is no doubt that scripture and the Church through most of its history have been patriarchal in their organizing systems and fundamental principles. This has created two opposing difficulties. There are thinkers who believe that Christianity is intrinsically and irredeemably patriarchal and sexist. It is committed to an understanding of women that sees them as subordinate and God as essentially male, certainly more male than female, more father than mother. So they have challenged women to abandon Christianity and form a religion that does not place these structural and theological inhibitions on them. There are Christians who agree with the main observation made by these post-Christian feminists but not with their conclusions. They believe that scripture is to be taken in its totality, that nothing in it is time-bound or to be interpreted in different ways by different people at different times. For them, women *are* subordinate to men because scripture says they are, in both the Old and the New Testaments, and that is that. There can be no argument, because the Bible is the absolute authority to which we must submit. We have already noticed the circularity in this way of arguing, because it is based on a non-provable assumption about the status of scripture itself. We want to contend for a dynamic understanding of Christianity that admits that it has been patriarchal for centuries, as it has been racist at times and has believed in slavery, but that these attitudes are not intrinsic to its nature; they are blots upon its record, not essential elements of it. We believe that the spirit that guides us into truth is calling us to identify and set aside the purely cultural elements and recognize the new thing, the new word that is being spoken to us. Inevitably, of course, this process will go on happening, because each generation has to enculturate Christianity for its own day. We believe, therefore, that the liberation of women into absolute equality in Christianity, both in structural and theological terms, is something that comes from God. This means that while we understand the historical difficulty of conservative people for whom change is difficult, and while we recognize that institutions cannot change as rapidly or be converted as urgently as individuals, nevertheless we have to acknowledge that the difference between these two attitudes to faith is of fundamental importance.

So it is no longer a question of affirming variety, but of challenging error. This is where we have to point out that the authoritarian, literalist approach to the Bible is dangerous. It has a static understanding of revelation and truth that contradicts actual human experience, and it puts Christianity on an unnecessary collision course with the best minds in the world. There have been many times in Christian history when the Church has appropriately and prophetically confronted the world and suffered for it. There have also been times when the world has shamed the Church, when God has sent prophets from outside the community of faith to challenge it. Any attempt by Christian reactionaries to impose an archaic world-view on people today is both vain and arrogant. It is a scandal in the technical sense of that word – an obstacle, a large rock placed in the way of people coming to faith, because it refuses to acknowledge the best insights of this generation and orders it to abandon the undoubted moral gains it has made if it wants to find God. This is to place a stumbling-block before people; it is to maintain not an allowable or colourful eccentricity in belief, but something that is repugnant and must therefore be opposed.

This recent episode in theological history underlines the importance of recognizing that only the truth of God has authority over us. Our predicament is that we have no guaranteed and infallible programme that dictates to us how we should live and what we should think down to the smallest detail. In the Christian tradition we are given a series of insights into the nature of God and God's creation that are both illuminating and challenging; but they leave us with the arduous task of using our minds to wrestle with a mystery that continuously encounters us in history, whose nature is prodigally creative of variety and change, and is always ahead of us, calling upon us to catch up. These Christian insights are called doctrines and they have been handled in history in a liberatingly selective way.

There seem to be times for a particular doctrine, a particular emphasis; and times when a doctrine is neglected or simply rests. There was a time when the doctrine of the Holy Spirit, the idea that God accompanies us in history and can erupt into the lives of individuals and peoples with spectacular consequences, was neglected. People talked about God the Father and God the Son with conviction and understanding, but God the Holy Spirit was treated as an awkward relative. Since the opening years of the twentieth century there has been a rediscovery and celebration of the Holy Spirit in a type of Christianity that is characterized by a religious excitement that expresses itself in praying in tongues, visions, ecstatic utterance, healings and wonders. So compelling was this for many Christians that it inevitably became unbalanced, and what was a corrective reassertion of a neglected element in Christianity became a new fundamentalism. This tendency is itself being corrected, and it brings us back to the puzzled believers who were dismissed as 'cafeteria Christians' because they could not eat everything on the menu with equal enthusiasm. In matters of faith it is better to build on the positive, to believe where we can, rather than mourn the fact that we have not been able to embrace everything. We can only believe what is available to us and go from there. In fact, we have always done this. We have been selective in the way we have emphasized particular doctrines, because the doctrines themselves are the result of a dynamic struggle in history to make sense of faith. In our generation we are struggling to achieve a new understanding of creation. In Stephen Hawking's language, we have come closer to an understanding of the mind of God. We are closer to the doctrine of God's Word, God's mind as expressed in the creation. We understand creation as being in some sense the result of a process of divine self-giving, a process of dynamic, creative loving. We begin to see a pattern in creation that corresponds to some of the insights we have received into God. We are given no answer to the ancient human question about suffering, but we do catch glimpses of a possible resolution. We now have an understanding of God's creative activity as continuously in operation, struggling to bring life and beauty out of violence and power.

The other Christian doctrine that illuminates the mystery of suffering is the doctrine of the Incarnation. This is the claim that the divine reality that continuously creates the universe and accompanies its history expressed itself in Jesus of Nazareth. The doctrine of the Incarnation has a particular and a general meaning for Christians. It is the way we express the unique significance of Jesus and the fact that for us he is the bearer of the truth of God, the way we understand God. The most helpful way to approach the mystery of Jesus is to follow the principle of availability. If the historic creeds still speak for us in a way that compels our honest assent, then we can use them. As we have already acknowledged, all our language about God is provisional. We only get into difficulties in describing the Incarnation if we become too defensive about the way we express it, or become too intent on making the mystery explicable. Being Christian means that we have committed ourselves to understanding God in the way revealed by Jesus Christ, but the doctrine of the Incarnation is also a way of saying that God continues to act in history through the Church, which has been called the extension of the Incarnation, the way Jesus is made contemporary, the place where the memory of Jesus is encountered. So we are committed to a continuing relationship with our creator through the adventures of our own day.

This way of expressing our experience of the divine is tragic as well as joyful. Here our words are at their least useful, though it is where the assured are at their most confident in the way they wield their metaphors. At the heart of the Christian story lies a death. Jesus of Nazareth who reveals God, who discloses the heart of God, is crucified. The crucifixion of Jesus stands at the very centre of our understanding of God. It rescues Christianity from moral superficiality and naïve optimism, because it identifies God with suffering, and links that suffering to human action. The crucifixion of Jesus is clearly documented. For Christians, however, though it is an event in history, it is an event of universal significance. It is a mythic event, remembering our previous understanding of myth, as an experience that is released into history to convey abiding truth.

Theories abound for the killing of Jesus, but two aspects of it are particularly compelling: one is the identification of Jesus with God; the other is that the deed was done in the name of God. This is an example of a reversal we see time and again in the history of the Christian religion, where truth gets inverted and value turned upside down. Christians have misused the fact, but the fact remains that the intellectual agents of the crime were the religious leaders whom Jesus consistently challenged. The nature of that challenge endures uncomfortably and confronts every community of faith. The challenge of Jesus to the religious leaders of his day was that they stood between humanity and God, and claimed control of the access points. They policed the frontiers and set up custom posts, letting some in and denying others entry; they categorized whole groups as being so far from official righteousness that it was a waste of their time to seek entry at all. This should raise uncomfortable echoes in our own minds. There are so many systems and tendencies today that do the same thing and make the same claims. They confidently claim to control access to the divine mystery. It has something to do with power, the very thing that was most passionately repudiated by God as made known in Jesus: religion as a system of control that tells us who is in and who is out, what is allowed and what is forbidden, what to believe and what not to believe, whom to consort with, whom to shun. It is there in our history, it is there today. This is religion as edifice and control, a human system, objective and manageable, that is distressingly close to what the Bible calls an idol. This seems to be what Jesus stood against. In their reaction to Jesus, the religious leaders showed the sort of defensive anger we all display when we know we are wrong and are, therefore, at our most dangerous. Criticisms that do not touch us, we laugh off and are relaxed about. It is the challenges that echo our own sense of failure and loss that are the dangerous ones. We see that in Peter's denial in the court-yard of the High Priest. It is precisely because he *is* one of Jesus' followers that he shouts most passionately that he is not. It is because the professionally religious know in their hearts they sometimes use God's gift for their own purposes, that they are so dangerously angry when challenged. That is partly what the crucifixion was about.

The Christian claim goes deeper than that, however. It boldly suggests that by enduring our defensive anger, Christ healed it, or offered it the promise, the possibility of healing. A metaphor that Christians have found useful in interpreting their experience of the cross comes from the system of slavery, where it was possible to release or redeem a slave by paying the owner the going rate. The metaphor of Jesus as redeemer, as one who pays the price of our wrongdoing, though dated, is abidingly helpful. It seeks to express the truth that God bears responsibility for the tragedy as well as the joy of existence. The crucifixion of Jesus of Nazareth is a symbol of God's struggle with the creation. God suffers it the way a patient teacher of a disturbed child responds to anger with love, and embraces and absorbs it into her own body. Christians offer no conceptual answer to the problem of evil, no words that resolve it neatly. Instead, they meditate on the death of Jesus because it sheds light on and offers meaning to their own condition.

One of the most compelling episodes in the story is the incident in the Garden of Gethsemane, where Jesus, having gone apart with his disciples, prayed on the night before he suffered. He is left alone with his uncertainties while his friends sleep around him. Which way should he go? Should he drink the cup of suffering, or escape from it? Confront the reality before him, or seek to deny it? This was the dilemma he wrestled with in Gethsemane. It is impossible for us to enter his consciousness or fully understand the spiritual logic of the crucifixion, but history shows that Jesus' surrender to his destiny has liberated and empowered millions of people down the ages, by a whole series of mysterious connections. One of the most powerful phrases in the dramatic narrative of the arrest comes when he tells his disciples to put aside their weapons, and addresses those who have come to arrest him: 'This is your hour', he says. He recognizes irresistible necessity, a situation that cannot be altered. At such moments when necessity confronts us, honesty and courage are required. We need to know when there is no way of escape so that we can turn and face what is coming and pray for the serenity to deal with it.

While he was still speaking, Judas, one of the twelve, arrived; with him was a large crowd with swords and clubs, from the chief priests and the elders of the people. Now the betrayer had given them a sign, saying, 'The one I will kiss is the man; arrest him.' At once he came up to Jesus and said, 'Greetings, Rabbi!' and kissed him.

(Matthew 26:47–49)

Life brings these sudden challenges. Lovers turn from us, society discards us, our own bodies betray us, and there is no escape. There is no secret passageway out of the Garden of Gethsemane, no regiment of angels that will suddenly blast its way into our midst and rescue us. There is only the raw fact that our betrayer is at hand and, since there is no escape from the event, meaning has to be found within the event. Since the betrayal cannot be undone, we have to allow our humanity to transcend it, even as the betrayer kisses us. This is easy to say, though difficult to do, because we do not want this reality that confronts us, this death, this loss. We experience these things as betrayals, and a voice within us says they should not happen, the universe should ban them, God should do something about them. This is what we quite properly feel, as anger and panic rise to our throat; but the fact remains that they do happen; Judas is constantly bringing police into the garden of our contentment to arrest us. And we have to deal with the situation that faces us, not waste energy wishing it away. Peace can only be reached by going through the experience to the other side. Somehow we have to say yes to it, look it in the eye and acknowledge it. When they come for us, we begin our triumph over their betrayal by standing erect and going with them to whatever awaits us.

There has been a lot of fantasy and denial in Christianity, but at the centre there is this picture of the young prophet of Nazareth saying yes to the very thing he wanted to escape from. And his surrender was the prelude to a surprise so transforming that the Christian Church still has difficulty in saying what it means by it. The mystery of the Resurrection of Jesus is one of those experiences that easily lend themselves to analogy. Preachers in the Northern Hemisphere find it easy to slip into horticultural metaphor and talk about the rebirth of spring after the death of winter. These analogies from nature suggest that the Resurrection is a particular instance of the general law of return that characterizes certain aspects of the natural cycle, and something can undoubtedly be made of that. But the heart of the Resurrection mystery is more surprising than that. It says something about the inescapability of much that confronts us. There are necessities we face, and we only compound their misery by seeking to deny them. Reinhold Niebuhr captured something of this in his famous prayer:

> God, give us grace to accept with serenity the
>   things that cannot be changed,
> courage to change the things that should be
>   changed,
> and the wisdom to distinguish the one from
>   the other.

Usually we would rather deny the reality of things we cannot change, and too often we acquiesce in things we ought to change, but Jesus was an example of human maturity. He challenged customs and traditions and caused them to be changed, yet when the hour came he accepted the thing he could not change and by saying yes to it, brought it into the realm of human freedom. He made it his choice, not something that merely overwhelmed him. When we make these choices we alter both the impact and the effect that overwhelming necessity has upon us. In the case of Jesus, the Galilean prophet who said yes to his own death, the testimony of history is that his act of serenity, his acceptance of the fate that was to overwhelm him, was the prelude to an enduring impact on history that continues to reverberate.

This is part of what we mean by the Resurrection of Jesus: his rising from the grave to be a continuing presence in the hearts and minds of his disciples. In interpreting the Resurrection we confront again the mysterious complexity of the great Christian symbols and metaphors. We have already seen that the power of religious mysteries lies in the narratives we use to encode and perpetuate them, so that they continue to be means of spiritual encounter. There is something elusive about the way they operate, but one way to understand them is to think of great works of art, whether in the theatre, music or painting. Art conveys truth through event, though it is almost impossible to describe exactly what is happening. We know that when we have confronted

great art we feel cleansed, uplifted, challenged, ennobled, sometimes through our tears. We use words like 'cathartic' and 'transcendent'
to describe their impact, because a mysterious exchange takes
place, inexplicable but undeniable. The mystery of the Resurrection
of Jesus, though it is located in a historical event, operates in
the same way. It is an event in history that has become myth, so
that it can now encounter us; and it will encounter us in different ways, according to how we understand it. For some, the
story of the stone rolled away from the tomb and the earthly
body of Jesus being transmuted to an eternal level of being will
be an event they claim to accept literally: the God who brought
the created universe into being from nothing can transfigure his
faithful servant from the nothingness of death into enduring
spiritual reality. But this is not the only way to find meaning in
the mystery of the Resurrection of Jesus. It can be used as a
metaphor for the transcendence of suffering and the determination to give it meaning by our response to it. In a short but
remarkable book called *Mary, Mother of Sorrows, Mother of
Defiance* Peter Daino, a Marianist brother and missioner who
works in Kenya, calls the anger and pain he feels as he confronts
the starvation of children in Africa 'apostolic grief'. He says
that the most helpful question one can ask about grief is,
'Whom will your grief serve?'[8] Apostolic grief asks not, 'Where
does the tragedy come from?' but 'Where does it lead?'[9] The
Christian response to suffering is not to account for it but to
challenge and transcend it. This is not the passivity of resignation,
though acceptance of inescapable necessity is part of it, but the
activity of defiance, the using of grief and anger to contend
against the forces that cause suffering. That is why faith, though
it may often reel under the hammer blows of evil, refuses to
submit to the interpretation of life as a pitiless absurdity and
persists in saying *no* to that. Faith protests against the alleged
lack of meaning in suffering by making it serve as an impetus to
action. This reaction to evil and suffering is also part of the
mystery of creation and has risen from within it. Who can be
certain that it is not also a response to an insistent purpose of
love that struggles to reveal itself through the joys and tragedies
of the universe?

PART II

Making Sense of Ourselves

CHAPTER FIVE

Unhappy Bedfellows

I

*I*n Chapter 1 we thought about the 'God of the gaps', the misuse of God, who is experienced, not as a reality to be encountered, but as a way of filling gaps in our knowledge systems. The result was that, as human knowledge continued to expand, the God of the gaps continued to shrink until, in Bonhoeffer's language, 'God was crowded out of the world.' If there is what we call God, then it must be a reality that is encountered through the world and not just at the limits of our knowledge. This means that there is no sacred sphere and no secular sphere, except as constructs for human purposes. God is encountered through reality as we experience it and not just in some reserved area, roped off from the rest of life.

The same thing happens in the sphere of morals and behaviour. There has been a constant temptation in religious communities to create an ethic of the gaps, though the function of the gap is slightly different. Here the separation is usually established by a moral theory concerning some aspect of human life that claims to be the final, authoritative approach to the subject. This was an approach to reality opposed by Jesus in his disputes with the religious leaders of his community. The system he opposed, and was opposed by, was a theory we might describe as exclusionary divinity. The motive behind the theory seems to have been a desire to protect or isolate God from infection by the morally and ceremonially impure.

Behind the system there probably lay a primitive understanding of the divine nature as a kind of radioactive force that could only be safely handled by strict attention to protective procedures. This primitive fear was originally physical. There is an intriguing story in the Second Book of Samuel, where David recaptures the Ark of the Covenant, then the most sacred object of Israelite religion, from the Philistines who had stolen it. Chapter 6 tells the story of the return of the Ark to Jerusalem:

> They carried the ark of God on a new cart, and brought it out of the house of Abinadab, which was on the hill. Uzzah and Ahio, the sons of Abinadab, were driving the new cart with the ark of God; and Ahio went in front of the ark. David and all the house of Israel were dancing before the Lord with all their might, with songs and lyres and harps and tambourines and castanets and cymbals.
>
> When they came to the threshing floor of Nacon, Uzzah reached out his hand to the ark of God and took hold of it, for the oxen shook it. The anger of the Lord was kindled against Uzzah; and God struck him there because he reached out his hand to the ark; and he died there beside the ark of God. David was angry because the Lord had burst forth with an outburst upon Uzzah; so that place is called Perez-uzzah, to this day.

(2 Samuel 6:3–8)

Behind the intricate ceremonial arrangements of Jewish religion, as well as other religious systems, there originally lay an understanding of the divine power as something that had to be handled with extreme caution by sacred professionals dedicated and trained for the task. Something of this superstition is still around in the Church. There are Christians who will not receive the bread or wine in the Eucharist from a lay person, because of their conviction that they should only be handled by a priest. This anxiety is attached particularly to the eucharistic bread. It used to be a convention in Catholic circles that it should not touch the hands of anyone except the priest, so it was placed straight on to the tongue of the lay person by the celebrant. Whatever genuine awe of the divine lay behind these anxieties, and whatever religious value there was in the mechanisms they produced, there is little doubt that at the heart of the dispute between Jesus and the religious leaders of his day was a profound disagreement over the nature of the relationship between God and humanity. In this dispute, Jesus placed himself in the dangerous company of the Hebrew prophets, in whom we find a scathing criticism of the ceremonial system, such as the famous passage in Micah 6:6–8:

> With what shall I come before the Lord,
> and bow myself before God on high?
> Shall I come before him with burnt offerings,
> with calves a year old?
> Will the Lord be pleased with thousands of
> rams,
> with ten thousands of rivers of oil?
> Shall I give my firstborn for my transgression,
> the fruit of my body for the sin of my soul?
> He has told you, O mortal, what is good;
> and what does the Lord require of you
> but to do justice, and to love kindness,
> and to walk humbly with your God?

The challenge of the prophets to Israel was always of this nature: they had substituted religion and ceremony for real knowledge of God, which had more to do with justice to the poor than with heaping up religious offerings or mastering complex rituals. Jesus was in the line of the prophets. He placed himself alongside those who were excluded from the inner circles of the chosen community by his words, his actions and, finally, by his death, which was itself a form of religious exclusion enacted outside the gate of the Holy City.

'This man receives sinners and eats with them' was the accusation that provoked his greatest parables as recorded in Luke's Gospel. What seems to have been at issue was the authoritarian attitude to religion as a fixed and objective reality to which people must conform, particularly in the area of ethics. There is an important difference between a fixed and unchanging ethical system and an approach that is based on human circumstances and experience. Are there fixed, objective laws that have to be applied in all circumstances to all people? Or is law as we know it a way of defining the accumulated wisdom of experience, while recognizing that, being human, it is provisional and revisable? In other words, is ethics as much about aspirations as about norms; is it designed to help us find the best ways of caring for one another?

Is ethics made for us and not us for ethics, as Jesus famously said about the Sabbath?

In one of Jesus' most famous parables, the Parable of the Good Samaritan (Luke 10:25–37), the status of law is directly challenged by Jesus in a way that probably increased the hatred of the religious establishment at whom it was aimed:

> Just then a lawyer stood up to test Jesus. 'Teacher,' he said, 'what must I do to inherit eternal life?' He said to him, 'What is written in the law? What do you read there?' He answered, 'You shall love the Lord your God with all your heart, and with all your soul, and with all your strength, and with all your mind; and your neighbor as yourself.' And he said to him, 'You have given the right answer; do this, and you will live.'
>
> But wanting to justify himself, he asked Jesus, 'And who is my neighbor?' Jesus replied, 'A man was going down from Jerusalem to Jericho, and fell into the hands of robbers, who stripped him, beat him, and went away, leaving him half dead. Now by chance a priest was going down that road; and when he saw him, he passed by on the other side. So likewise a Levite, when he came to the place and saw him, passed by on the other side. But a Samaritan while traveling came near him; and when he saw him, he was moved with pity. He went to him and bandaged his wounds, having poured oil and wine on them. Then he put him on his own animal, brought him to an inn, and took care of him. The next day he took out two denarii, gave them to the innkeeper, and said, "Take care of him; and when I come back, I will repay you whatever more you spend." Which of these three, do you think, was a neighbor to the man who fell into the hands of the robbers?' He said, 'The one who showed him mercy.' Jesus said to him, 'Go and do likewise.'

There are many aspects of this parable that need to be uncovered if its meaning is to be made plain to a modern reader, but the one that concerns us at the moment is the way the story challenges the listeners' understanding of what is appropriate ethical behaviour.

Luke tells us that the man who fell among the thieves had been stripped naked and left unconscious. These are not just colourful details, there to give the narrative pace and drama: they are crucial to the meaning of the story. The question asked by the lawyer was a genuine question: whom may I appropriately help? According to the received tradition, well known to the hearers of the parable, there were severe constraints upon the answer to that question. One of them was ethnic: a Gentile was not a neighbour. Another was moral: a sinner was not a neighbour. And yet another was cultic: an unclean person could not be a neighbour. In other words, in order to help the man who fell among thieves a devout Jew would have to establish that he belonged to the correct community and that he would not be a source of ritual pollution.

This was particularly true of priests, who had to be in a permanent state of cultic purity. The priest in question, returning to Jericho after duty in the Temple at Jerusalem, would be in a state of purity. His purity would be destroyed by touching a corpse, necessitating a burdensome series of rituals, back in Jerusalem, that would have prevented him from returning home or conducting his professional duties, until his state of ritual purity was recovered. He was not allowed to come closer than five feet to a corpse. How could he tell if this man was dead or alive? He approaches as far as his code will permit and sees that he is not only either dead or unconscious but naked. Now his predicament is doubled: he cannot tell if he is a neighbour by his dress and he does not know if he is even alive, because there is no sign of life. He runs a double risk of falling into a state of impurity.

Those who were listening to the parable would have been in no doubt about the most prudent course to follow. They are not surprised when the priest, after checking out the situation, passes by on the other side. The Levite followed the same code as the priest, though his purity requirement was less rigorous. He makes the same calculation as his superior and moves on. The listeners would have approved his prudence. The appearance of the Samaritan in the story would have shocked them, because he was precisely the kind of person who could not be a neighbour. The presumption in the story is that the man by the roadside is a Jew and, therefore, no neighbour to the Samaritan. Had he woken during the Samaritan's ministrations he would probably have sent him away. The point to remember is that the Samaritan, while a hated heretic to the Jews, followed the same code and was bound by the same ethical system. Had he been a prudent observer of his own code he, too, would have passed by on the other side, after checking out the ethical complexity of the situation. We are told, however, that he was moved with pity. The verb is a strong one. The suggestion is that his compassion at the plight of the man bleeding by the roadside is so strong that it overrides his code. The need to respond personally to the crisis is stronger than the pull of the ancestral code that binds him. There are other layers of meaning in the Parable, but we need not pursue them here. The main point of the parable establishes the primacy of the personal in the ethical sphere. Compassion overrides other considerations, no matter how strongly our code binds us. In Chapter 3 we noted the Russian thinker Berdyaev's observation that in the field of Christian ethics every case has to be taken as an exception. He was making the same point as the Parable of the Good Samaritan: the human in its need and necessity always has primacy over the legal. The law is there to help us; when it ceases to do so, or gets in the way of human compassion, it is to be overridden. This is partly what Paul meant when he told us that love was the fulfilling of the law.

We need to get away from the legal approach to thorny questions in which life is seen as a sort of board game: if we stray onto some squares we are sent immediately to jail or fined. We are better helped by an ethic of understanding and aspiration that guides us by persuasion rather than by police work. There is a tendency in Christianity to claim too much for its approach to complex issues and to transform them from guiding principles into positive law. This authoritarian style does not commend itself today. Ethical guidance works best where it is able to persuade people by its intrinsic usefulness and value. However, we have already seen that people who do not understand the provisional nature of human constructs, including morality, are made anxious by these transitions. They talk bitterly about objective or absolute morality and are led to despise and reject whole categories of people as a result. In one of his most recent poems R. S. Thomas alludes to this kind of religion:

Who was the janitor,
with the set face, wardening

the approaches? I had prepared
my apologies, my excuses
for coming by the wrong
road. There was no one
there, only the way
I had come by going on and on.[1]

The Scottish philosopher David Hume said you could not derive an 'ought' from an 'is', except on the basis of a fixed theory of the authority of revelation. It is against too exclusive a claim to revealed authority for what are obviously human judgements and misjudgements that we are attempting to argue. It is one thing, of course, voluntarily to submit ourselves to an authority system; no one can object to that, provided it does not damage or oppress others. But the voluntary principle is not what we are arguing against, so much as the misuse of authority to condemn and shame others, used with particular vindictiveness in the area of sex.

The historical picture of relationships between men and women is less clear than many passionate advocates make out. For example, although many claim the authority of scripture for what they describe as Christian marriage, it is extremely doubtful if anything like our current system can be found there, except by reading back into the text our own experiences or preferences. Originally, Judaism made no distinction between cohabitation and marriage:

> There is no formal marriage ceremony in the Pentateuch. The act of marriage in Biblical times was called 'taking', which was synonymous with sexual intercourse. Put bluntly sex meant marriage. To be precise, this is in the sense of a couple living together in a stable relationship (as in the modern sense of cohabitation) rather than having a one-night fling. Jewish law subsequently added two extra dimensions – the purchase/bride price and a written contract. However these are both later additions. Technically, Jewish law regards cohabitation as a legitimate form of marriage, although it would today prefer a formal marriage ceremony in a synagogue.[2]

We know, moreover, that the great patriarchs and exemplars of faith, such as Abraham, were polygamists. The role of women in the period described in the first five books of the Old Testament is not easy to define. The account of the Fall in the Book of Genesis suggests that women were held to be disproportionately responsible for human sin: 'The woman gave me and I did eat,' said Adam to God. We know from the legal codes represented in the Old Testament that women were held to be of lesser value. We know that the pollution taboos that were such a mark of Hebrew religion separated women from the sacred. This was exemplified dramatically in the layout of the Temple, which limited women to their own reserved area or court, like the one reserved for Gentiles. In fact, the woman was thought of as 'the Gentile within' the community of Israel. Nevertheless, the Old Testament does not lack strong women in positions of leadership, if not exactly of equality, such as Miriam, the sister of Moses. In the famous passage in Proverbs beginning, 'A good wife who can find?' (Proverbs 31:10ff.), a picture is painted of an indefatigably productive woman, who not only cares for her family, but trades in land and farming, as well as caring for the poor. A less attractive account of the effect on women of the social system of the Old Testament is the story of Hagar, the Egyptian slave woman whom Sarah gave to her husband when she herself was unable to conceive. Years later, seeing Hagar's son playing with her own son, Isaac, she was filled with jealousy and forced Abraham to expel Hagar from their extended family. Another unpleasant little vignette in the Pentateuch is found in Genesis 19, where the fate of the famous city of Sodom is described. Sodom brings down God's wrath upon itself, not for homosexuality, which is usually alleged, but for lack of hospitality to strangers. When two strangers come to visit Lot the men of Sodom order them to be sent out of the house, so that they can rape them. This is so much a breach of the law of hospitality that Lot offers them, instead, his two daughters, both virgins: 'do to them as you please; only do nothing to these men, for they have come under the shelter of my roof.' Reading this story, one feels a complicated sort of revulsion: admiration for Lot for maintaining the law of hospitality; disbelief that he volunteered his daughters for a gang-rape instead. All things considered, it has to be admitted that the Old Testament doesn't help us much in dealing with our problems today, nor should that surprise us. It reflects the experience of a long period of transition and violent change. It is not interested in answering the questions we put to it, nor does it reflect our own preoccupations.

When we turn to the New Testament the picture is clearer, but it is still not interested in our preoccupations. We can assume that our Lord's followers, the first Christians, certainly the first Jewish Christians, followed the social patterns of their own community. Jesus did not lay down specific laws on the subject, though he did say that women ought to have the same rights in marriage as men, contrary to the Law of Moses, which gave the husband the power of unilateral divorce. We also know that, contrary to the customs of the day, Jesus had women disciples who followed him and provided for him and his band from their own substance. One commentator interprets the famous story of Martha and Mary in Luke 10:38–42 as an account of an older sister who is worried in case her young sister, clearly enthralled by Jesus and his teaching, compromises her reputation and the possibility of respectable marriage, by becoming one of his followers:

> Now as they went on their way, he entered a certain village, where a woman named Martha welcomed him into her home. She had a sister named Mary, who sat at the Lord's feet and listened to what he was saying. But Martha was distracted by her many tasks; so she came to him and asked, 'Lord, do you not care that my sister has left me to do all the work by myself? Tell her then to help me.' But the Lord answered her, 'Martha, Martha, you are worried and distracted by many things; there is need of only one thing. Mary has chosen the better part, which will not be taken away from her.'

In the early Christian community women held positions of leadership as prophets and apostles, such as Junia, mentioned by Paul in Romans 16:7. Although there is little explicit formal teaching by Jesus in the Gospels on the structured relationships between men and women, he himself provides a model of relational equality. He was remarkably free in his relationships with women, neither sexualizing them nor excluding them from his followers out of fear of their gender. This was a dramatic transformation of and challenge to the dominant social pattern. It reflected the compassion of Jesus for people on the edge. In his parables he taught that the despised go into the Kingdom first. The crucifixion stories reflect this reality. When the male disciples forsake Jesus and run away, it is the women who remain at the cross. The new, prophetic status of women in the early Christian community did not long survive the pressures of the surrounding culture, and the Church soon reverted to the prevailing pattern.

In Paul's letter we look in on something of this struggle. Some commentators believe that behind Paul's famous statement in Galatians 3:27–28 there lies an early baptismal formula: 'As many of you as were baptized into Christ have clothed yourselves with Christ. There is no longer Jew or Greek, there is no longer slave or free, there is no longer male and female; for all of you are one in Christ Jesus.' Part of the difficulty in interpreting Paul arises because of the apocalyptic background against which he thought and taught. Paul and the early Church, because of a mood in religion and society, fortified by the memory of certain mysterious predictions which Jesus had made, expected the imminent return of Christ to inaugurate the Kingdom of Heaven on earth. This expectation strongly influences much of Paul's teaching, resulting in what C. H. Dodd called the provision of 'an interim ethic' for the early Christian communities. Paul was ministering mainly to Gentiles, probably against the background of their own social arrangements, but he is less interested in those arrangements than in the imminent return of Jesus. It is this eschatological preoccupation that probably accounts for his tolerant attitude to slavery.

In 1 Corinthians 7:29–31 Paul provides us with enduring principles, but the guidance he gives is modified by his eschatology:

I mean, brothers and sisters, the appointed time has grown short; from now on, let even those who have wives be as though they had none, and those who mourn as though they were not mourning, and those who rejoice as though they were not rejoicing, and those who buy as though they had no possessions, and those who deal with the world as though they had no dealings with it. For the present form of this world is passing away.

His advice concerning relations between the sexes could be summed up in this way: since the end of the world will soon be upon us, it is not worth entering a new marriage or undoing an existing one. Nevertheless, if you are burning with desire, go ahead and get married, even though the time is short, because it is better to marry than to burn with lust. Inevitably we read into the biblical narrative our own experiences and expectations. It has even been said, during current debates, that the nuclear family as we know it today was invented by Jesus 2,000 years ago. As a matter of fact, Jesus sat rather lightly to his own family and claimed that there were more important relationships; but the main point to notice is that the households of those days were more like the extended families found in Africa today than anything known in suburban Britain or America. It therefore makes sense for us to find appropriate arrangements for our day that suit our social and cultural environment, just as our forebears did in their time.

When we turn to the early Church we find that, as it emerges as an institution in its own right, seeking approval and offering society support for its own institutions, there was a gradual enculturation of the gospel to suit the norms of the day. One aspect of this was the gradual marginalizing of women and their removal from positions of leadership in the early Christian community. The plight of the female apostle Junia in Romans 16 is an example of this. So convinced was the later Church that a woman could not have been an apostle that the name Junia, a woman's name, was replaced with the name Junias, an allegedly masculine name, that does not exist as a male name in the literature of the time. The pattern that emerges is of a gradual transition from a community that operated within the structures of the Jewish religion, with a radical tendency towards a more open acceptance of women, to one in which the place of women is increasingly sexualized in a negative way. The Jewish attitude to sexuality is matter-of-fact and accepting, recognizing both the pleasure and inevitability of the sexual relationship. With unsentimental realism, it seeks to protect itself against the dangers and excesses of sex, rather in the way we value electricity, but have an intelligent appreciation of its dangers, unless it is appropriately guarded.

This Jewish pragmatism is gradually replaced by what has been called an hermeneutic of suspicion and a subsequent misuse of the biblical material in the early Church, so that sexuality is seen, not as a human energy to be used with appropriate care, but as a problem in itself. The origins of this fateful twist in the history of sex in Christianity may have lain in some of the dualistic religions of the time that despised the body and sought redemption not in it but from it. Whatever the precise origin of the new approach, we reach the point where sex is perceived as the mechanism that conveys original guilt. During this phase of the Church's history there were some men of genius who put a fateful stamp upon the whole debate, mainly because of their own intricate psychology, and none more powerfully than St Augustine of Hippo. Augustine claimed that Adam and Eve, had they never fallen, would have propagated children without what he called 'concupiscence', the fateful desire that accompanies sexuality:

> An urge which burns quite indiscriminately for objects allowed and disallowed; and which is bridled by the urge for marriage, that must depend upon it, but that restrains it from what is not allowed ... Against this drive, which is in tension with the *law of the mind*, all chastity must fight: that of the married couple, so that the urge of the flesh may be rightly used, and that of continent men and virgins, so that, even better and with a struggle of greater glory, it should not be used at all. This urge, had it existed in Paradise ... would, in a wondrous pitch of peace, have never run beyond the bidding of the will ... It would never have forced itself upon the mind with thoughts of inappropriate and impermissible delights. It would not have had to be held upon the leash by married moderation, or fought to a draw by ascetic labor. Rather, when once called for, it would have followed the will of the person with all the ease of a single-hearted act of obedience.[3]

Peter Brown, in his magisterial book *The Body And Society*, points out that Augustine would have appeared dangerously revisionist and pragmatic to other Christian fathers, such as Ambrose, Jerome and Gregory of Nyssa:

> All three had shared an instinctive, largely unanalysed, assumption about the origins of marriage and of sexuality. Marriage, intercourse and Paradise were as incompatible, in their minds, as were Paradise and death. Of that, at least, they felt they could be certain.

This meant that sexuality, hence marriage and the creation of the family, could only have followed the Fall of Adam and Eve. They were the result of a sad decline, by which Adam and Eve had lapsed from an 'angelic' state into physicality, and so into death. A question mark was allowed to hover over human society. Marriage, and the structures that sprang from it, could not be derived from the original nature of the human person. Ascetic exegesis of the Fall of Adam and Eve tended to preserve, at the back of the minds of its exponents, a lingering doubt: society, marriage, and, if not those, certainly sexual intercourse, were fundamentally alien to the original definition of humanity. They had come as an afterthought. They had imposed limitations on the first angelic majesty of Adam and Eve.[4]

This attitude lies behind the cult of virginity in the early Church. Marriage, to quote the Prayer Book, which reflects the view of sexuality as disease, was a remedy for those who did not have the heroic gift of continence. Marriage was a necessary but regrettable mechanism for procreation and the control of lust; but, as Saint Jerome observed, the only good thing that could be said about it was that it produced virgins. Even as warm-hearted a saint as St Francis de Sales, at the beginning of the seventeenth century, who had a more positive approach to sexual intercourse in marriage, encouraged Christian couples to imitate the elephant's sexual habits:

> The elephant, not only the largest, but the most intelligent of animals, provides us with an excellent example. It is faithful and tenderly loving to the female of its choice, mating only every third year, and then for no more than five days and so secretly as never to be seen, until on the sixth day, it appears and goes at once to wash its whole body in the river, unwilling to return to the herd, unless thus purified. Such good and modest habits are an example to husband and wife.[5]

It is important to remember that this emerging attitude to sex in the Christian community, leading to the cult of virginity and the compulsory celibacy of the clergy in the Western tradition until the Protestant Reformation, had a profound effect on male attitudes towards women, and women's attitudes towards their own bodies and sexuality. The idea of sex as disease went very deep in the Christian consciousness. When the Reformation promoted the marriage of clergy, the rhetoric that surrounded marriage and influenced the new marriage liturgies still treated sexuality as a disease, for which marriage was, if not a remedy, at least a palliative. As the Book of Common Prayer expressed it, marriage was 'Ordained for a remedy against sin, and to avoid fornication; that such persons as have not the gift of continency might marry, and keep themselves undefiled members of Christ's body.'

It is worth observing, of course, that this theology and the understanding that lies behind it, reflects the male rather than the female experience of sexuality in the Christian tradition. This dualistic understanding of sex resulted in what has been called the Madonna Whore Complex, a male ambivalence towards the female in the Christian tradition, that treats women as objects of desire, there to test the strength or prove the downfall of the struggling male; or as impossible objects of purity in the form of virgin mothers who give birth without being sullied by the reality of sexuality. History has burdened the Christian experience of sex with unusual tensions, loading a natural reality with too much supernatural consequence. The famous double standard for men and women has some of its roots in this dualism and has made it even more difficult to talk about the subject with ease and straightforwardness. This is particularly true of ordained ministers in the various Christian traditions who are expected to inhabit doubt-free zones in their life of faith and be uniquely controlled and untroubled in their sexuality. We now know that this is an ideal which is hardly ever realized.

The major complicating effect of all this upon Christians is probably more psychological than moral or legal. It is true, of course, that all societies need wisdom in handling this human reality that we have already likened to electricity, a vital energy that brightens our lives but needs to be treated with care. Most of these codes and systems are grounded on the normativeness of the male experience and are usually less sensitive to the women's needs. The most extreme example is probably the practice of female circumcision, as an intervention that secures the fidelity of women by removing their ability to experience sexual pleasure, without impeding their use by the male. Complicated as sexuality is everywhere, it seems to have a particular momentousness in Christianity, which makes sex itself problematic and productive of enormous psychic tension. We have already noted how the Reformation accepted the understanding of sex as disease, so that this instinct, above all the other instincts, is thought of as uniquely flawed and only to be indulged within licensed arrangements. That, at least, is the theory. The facts rarely fitted the theory. The question now is whether we should attempt any longer to make them fit.

2

One of the constant paradoxes of human nature is that we tend to treat our own era as uniquely corrupt and disintegrating: standards are falling and all the great institutions that hold human community together are under a state of pitiless assault; yet, at the same time, we treat the institutions we have inherited and the assumptions we make about meaning and society, religion and love, as if they were eternally normative. This kind of dilemma is almost unavoidable. As we have already seen, one of the ways we operate is by interiorizing, making our own, the going value systems or paradigms that undergird our sense of ourselves and the meaning of life and society. We tend to think that the way we handle these things has been around forever, and that the institutions we have inherited have been unchanging through the ages. A reading of history illustrates how false this view is. Nevertheless, it is persistent. The one unchanging reality in the human condition is change. It is true that there have been long periods when culture and society achieved a kind of stability, but these are precisely the periods few of us would want to visit. Maybe it would have been pleasant enough to have been lord of the manor in one of those draughty fortresses, but we certainly would not have enjoyed being peasants on the estate, never knowing when a bad harvest would bring destitution. There has been a tendency in the Church down the ages to sacralize the different stages of human evolution and treat them as eternally fixed. For a long time the Church taught that the divisions in society between the powerful and the weak, the rich and the poor, the nobility and the peasantry, were not arbitrary human inventions, but divinely given, unchanging realities. That is a cautionary prologue to what will be a swift review of the history of marriage, because it is one of those institutions about which we continue to make enormous, though rarely justified, claims.

The first thing to note is that the modern understanding of marriage is very recent and is peculiar to our culture. Let me quote from a lecture delivered by Janet Walker, Director of the Relate Centre for Family Studies at the University of Newcastle Upon Tyne:

> Until well into the seventeenth century love and companionship were secondary considerations in the marriage relationship. Marriage created an economic union, an alliance between families and kinship networks. As far as the law was concerned, husband and wife were one, *'the very being or legal existence of the woman being suspended during the marriage ...'* (Blackstone, 1765). But as parents played a less dominant role in the choice of their children's marriage partners after the mid seventeenth century, the socially accepted criterion for choice laid increasing emphasis on the affective bonding of the couple. By the eighteenth century parents were warning daughters not to read novels lest they develop unrealistic notions about the joys of marriage – there was awareness already of the connection between the search for romantic love and marital unhappiness. In the late twentieth century, our increasing emphasis on personal emotional satisfaction has dramatically changed our expectations of marriage, and our tolerance of unhappy relationships. A strong emotional bond is no longer viewed as a bonus – rather it is the key aspiration in marriage.[6]

Marriage, like all other human institutions, has been subject to change and evolution, and our expectations of it today are very different to those of our ancestors in the seventeenth century. Indeed, our expectations of it may be impossibly high.

DANCING ON THE EDGE

Let us turn to the role the Church has played. The facts are interesting. If we read the studies of marriage and divorce written by Lawrence Stone, we discover just how varied marriage practices were, how changeful has been the approach of the Church and how indifferent it has been at certain periods.

> For its first thousand years the Church in the West took very little part in marriage, offering blessings only to priests and well-to-do lay people. But even by the early nineteenth century only about half of the adult population was formally married. It was only a matter of concern for those who sought to retain their social standing and avoid the dreaded state of poverty ... The Fourth Lateran Council (1251) ordered banns to be read and weddings to be held in public but did not insist on ecclesiastical benediction. The whole matter was eventually officially resolved in the Roman Catholic Church at the Council of Trent, when it was decided that a marriage must take place in the context of a public Christian ceremony and marriage came to be regarded as a sacrament. Therefore public Christian ceremony combined with the much-debated consent and consummation as the basis of validity.[7]

From this encapsulation of a long period of history we can see that the Church has varied its attitude to marriage and marriage discipline over the centuries. We might describe the evolution of marriage in Western understanding as a move from a contractual economic arrangement, from what Jack Dominian calls 'task orientated togetherness', to modern marriage, which he describes as 'an interpersonal encounter of intimacy'. Today we marry for love, and this is where new difficulties arise. Because of the high expectations many people bring to marriage, they experience the reality too often as a major disappointment. A headline in one of our national newspapers put it like this: 'Lovely idea – shame about the reality'. Elizabeth Stuart provides a good summary of the statistics:

> Despite dramatically declining figures for those over 16 marrying for the first time, nine out of ten people marry before they are 30 and two-thirds of all marriages

are between those who are marrying for the first time. In Britain one in three marriages ends in divorce; in the United States the failure rate is worse. The average span of what is supposedly a lifelong relationship is nine years. 9.5 per cent of marriages in Britain end in divorce in the first two years of marriage.[8]

These are the sort of statistics that send politicians and clergy to the microphone, but we must not allow them to scare us into a panic, wringing our hands and crying that our days are uniquely evil. They are not; and a reading of history can be a cordial for drooping spirits. Let us turn again to Janet Walker:

> Until the twentieth century divorce was not a feature of daily life. But we must not be tempted to believe that in the past there were proportionately fewer unhappy marriages – in reality, there were probably more. There were, however, economic, social and emotional constraints that served to keep couples locked into intensely unhappy, often violent relationships. Death provided the most common way out. In the mid nineteenth century as many marriages ended through death in the first 15 years, as ended in divorce in the 1980s ...
>
> In the nineteenth century two in every five children lost their father and almost the same proportion their mothers by the age of 15. One in 25 would have lost both. The only difference is that for those children the loss was absolute. Step-parents were just as much a feature of Victorian family life as they are today, as was living in a lone parent household. Indeed in 1851 about one in eight children under the age of 15 lived with a lone parent – a figure very similar to that recorded in the 1981 census. Add to these the children who were in institutional care, and those who lived with other relatives, then the proportion of children being brought up outside the two-parent family unit was the same in 1851 as it is today.[9]

The modern paradox is that people divorce today not because marriage has become unimportant to them but because it has become so important that they have little tolerance for an unhappy union. Janet Walker reminds us:

> Ending a marital relationship is far from easy. It can be deeply damaging for adults, but there is no evidence to suggest that couples entering a marriage anticipate divorce – it is something which only ever happens to other people. Marriages disintegrate over time, often years, and people remain in deeply unhappy marriages often for the sake of the children, or in the hope that things might improve, simply because ending a marriage is such a serious step to take. Divorce is the second most stressful life event for adults, after the death of a spouse.[10]

It can be seen, therefore, that, while there are many things to give us pause, the picture is not as straightforward as some commentators would have us believe. It is certainly not helpful to denigrate single-parent families as if they were a recent invention or were a particularly potent cause of social disintegration. The evidence would suggest that they can be as good as some marriages, better than some and worse than some, just as some marriages are good, some are tolerable and some are awful. Even the Bible offers us variety here. Elizabeth Stuart finds 40 different forms of family mentioned or implied in the Hebrew Christian scriptures. These include: patriarchal extended families; polygamous marriage; female-headed extended families; single parents and children; monogamous marriage; cohabitation without marriage; surrogate motherhood; unrelated adults sharing a home; women married by force; cross-cultural adoptive families; cross-class adoptive families; and even commuter marriages. She comments:

> The Hebrew and Christian scriptures actually speak a great deal more accurately and honestly about family life than most Christian Churches. They do not idealise or sentimentalise but present us with a quilt of images which we can recognise in our own experience of family life and which cries out in defiance of those who seek to claim it as the source and demander of 'traditional family values'.[11]

When all has been said and every concession and explanation has been offered, we should recognize that the human community ought to help and encourage people to relate wisely and kindly to one another. We know that the breakdown of these covenants of marriage or friendship do enormous damage. How, therefore, can we help one another to stay within our covenants and to make them emotionally more rich?

Karl Barth said that there was no Christian doctrine of marriage; there was only a doctrine of the marriage service. The actual business of staying married and growing in marriage was something that we took too much for granted, paid little attention to, and imposed certain stereotypes upon. Marriage was late on the Christian scene, and when it appeared the focus tended to be upon the theological or legal status of the marriage service itself, the promises that were taken and the intention that lay behind them. Little attempt was made at understanding the interpersonal dynamics of the marriage relationship. Today the scene is different. To quote Jack Dominian again, we have moved in our understanding of marriage from 'task orientated togetherness to an interpersonal encounter of intimacy', and it is this new expectation that imposes the greatest strain on marriage. Sometimes that strain focuses upon gender differences, the subject of Deborah Tannen's impressive book *You Just Don't Understand*. Men and women use language differently and for different purposes, she claimed: women use it for rapport and men for report; women use narrative in an almost sacramental way to share themselves with others, to share their day; whereas men tend to use language instrumentally and purposively, for report. Many of the misunderstandings that afflict the average marriage are to do with the different ways we express ourselves emotionally and the different force conversation has for us. There are exceptions, of course. Some women are reserved and stoical, and some men are emotional cauldrons. The importance of this insight, anyway, does not lie in some theory of gender relations, but in acknowledging that negotiating differences between human beings, keeping channels of communication open, building up relational intimacy, all require work and are not easy; and men and women very often have different capacities for the work of staying married as opposed to getting married. It is obvious, therefore, that we should spend more time understanding the forces that break relationships and assist people to deal with them; and we should learn the disciplines that help to fortify and restore relationships that are close to breakdown.

The fundamental insight is that marriage is a difficult relationship to sustain and it should not be entered, as the Prayer Book warns us, lightly or inadvisably. Once entered, it cannot be assumed that it will automatically flourish, deepen and develop. We can learn much about covenants from scripture. The story there is of the faithfulness of God and the faithlessness of Israel, and about God constantly calling his people back into relationship. Christians should help others with their covenants, and there are a multiplicity of covenant relationships in our culture. We should assist people to remain faithful to their friendships as well as the covenant we call marriage, without insisting upon one pattern of relationship to the exclusion of all others. The Church has always had an ambivalent relationship with society and culture. On the one hand, it adapts itself to the culture in which it finds itself, in a more or less approving, more or less critical way. It has adapted itself to political arrangements that modern democrats would find impossible to approve; but there is wisdom as well as compromise in these arrangements. All human arrangements are provisional and revisable, but they can, in their way and in their time, serve humanity and keep it in some sort of equilibrium, especially if they are legitimated by the consent of the society itself. The Church has usually recognized that the best can be the enemy of the good and, since the best is rarely available to human beings, they usually have to content themselves with structures that are good enough to do the job, though imperfect. In relationships between the sexes, the Church has adjusted to a variety of forms, even if it has retained an idealized norm in its tradition. It has always lived with a degree of tension between responding to people as they actually are, and holding before them the ideal. It is a difficult tension to hold, especially if we are unsure what the ideal is in the relational sphere. Western society has moved into a culture that has a variety of ways of organizing its sexual arrangements. As well as the traditional estate of matrimony, however beset by divorce, most people see nothing wrong in cohabiting before marriage (and in this they reflect a permanent human tradition) or in cohabitation as an alternative to or a variant of marriage. This is not necessarily evidence of moral disintegration.

Surveys show that faithfulness is still a strong value for most people, certainly in intention. The new, more relaxed attitude to official approval or legitimation may even be evidence of a laudable desire to maintain personal independence and integrity in the face of social pressure. The Christian community ought to respond to people where they find themselves. It should try to avoid becoming a support for bourgeois values, rather than an instrument of the gospel of a grace that meets people where they are, without waiting till they have gained access to the official enclosure. But we have not yet looked at the meaning or nature of the sexual act itself, only at the various contexts in which it occurs. What can science tell us about the subject?

CHAPTER SIX

Sex and Why It Bothers Us

At the end of the twentieth century the human community is in a crisis of relationships. The statistics are well
known to us all: the increase in divorce, the number of
people who cohabit, choosing not to get married, the number of
children brought up in single-parent families, the uneasiness that
sometimes characterizes relations between men and women at the
tail end of the second millennium, and the complex debate about
same-sex relationships. It is a situation that is not patient of a simple description or diagnosis, nor are there any obvious cures. In
this chapter we shall examine the background to the current
predicament and discuss some responses to it.

In entering a debate of this sort, we look for an instrument of
interpretation, however symbolic it might be; some key that will
help us to enter the discussion. For instance, in Milton's great poem
Paradise Lost, the first evidence of the new state of sinfulness of
Adam and Eve after they have eaten the forbidden fruit is that they
sexually arouse each other for the first time, the implication being
that their straightforward companionship has now been tainted by
passion and desire.

> *Adam took no thought,*
> *Eating his fill, nor Eve to iterate*
> *Her former trespass feared, the more to soothe*
> *Him with her loved society, that now*
> *As with new wine intoxicated both*
> *They swim in mirth, and fancy that they feel*
> *Divinity within them breeding wings*
> *Wherewith to scorn the earth: but that false fruit*
> *Far other operation first displayed,*
> *Carnal desire inflaming, he on Eve*
> *Began to cast lascivious eyes, she him*

As wantonly repaid; in lust they burn:
Till Adam thus gan Eve to dalliance move.[1]

The Adam and Eve story is certainly an instructive myth, but it does not explain why human beings are the way they are; rather, it is a colourful way of describing how they are. In the Genesis story we see the relationship between man and woman characterized by the dominance of the man over the woman and the woman subjected to the pain of childbirth and a life of drudgery. In the text there is a disproportionate emphasis upon the responsibility of Eve for the first sin, but there is no suggestion that sex itself is the cause of this tragic abandonment of Eden, though there is more than a hint that sex is a consequence of the Fall, since the original couple now know they are naked and hide themselves from God. The idea that sex is the cause as well as the consequence of the Fall came into the Christian system much later. The doctrine of the Fall, the idea that all human relations are vitiated by a psychic virus, clearly applies to everything, including sex; but it is more descriptive of the fact than helpful in accounting for it. Scripture describes human beings as complicated, fallen creatures who struggle to be righteous and chaste; it does not say *why* they are the way they are, except through this myth of decline from a previous golden age of innocence because of an act of primordial disobedience. The myth of the Fall is illuminating and suggestive, especially in the way it captures the moral tension in humanity and the complicated relationship between men and women; but there are other ways of explaining the human predicament and accounting for the dilemmas we find ourselves in.

One that is instructive comes from the comparatively new science of evolutionary psychology, which tries to account for human behaviour by studying our genetic drive, the compulsion to replicate our genes. Without necessarily agreeing with every aspect of this deterministic theory, we can learn much from it. We already know that as human beings we are curiously dualistic. An old Jewish commentary on the Creation points out that in the Book of Genesis all parts of creation are pronounced good or completed by God, except humanity. Humanity is not yet fully created; it is a dynamic, evolving reality. Modern science has taught us much about the long process of evolution that has brought us, after

DANCING ON THE EDGE

billions of years of development, to what we are today: conscious creatures who try to understand our nature and the universe we inhabit. We are what Pascal called 'thinking reeds', reeds so fragile that nature can easily crush us, but reeds that transcend nature, because we have minds that seek to understand and look for answers; in us nature has become self-conscious. The picture that emerges is of a divided humanity, part of which is governed by the dynamism of our genes and their determination to replicate; and part of which points to another side of our nature, the rational ability to study ourselves so that we can learn how to modify our instinctual drives. We are not driven entirely by blind nature, like the sub-rational creation, which is programmed to feed, breed and die. We share many of these characteristics, but in us nature has been given sight, so we are able to see what is going on, to stand apart to some extent, and transcend nature. Being human is not straightforward, because the rational side of our nature is in tension with, though never entirely in control of, our instinctual nature.

These two aspects of our humanity are often experienced in a struggle that is seen with particular clarity in the area of male violence. In the early stages of our evolution the ability to fight, to defend ourselves against neighbouring bands of hunter-gatherers, had high survival value. The strong man, the fighter, became the prototype of the classic male. We have long since left the environment in which *that* drive was necessary for survival, but it still lurks within us. Male violence has scarred our era with the most horrendous wars history has ever known; it ruins relationships between men and women; and it can even destroy the innocent enjoyment of football spectators. Being a male continues to be dangerous. Steve Jones points out that at birth there are 105 males to every 100 females, though this drops to 103 to 100 at the age of 16; but by the age of 70 there are twice as many women as men. Men have more accidents than women, suffer from more infectious diseases and kill each other more often. Crime and random violence is mainly the preserve of young males.[2] Traditional male sports contain a high level of violence and danger, which is why many men, to the bafflement of most women, support boxing against those who campaign for its prohibition. Everywhere, we see male aggression in contention with the desire for peace, our need to live with our neighbours in harmony. Males often find themselves caught in a struggle between their impatience, anger and violence, and their desire for tenderness, their longing to build up communities where children flourish and peace may prevail.

The science of genetics and the new discipline called evolutionary psychology, a particular application of Darwin's theory of evolution, have shed new light on why we are the way we are. According to David Suzuki and Peter Knudtson:

> A gene is life's way of remembering how to perpetuate itself. That memory is chemical. It is woven into the intricate internal structure of a family of biological molecules, called *nucleic acids* found in *chromosomes* and other gene bearing bodies in organisms ranging from viruses and bacteria to human beings.[3]

Genes are the vehicle of biological inheritance through which living things transmit information from one generation to the next. In 1953 Watson and Crick discovered DNA, a molecule that stores vast amounts of coded information – our genes – and replicates itself in order to make new cells loaded with the same information and self-replicating capability. These self-replicating genetic molecules are essential to life. Scientists believe they appeared with the first stirrings of life on our planet. Most of the matter in the universe seems to be dead or inert, which is why we speculate about whether there might be life on other planets in other parts of the universe. One definition of life is the ability of a thing to reproduce or replicate itself. This process of self-replication is the miracle of life itself. The first gene is thought to have appeared more than 3.5 billion years ago in the lifeless, saline seas of the young planet earth. According to Suzuki and Knudtson:

> Any attempt to reconstruct the origin of genes must deal with a paradox. The first organism had to have some sort of genetic mechanism to ensure the continuity of its kind. Yet even the simplest genetic mechanisms found in modern organisms are fairly complex. How could heredity have been handled in early life forms during the gradual transition from non life to life?[4]

The earth's atmosphere was composed of gases in concentrations that would poison most modern organisms. Poured from erupting volcanoes, the atmosphere was a mix of methane, ammonia, nitrogen, carbon dioxide and other gases; it was dark with clouds that poured

DANCING ON THE EDGE

down rain to feed the shallow, emerging seas. Scientists speculate that a combination of powerful natural forces, such as sunlight, geothermal heat, radioactivity and lightning, provided the critical jolts of energy that made chemical reactions possible. These flashes of energy resulted in the emergence of more complex molecular structures. This march towards greater molecular complexity, or chemical evolution, gradually enriched the seas with a mix of spontaneously formed organic chemicals. Among these were small pools of nucleotides and sugars, the basic ingredients in modern gene bearing nucleic and amino acids, the building blocks of modern proteins. Over millions of years these ingredients formed and reformed into countless random combinations. The primal gene may have been a product of this chemical roulette. This time, however, there was a difference: it possessed the power of self-replication and was, therefore, the beginning of organic life and its development on our planet.

With the appearance of this self-replicating molecule the engines of biological evolution stuttered into action:

> The primitive genetic mechanism allowed a molecule to produce a wild profusion of chemical offspring, transforming raw marine resources into replicas faster than any other molecule. This self replication, in turn, permitted its 'kind' to command an increasing share of the pool of small-molecule marine resources in its surroundings at the expense of less innovative competitors.[5]

From the beginning this process of self-replication was prone to error. In each new generation an element of chemical imperfection, and therefore of genetic diversity, was introduced. With this molecular innovation came biological evolution:

> for not only did this first genetic molecule possess the memory for its own duplication, it also retained a memory of any accidental lapses that fortuitously enhanced its survival. The primal gene thus met the two prerequisites for evolution: possession of a hereditary system and possession of a source of heritable change.[6]

So far, these primitive life forms are self-replicating or sexless. Steve Jones, in his book *The Language Of The Genes*, asks why sex appeared on the evolutionary scene. It is a late arrival, but why is it here at all? He points out that some creatures manage with just females, so that every individual produces copies of herself. Why do any bother with males? Jones defines sex as

> a way of producing individuals who contain genes from more than one line of descent, so that inherited information from different ancestors is brought together each generation. In an asexual creature everyone has one mother, one grandmother, one great-grandmother, and so on in an unbroken chain of direct descent from the ur-mother who began the lineage.[7]

One theory about why life is not female, and therefore sexless, has to do with mutation. If a sexless organism had a harmful change to her DNA it would be handed on to all her descendants, none of whom would ever get rid of it, however destructive it might be, and the decay of the genetic message would set in as one generation succeeded another. Jones points out that in a sexual creature the new mutation can be purged as it passes to some descendants but not others. He says that sex has a positive effect on evolution, because the new combinations of genes are better able to cope with the challenges of a changing environment. In fact, creatures that have given up males have problems:

> Nearly all asexual plants can only be used for a few years. They become so loaded with genetic damage that they no longer thrive, or they cannot keep up in the evolutionary race with their parasites, who in time prevail. Their lineage has become senescent.[8]

Sex means that new mixtures of genes arise all the time, as the chromosomes from each parent combine. Sex reshuffles life's cards continuously. Jones reminds us that sex has always been filled with strife; 'the battle of the sexes' is more than a cliché. The very existence of males and females is the resolution of a war to pass on cytoplasmic genes. There is conflict between males for females. There is also conflict between males and females, as they invest time and effort in bringing up their young.

As far as sexual relations are concerned, Jones points out that our closest relatives have very contrasting lifestyles. From the human perspective, 'chimps are deplorable but gorillas dull'. The male chimpanzee copulates hundreds of times with dozens of females each year, while the gorilla has to wait for up to four years for his female to be ready to mate after she has given birth. Even then she is available for only a couple of days each month. It is no surprise, therefore, that there is intense competition among gorilla males for access to females. In his book *The Moral Animal: The New Science Of Evolutionary Psychology*, Robert Wright says that by examining the physiology of primates we can learn something about our own evolution:

> Just how far from being naturally monogamous is our species? Biologists often answer this question anatomically. There is anatomical evidence – testes weight and the fluctuation in sperm density – to suggest that human females are not devoutly monogamous by nature. There is also anatomical evidence bearing on the question of precisely how far from monogamous males naturally are. As Darwin noted, in highly polygynous species the contrast in body size between male and female – the 'sexual dimorphism' – is great. Some males monopolise several females, while other males get shut out of the genetic sweepstakes altogether, so there is immense evolutionary value in being a big male, capable of intimidating other males. Male gorillas, who mate with lots of females if they win lots of fights and no females if they win none, are gargantuan – twice as heavy as females. Among the monogamous gibbons, small males breed about as prolifically as bigger ones, and sexual dimorphism is almost imperceptible. The upshot is that sexual dimorphism is a good index of the intensity of sexual selection among males, which in turn reflects how polygynous a species is. When placed on the spectrum of sexual dimorphism, humans get a 'mildly polygynous' rating. We're much less dimorphic than gorillas, a bit less than chimps, and markedly more than gibbons.[9]

In our species, males are about 15 per cent bigger, enough to suggest that male departures from monogamy are not just a recent cultural invention. Jones suggests that humans, with men just a little larger than women, have a history of mild polygyny intermediate between that of the gorilla and the chimpanzee whose 'more relaxed lifestyle has taken the pressure off sexual hostility and males and females weigh about the same.'[10] Wright is not so sure:

> One problem with this logic is that competition among humans, and even prehuman, males has been largely mental. Men don't have the long canine teeth that male chimps use to fight for alpha rank and supreme mating rights. But men do employ various stratagems to raise their social status, and thus their attractiveness. So some, and maybe much, of the polygyny in our evolutionary past would be reflected not in gross physiology but in distinctively male mental traits. If anything, the less than dramatic difference in size between men and women paints an overly flattering picture of men's monogamous tendencies.[11]

Even Jones is not too sure. He points out that among different species of primate there is a good fit between the size of the testes and the extent of male promiscuity:

> Chimpanzees, the Lotharios of the primate world, have enormous testes, while gorillas, in spite of rumours, are far less well endowed. Humans are not too different from chimps in this respect – which may say some startling things about our past.[12]

Further evidence to support this account of human sexual behaviour is claimed by Dr Robin Baker, a research biologist, who argues in his book *Sperm Wars*[13] that 4 per cent of people are conceived during sperm warfare: 1 in 25 owes their existence to the fact that their genetic father's sperm out-competed the sperm from other men in their mother's reproductive tract. The act of conception is the culmination of a fight to the death between killer sperm which are programmed to eliminate the competition. According to Dr Baker, there are three types of sperm: blockers, killers and egg-getters. Most male sexual behaviour can be seen as an attempt to prevent the female from exposing his sperm to competition or to maximize his own sperm's chances of winning. Most female sexual behaviour can be seen as an attempt to out-manoeuvre her partner and other males, or to influence which man's sperm has the best chance of winning any competition she promotes. Even reproductively useless sexual activities, such as male and female masturbation and nocturnal emissions, are part of nature's technique for preparing for sperm warfare and are, therefore, not 'unnatural' but part of an overall reproductive strategy. According to Baker, even the bodies of the monogamous spend a lifetime on alert for a sperm war that may never happen. The obvious trouble with Baker's claims is that they are impossible to verify. Setting up appropriate clinical conditions to measure and assess these claims would be impossibly intrusive, so most of the evidence remains anecdotal. The most that we can claim is neither new nor surprising. Without pushing the evidence too far, the picture of human reproduction which science presents, of unconscious natural forces that programme our behaviour in ways we neither understand nor ever completely control, seems to conform to human experience.

But it would not be correct to claim that the engine of genetic self-replication programmes us in a way that amounts to complete determinism. It is the fear of determinism, the claim that human beings have no freedom and therefore no responsibility for their behaviour, that disturbs many people when they study scientific accounts of human nature. In a recent Green College lecture, Dame Mary Warnock, Mistress of Girton College, Cambridge, says there is no reason to be appalled by determinism, whatever system of explanation for human conduct we adopt. She points out that the bugbear of determinism has always been that if our actions are predictable, then we are no longer true agents – we have lost our power to choose and manage the world according to our wishes or our visions. She writes:

> If we think about the nature of human choice we must recognise that, though what people want and choose may in some sense be explicable, it cannot be completely predictable because of the innumerable contingencies within the context of which a choice is made.
>
> If everything were known and if I lived in laboratory conditions where the contingencies and chance happenings could be kept on record from the moment of my birth, then my choices might appear foregone conclusions

if anyone could be bothered to draw them. But we do not live in such conditions and never could. We could never know all that happened in the past to influence me, nor what was even now happening to limit or guide my choices. We feel free because we act against a background of ignorance, including ignorance of our own genetic system and of the input of circumstances and environment on the computer that is our own brain. Spinoza said that freedom was the ignorance of necessity. It is the combination of consciousness, ignorance, and language which make up what we call freedom of the will.[14]

Another way of putting this is to point to the effect of the influence of environment on our minds and the development of our characters. The evolution of our species over the ages has given rise to an interacting biological and psychological environment that influences us, which we ourselves influence and within which we operate as agents who are partly but not wholly determined by all our previous history. This tension is fascinatingly similar to the distinction between the theological categories called original sin and original righteousness, our tendency to get things wrong and our longing to make good and appropriate choices. We experience ourselves as being tethered but not entirely bound, which is why we usually find excuses for behaving badly while, at the same time, owning that we are at least partly responsible.

Wright, who is a dialectical sort of determinist, understands the situation well:

The basic paradox here – the intellectual groundlessness of blame, and the practical need for it – is something few people seem eager to acknowledge. One anthropologist has made the following two statements about divorce: (a) 'I do not want to encourage someone saying, "Well, it's programmed in and I can't help it." We can help it. While these behaviours may be powerful, many people in fact resist them quite successfully'; and (b) 'There are men and women walking the streets today saying to themselves, "I'm a failure! I've had two marriages, and neither of them has worked." Well, that's probably a natural human behaviour pattern, and they feel a little better when they hear

DANCING ON THE EDGE

what I have to say. I don't think people need to feel failure following a divorce.'[15]

He goes on:

> Each of these statements is defensible, but you can't have it both ways. It's accurate, on the one hand, to say that any given divorce was inevitable, driven by a long chain of genetic and environmental forces, all mediated biochemically. Still, to stress this inevitability is to affect public discourse, and thus to affect future environmental forces and future neurochemistry, rendering inevitable future divorces that otherwise wouldn't have been. To call things in the past inexorable makes more things in the future inexorable. To tell people they are not to blame for past mistakes is to make future mistakes more likely.[16]

There are extraordinary echoes here, not only of Paul's 'The good that I would, I do not; the evil that I would not, I practise', but also of the central paradox of the Christian religion, that we are both forgiven for our weaknesses and strengthened to overcome them. The self-acceptance that forgiveness brings gives us the desire to resist the pressures within our own nature and its ancient history that try to control us. Part of the resolution of our dilemma lies in understanding it and in developing appropriate strategies for handling it. These strategies involve what Christians call the conversion of the mind, the turning of it, by degrees, from unreflective to reflective living, from blind instinct to clarity of reason. Again, Wright is fascinating on the subject:

> Natural selection 'wants' men to have sex with an endless series of women. And it realises this goal with a subtle series of lures that can begin, say, with the mere contemplation of extra marital sex and then grow steadily more powerful and ultimately inexorable. Donald Symons has observed, 'Jesus said, "Whosoever looketh on a woman to lust after her has committed adultery already in his heart" because he understood that the function of the mind is to cause behaviour.'[17]

This can work both ways. We know that the mind is the engine that causes behaviour, but we also know that the mind, however slowly and painfully, can be changed or formed into different patterns of behaviour. The tragedy of life is that we live heedlessly, allowing patterns of behaviour to settle firmly in our personality, and we discover the longing for change when it is almost too late to achieve it. Thought dyes character for good or ill and it is difficult to change the colour of our spots once they have become fixed. The 'adultery of the heart' that Jesus referred to is the recognition that our mind, consciously or unconsciously, can have as much effect on our behaviour as our genetic drive. The battle between our desires, the recognition that certain kinds of behaviour bring pain and complexity to our lives, our tendency to act without reference to the consequences, are all real and can be violent, but the struggle can be resolved one way as well as the other. We can exert some influence on our inner environment and by our choices influence the larger, external environment. One of the necessary disciplines of human maturity is to train the mind to understand the behaviour it causes and so help it to make right choices, but there is little point in moralizing over these matters. A realistic estimate of the human predicament should result in a compassionate realism about ourselves and others, based on the knowledge that when the human community moved away from ancestral systems to more complicated societies, acute difficulties of adjustment arose. We are certainly more than gene-propulsion machines; we are also value-seeking beings; but there is a clear tension between our sexual nature and the need for relational concord in human communities. Inevitably, there developed over the centuries a series of codes that ordered this potentially chaotic tension in a way that achieved remarkable stability in some cultures for centuries. From our twentieth-century point of view, however, the most unattractive aspect of these codes was that they treated women as sexual property rather than as human beings with the same rights and opportunities as males. Some of the most successful of these cultures were also the most severe, in which the external environment was entirely desexualized. Women were literally covered up or hidden away, so that only their masters had access to them.

In modern Western culture we face a complex constellation of factors that makes it impossible as well as undesirable to return to the old arrangements. The most obvious and potent is the emancipation of women, which is historically and inextricably linked to the availability of reliable methods of contraception. Another powerful element in contemporary society is the overt sexualization of culture, so that our sexual preoccupations are explicitly exploited in theatre, film and advertising. The role patterns that prevailed for centuries have been eroded and people are increasingly wary of or unsuccessful at achieving permanent relationships. The heightening of expectations about the sexual relationship itself also militates against stable unions. We no longer follow a stoical code; we no longer find it easy to endure pain or frustration or less-than-perfect relationships. The prevailing ethos is one of individualistic hedonism in which we seek, usually at the expense of community and the relationships that are essential to its health, personal fulfilment, private delight and relational equality. This rising tide of expectations places increasing strains upon marriage, which is now marked, as we saw in the previous chapter, by increasing divorce in our culture, leading to serial monogamy in which men and women marry several times throughout their lives, creating new versions of the extended family and new opportunities for stress and conflict. Another powerfully complicating aspect of contemporary culture is the way an increasing number of women are deciding that men are not worth the trouble they bring. This is particularly true of that small but significant percentage of men who have very little stake in society, the unemployed, the rootless, who father children but do not have the stability or maturity to commit themselves to the parenting role.

This quick sketch of the human sexual odyssey offers little to cheer us, but it is always futile to be pessimistic. It will be useful to return now to our earlier discussion of determinism, the theory that we are programmed by forces beyond our control to act the way we do. The debate about determinism is one of those philosophical puzzles that moves in circles. Most people probably find themselves somewhere between the extreme protagonists who argue either that we are determined and not free, or that we are free and therefore responsible. Since we want to change human nature as well as understand it, the theoretical resolution of the debate is less important than its practical resolution: what must we do?

Our reading of contemporary science, as well as our own experience, points us in the direction of a moderate determinism. We are programmed by our genes to propagate, and it is obvious that many aspects of this reproductive necessity operate in a way we can do little about. At the level of the external human environment, we are determined by factors beyond our control. We did not choose our own parents and we had little control over the way they reared us. We know, for instance, that our experience of nurturing love or its absence in our earliest years has profound and lifelong consequences. We also know that our social context profoundly influences us, and that much in our life depends on the choices and opportunities it brings. Young men from communities where there are few exemplary male role models, where there is high unemployment and poor educational opportunities, are more likely than their middle-class counterparts to end up in the prison system. It is also a fact that among homeless teenagers a high proportion has been brought up in local authority care and graduates to the streets when they are forced to leave the system at 16. We also know from research into the distressing phenomenon of child abuse that compulsive and incurable abusers were themselves usually abused and sexualized from a very early age. The contemplation of these facts should not immobilize us, but it should temper our eagerness to judge. Compassion is a more appropriate response to human behaviour than contempt, and it will equip us better for the task of changing it. What we might call a compassionate determinism will immediately recognize that if we are programmed by forces in one way we can, however slowly, be turned in another direction. What we have to learn to do is alter the determinants. We know from human experience of healthy change that this can be done, however imperfectly. By taking children at risk in one environment and placing them in a better one we increase their chances for healthy development. We know that education is a great modifier of social determinism, which is why humane societies create special educational opportunities for those who benefit least from the social roulette of the present system.

How do we alter the determinants in the sexual sphere? Our difficulty lies in choosing between appropriate and inappropriate methods of modifying behaviour. In authoritarian societies sexual behaviour is modified radically by harsh penalties, such as capital punishment for adultery. Just as influential has been the internalizing of a particular religious code. According to traditional Christian canons of behaviour, any sexual activity other than intercourse in marriage was a mortal sin, punishable by damnation, unless repented and amended. To internalize such a system, as generations did, had a profoundly inhibiting effect on human sexual behaviour.

It promoted guilt, hypocrisy, blackmail and neurosis, as well as chastity, but the janitors who wardened the approaches to God thought it a price worth paying for salvation. As a system, however, it only works if people offer it the consent of their hearts and minds. Plausibility structures cease to work when people no longer find them believable. Indeed, when they see through a plausibility structure they may reject it with a reactive ferocity that denies even its virtues. Time and again we see this drama played out in human affairs: an idea is imposed by force, moral or physical, sometimes both; when it loses its plausibility in the minds of those upon whom it was imposed, it is totally rejected and leaves a vacuum behind, because the people in control spent all their energy protecting a crumbling theory rather than searching for a valid replacement. This is what has happened to traditional Christian attitudes to sex. Because they were imposed or asserted by reference to authority, rather than reason or utility, when the authority was rejected the whole system collapsed. The result is a state of moral confusion that is not unlike the chaos in Russia since the collapse of communism in 1989. In the resulting turmoil, some voices call for the forcible reimposition of the previous paradigm, while others profit from the confusion by an opportunistic amorality. For those who are still able to offer a sincere allegiance to the traditional Christian sexual paradigm there is little more to be said, apart from wishing them well and hoping they will follow their code with compassion and resist the temptation to denounce as damned those in search of another, perhaps less clear-cut, way.

The basis of a new ethic is more likely to be found in some version of utilitarianism than in authoritarianism. It will be self-commending, intrinsic rather than extrinsic in its authority. It will be based on a clear-eyed estimate of the consequences of behaviour upon human happiness and well-being; and it will commend principles of restraint on pragmatic rather than on penal grounds. Nor will such an ethic be necessarily less rigorous than the ethic it replaces; indeed, it may be held to be more rigorous because it will be based on principles of self-restraint for the sake of the common good, rather than on anxiety about the effect of one's sexual behaviour on one's eternal destination. The outlines of such an ethic will be looked at in the next chapter.

Meanwhile, we can at least acknowledge that, as far as our sexual nature is concerned, there are unconscious, natural forces that pour through us; if they are unmodified by the conscious values of love and faithfulness they can bring enormous pain to the human community. We need to educate people into an ethic that understands their own nature and its compulsions, while acknowledging the importance of learning principles of restraint. The breakdown of relationships is immensely productive of pain, anguish and social damage. How do we, in a plural culture that adheres to no single moral system, assist men and women to manage these compulsions wisely and compassionately; and what, if anything, can Christianity contribute? Christianity has a high ethic of holiness and commitment, supported by an understanding of God as unconditional love, as one who is compassionate towards the human predicament. Our Lord's word to the woman taken in adultery is normative. He set himself against the condemnatory lynch mob that wanted the death penalty and, at great risk to himself, sided with her against them. He gave the woman the understanding and forgiveness that enabled her to be strengthened against temptation in the future. This is always how the gospel of Christ works upon our moral impotence and hopelessness. God meets us in our confusion, shame and sinfulness and assures us that we are still loved; that knowledge gives us strength to repent and to try again.

Christianity has much to offer society in its current predicament, but it will not commend itself to troubled and confused men and women if it hectors and condemns them. Unfortunately, this is the prevailing tone in certain sections of the Christian community that are intent on forcing people to conform to ethical systems that are commended on authoritarian, not utilitarian grounds. They divert people from the crucial work of creating an appropriate ethic for today, by insisting that they accept codes devised for a very different time. The tragedy is that, by exaggerating the claim to divine inspiration, they fail to commend some of the enduring values in the traditional Christian ethic, such as restraint. We can make a case for an ethic of self-control by patiently showing people that letting our sexual nature express itself without reference to the consequences is productive of enormous human pain and guilt. If we get it right, such an ethic will commend itself to men and women of good will because of the benefits it bestows rather than because of the penalties it avoids. It will, for that reason, be a more honest ethic than the one it replaces.

CHAPTER SEVEN

Making Sense of Sex

*I*t will be useful at this point to summarize the discussion so far and to bring some of the elements together again before going on to look at some possible solutions. What theologians call Original Sin is a determining reality in human experience. This is not to stake a position on some theory of human origins, but to accept a mythical description of actual experience. Even if we use the evolutionary paradigm, instead of the idea of descent from a previous perfection, and describe humanity as being in a state of incompleteness, the human as a developing, unfinished reality, the term Original Sin is still extremely useful. We can claim biblical precedent for the idea of incompleteness from the Genesis story itself. We have already referred to the commentator who pointed out that in the creation narratives everything is declared good by God except humanity, because it is not yet finished and co-operates with God in its own perfecting. However we describe it, we experience ourselves as incomplete. We find ourselves in a state of struggle between our determined nature and our rational choices; the unalterable facts of our life as we find them and our aspiration towards something better or more fulfilling.

Sex is a particularly powerful expression of this dilemma, because we are obviously programmed by forces we are not totally in command of. In the ancestral environment things were probably less complicated. The rituals of initiation at puberty and the entrance into a sexual relationship that followed probably removed much of the tension we now associate with our sexuality. The pairing arrangements would vary in significance and understanding, but there would be a recognition, however tacit, that delaying sexual experience would be inappropriate if not dangerous, though we can safely assume that even in the ancestral environment there would be conflict and experimentation.

A particular area of tension in Christianity and the cultures it has influenced has been provoked by the dilemma over what to do with sexuality between the onset of puberty and the establishing of the permanent relationship that licensed its expression. An obvious theme in fiction and biography, certainly from the male angle, has been the search for sexual experience in cultures where it was severely circumscribed or forbidden outside marriage. Christianity added an extra burden to the human experience of sex by treating it as uniquely sinful. Other aspects of the search for virtue in Christian experience were treated incrementally or developmentally, but this practical wisdom was usually denied in the sexual sphere. The scope for experimentation with something as momentous as sex was severely circumscribed. Though Christianity may have developed a particularly harsh and humourless sex ethic, we have to recognize that most cultures developed some sort of code for controlling sexuality. Our review of the history of marriage has already demonstrated that marital arrangements originally had as much to do with dynastic and economic relations between families and tribes as with the policing of sex itself. The procreative aspects of sex were taken for granted, and in most societies were integrated without much difficulty into the current social arrangements. In cultures where the family is extended and children are valued and blessed, no matter their origin, the arrival of a new child and arrangements for its upbringing are more easily accommodated than they are in societies where sexuality is severely licensed and arrangements for its practice are policed, if only by social disapproval. Shame was the great deterrent against unlicensed sex. We have moved far from these days in Western society, but official Christian attitudes are still held captive by the previous paradigm.

If we recognize that the revolutionary insight that characterized the message of Jesus was the idea of Grace, the conviction that our folly and failure is met by the unconditional love of God, then ethics, including sexual ethics, become easier in some ways and more taxing in others. Easier, because our acceptance by God is not dependent upon achieving a maturity and perfection we are not given at birth and are unlikely to achieve if the consequence of failure is eternal punishment. We need to make a distinction between aspiration and compulsion in the moral and spiritual life. Christianity has often been unable to make up its mind about the difference. It is certainly interested in helping men and women aspire to goodness and loving kindness, but is it, in Augustine's words, 'a school for sinners' or 'a museum for saints'? Does it take people where they are, as Jesus did, and help them to grow; or does it establish perfection as the criterion of membership and advertise itself in such a way that sinners need not apply? Christians create particular difficulties for themselves, because for them each sexual act is morally complete in itself; by the perfectionist calculus it is already good or bad; whereas a developmental approach takes the character as a whole and not simply one aspect of it in evaluating its progress. Here the model is not the competition in which we can be disqualified from the whole match by a single infringement, but life itself, an evolving human experience with many false starts, moving towards an end which, in the case of the human person, is a realized nature in which compassion towards others is a dominant value, a compassion that avoids harm to the neighbour. The strength necessary for embarking on the moral adventure is provided by the God who already loves us in our imperfection. This does not excuse us from the difficult task of struggling to find and apply appropriate principles for conduct; indeed it adds a particular intensity to that quest, but it is no longer a search whose success or failure qualifies or disqualifies us for the divine mercy: that is already guaranteed. What, then, is the best way to live, and what constraints upon that aspiration are there, where do they come from and what might we do about them?

Those are appropriate questions, though not easy ones to answer. We would expect to find wisdom as well as error in the accumulated human experience, including the Christian part of that tradition. The high Christian estimate of marriage and chastity will have obvious survival value, to use the evolutionary metaphor, so we will want to learn from that, but we will be reluctant to fall into the trap of permanently setting in place particular historic expressions of the human experience of sex. Our governing principle will continue to be pragmatic: in our time and the circumstances that characterize it, what way of ordering our sexuality will best benefit humanity?

We will recognize that room for manoeuvre is limited in human experience, because large areas of our life are determined in ways we can no longer control; but we will also remember that we can work to modify the factors that determine us, and try to mould them in a different direction. Our governing ethical principle will have positive and negative consequences: good persons try not to harm their neighbours and will, indeed, seek to do them good. If we apply this principle to sexuality we immediately arrive at certain types of behaviour that are obviously harmful and must, therefore, be avoided. The most obvious of these is rape. One of the most important elements in an appropriate human sexual relationship is consent. Rape fails this test because it is, by definition, an act of non-consensual sex. This is why defences against the charge of rape usually try to prove that the victim consented to the act. Rape is obviously non-consensual and it is just as obviously harmful to the victims, who experience the act as a profound psychological as well as physical violation.

Most societies have a law that governs the age of consent to sex, recognizing that the young are not only less equipped to make true choices but are also vulnerable to exploitation by their elders. Both rape and sex with children below the age of consent obviously fail the test of behaviour that is based on consent, not exploitation. It also follows from the principle of consent that people in positions of power who use their status to exact sexual favours, either by physical force, the pressure of personality or by exploiting the opportunities provided by their position, offend against a code of conduct that seeks to do good and not harm to the neighbour. In recent years we have become more aware of sexual exploitation in a whole host of relationships. The most distressing is the incidence of sexual abuse in families. It is likely that this has been a constant in human relationships rather than a recent invention, but there is no doubt that developments in society now make us more aware of it and offer opportunities for its detection, difficult at any time, that were not so available to previous generations. A variant on abuse within families is the phenomenon of abuse of children in their care by adults, either as social workers, youth club leaders or clergy. In all these areas we know that children are open to sexual exploitation and that adults operating in these situations have to be helped to identify abusive tendencies and develop codes for their avoidance and detection.

Paedophilia, the sexual love of children, is one of the most tragic and intractable of human conditions. There is no legitimate sexual expression for these urges, though they can be sublimated into creative work with young people, as long as appropriate disciplines are practised. The abuse and exploitation of children is the most distressing aspect of human sexual history, and it is one of the most difficult to deal with. There is some evidence that compulsive paedophilia can be altered by intensive therapy, though very few penal institutions anywhere offer this service. To use a genetic analogy, the only really hopeful approach is to purge this distressing mutation from the human system by taking all possible steps to remove children from situations of abuse so that they will not, as adults, replicate the behaviour that scarred them as children.

Related to these types of exploitation of the young and the weak is the abuse of professional relationships that offer privileged access to people at their most vulnerable. This is a particularly difficult area to deal with, and this is why most professions have specific ethical codes that prohibit sexual relationships with clients. Seduction by the professional of the client, or by the client of the professional, spells the immediate death of the pastoral relationship. This is an area in which most professionals are both vulnerable and prone to self-deception. It is important to understand that the problem in these relationships is not only with the sexual act, but in the impossibility of its ever being a mutually consensual act that has not been influenced, however unconsciously, by the power relationship. Most sexual misconduct by the clergy comes under this rubric: it is as much an abuse of power as of sex and, even when it is an apparently mutual act, it invariably leads to pain, unhappiness and a deep sense of shame and anger in the exploited person. This, again, is a phenomenon that is unlikely to be a modern invention, though it is more likely to be openly acknowledged and dealt with today.

It is worth observing that in all these abuses of sexuality the real heart of the offence lies in an abuse of power that robs the victim of the freedom to choose or reject the sexual advance. Because of the unbalance in the relationship, its lack of symmetry, no free choice is possible. This is most obvious in the case of rape, but it is also true of the abuse of the young, even if they appear to consent, or of people in a subordinate relationship to the person making or responding to the sexual advance. It is possible to apply this logic to sexual encounters in a way that would invalidate most of them. There seems to be an intrinsic asymmetry in the sexual styles of men and women. Men seem to be more predatory or activist in their sexuality than women. Rape is almost exclusively a male crime, and males are the main consumers of pornography and the main users of prostitutes. In traditional societies males were the active initiators of the sexual encounter; and the process of seduction and possession could be interpreted as intrinsically exploitative because of the imbalance in the power relationship between men and women. This was not always a case of 'rough wooing'; the smoother arts of the practised seducer can also be thought of as intrinsically exploitative. Sex is certainly a rough business in nature, and human beings are animals as well as creatures who aspire to rational morality, so it is unlikely that the sexual imperative is ever going to be completely tidy and controlled. The drama of the human adventure is our constant attempt to transcend the purely natural and, in some sense, hallow and gentle it. This is partly what the Christian tradition means when it talks about the sacramental nature of sexuality: as well as being a blind force of nature, the drive towards genetic replication, it is also one of the most effective ways for establishing and maintaining deep relationships. Sex, like Hobbes' definition of human life, can be 'nasty, brutish and short'; but it can also be an activity of great joy and tenderness. Like sacraments in general, sex can effect what it signifies: it is the outward and visible sign of human union, but it is also a way of establishing that union. This is why fraudulent sexual encounters are so damaging. If one of the partners in a relationship is acting the role of lover and pretending that it is a genuine act of union, rather than a nakedly sexual encounter, the offended but trusting partner feels deceived. The act is diminished and cheapened by the deception, and the victim feels violated. It is possible, of course, for sexuality to lack this profundity and to be sought and experienced by both parties simply for the pleasure and relief it brings. Whatever we think of this sort of sex, it is certainly not exploitative by one person of the other, and it can contain elements of friendship and tenderness that remove it from the clearly abusive versions of sexuality we have been considering.

One of the problems of our own era is that the negotiation of these complex relationships has become particularly difficult. Certain university campuses in the USA impose a code of conduct on students that makes the sexual relationship as awkward as negotiating a minefield, with an elaborate system that requires 'verbal consent with each new level of physical or sexual conduct in any given interaction and the request for consent must be specific to each act.' While this must increase anxiety, never a helpful element in sexual matters, it may offer some kind of protection to women from unwanted overtures. Inevitably, as with all human arrangements, there are losses as well as gains, over-compensations as well as appro-priate adjustments, but it does not sound like a whole lot of fun. In the endless process of adaptation that characterizes the relationship between the sexes, this phase may pass, having achieved some shift in consciousness and conduct in the intricacies of human sexuality. It could just as easily, however, herald an enduring era of suspicion in the war of the sexes that will profit none but the lawyers.

So far, in our ethical calculus, we have been on reasonably firm ground. The ground gets marshier from now on. We have identified consent as a key element in validating a sexual act, but it is clearly insufficient on its own if we are to develop an ethic of any subtlety and usefulness. The consent test works best as a negative criterion: without consent, we know that any sexual act is clearly wrong. Is there a criterion that will help us to establish when a given sexual act is right? In continuing to follow this path of ethical calculation we must resign ourselves to thinking our way through the issues rather than dealing with them in an *a priori* way. *A priori* approaches to these matters have important advantages. By ruling out whole categories of behav-iour in advance, usually on the basis of an authoritarian ethical system that claims special insight into the mind of nature or of God, this approach removes uncertainty at a stroke and gives the follower a clear set of rules to live by. In the area of sex the most famous of the *a priori* rules simply states that sexual intercourse outside marriage is wrong. Even that blanketing proposition, however, was capable of subtleties of interpretation. Was every kind of sexual encounter forbidden, or only intercourse? If some things were permitted and not others, how far could we go? That question expresses the quality of the sexual debate in my own adolescence. We knew that sexual intercourse was wrong outside marriage, but how far could we go before we crossed the line of mortal sin? Various guides were offered by counsellors in the days before the sexual revolution. Some said that touching above the waist was permitted, but nothing below; and kissing was fine as long as it did not go too deep. Some of these calculations were ethical but many of them were prudential in the days before easy access to contraception. It is hard to decide which factor has been more powerful in eroding the traditional ethic: the humanist reaction against the Christian teaching about sex, or the invention of reliable methods of contraception that gave women control of their own reproduction. Even the *a priori* approach was not as straightforward as it appears and it certainly did not exclude all sexual experimentation, though it did cloud it with a sense of guilt and danger that was far from helpful in establishing an honest sexual ethic.

For those for whom the *a priori* approach is not convincing, much more has to be said and some of it will involve serious thinking. So far we have been ruling out rather than ruling in. How do we begin to think our way towards an ethic of responsibility that will offer us a way through complex terrain? If we reject the idea that there can be or ever has been an authoritarian sexual ethic that was both honest and useful, what can we replace it with? A useful alternative to the authoritarian approach might be one in which the test is both ethical and practical. An ethic of this sort will involve us in a calculation of the consequences of our acts that will enable us to judge their impact on ourselves and on others. *A priori* ethicists sometimes try to steal the arguments of those who adopt this approach. Their essential position is that a particular activity is wrong because it is forbidden by God, but they often follow the assertion by smuggling in an argument based on consequence and utility: God forbids it because it will make us unhappy and damage the lives of others. In other words, it is not just a case of God forbids it therefore it is bad; but because it is bad for us God forbids it. If the argument goes that way, however, we are left trying to justify the claim on utilitarian grounds and it lays itself open to challenge on the same grounds. It seems more helpful, therefore, to jump straight to the consequentialist calculus, since it offers us a way of commending the ethic through consent rather than by obedience to authority.

An immediate and obvious application of the consequentialist approach would be to say that responsible humans accept the consequences of their actions, no matter how far-reaching they may be. If we engage in sexual acts that lead to the birth of children, then we have an abiding responsibility for them. That is one of the easiest deductions to make within the utilitarian calculus, though it is one that is often and tragically repudiated. At the basic level, the responsibility for a child involves the parent in its physical and economic support; at its most complete, it commits the parent to a lifetime of nurturing love and, in the earliest years, supervision. There are other consequences of the sexual act that may not be as obvious and important as the birth of a child. The sexual act, even if engaged in casually, almost invariably has emotional consequences and these, too, have to be acknowledged and dealt with. Married men who engage in casual affairs have to reckon on the possibility that their new partner will become emotionally as well as sexually engaged by the affair, leading to the classic love triangle in which everyone gets hurt and someone always comes off worst. These are easy versions of the calculus to work out: what about relationships between the unmarried? In the next chapter we shall look at marriage and same-sex relationships; now let us turn to sexual relations among the unmarried.

One of the most controversial aspects of the new arrangements is the enormous increase in teenage sex. Most cultures have an age of consent for sex, below which sexual relations are illegal. This is a tacit recognition that the biological capacity for sex is not necessarily a sufficient justification for having it. Most developed societies will want to protect the immature from the consequences of sex at too early an age. We also know that many young people in our society have sex before the age of consent. While the law is usually brought to bear when one of the partners in these affairs is an adult, it is difficult to invoke when both the participants are children. Here the arguments against the exploitation of minors by adults can be adapted to the case of sex among children: if they are too young to make responsible choices as far as sex with adults is concerned, then it is just as irresponsible where both partners are children. Simply asserting that, of course, will not of itself influence the behaviour of children. What we need is an approach to values that will win their consent. Consent to a system of values is not the same thing as the ability to conform to it, but it is where we ought to start.

A moderate version of what is called utilitarianism could provide us with a basis for a moral ecumenism that might win the co-operation of many people in our society. They might not themselves accept utilitarianism as a sufficiently rigorous principle on which to build a valid theory of conduct for themselves, but they might see some value in co-operating with it if it could be shown to establish a route through the moral maze that faces us. The basis of utilitarianism is the pursuit of the greatest happiness of the greatest number. We should immediately recognize that we are not trying to establish this as an absolute principle beyond criticism, but as an experimental method that might yield helpful results if used wisely and modestly. We know that the principle is abusable, as is any principle, and dictators in our own century have claimed that achieving happiness for the many could be used to justify the oppression or extermination of the few. This is an arithmetical, not a moral way of arguing and it falls into the most basic of moral traps, which is to treat people as means, not ends in themselves. The value of the utilitarian approach is that it can help us to measure results in actual situations. The misuse of the principle does not deny its value, although it should make us wary of turning it into an absolute. Let us, if only for the sake of argument, posit the pursuit of happiness as an ethical end that might help us judge between various types of conduct.

Using this approach in what is called 'values education' with young people could open up some interesting discussions. People want to be happy themselves and believe that other people should be allowed to find happiness. On exploration, however, the pursuit of happiness turns out to be subtle and complex. This is certainly the case in the area of sex. Most people find sex a pleasure, but there is an obvious distinction between pleasure and happiness. Pleasures are immediate satisfactions that may, in the long run, lead to intense unhappiness. Happiness is a strategic end for humanity, long term, something that may involve delaying gratification or even denying it altogether. The mature understand this, though they may not find it easy to act accordingly; but the immature seek immediate gratification, just as the hungry child seeks her mother's breast and will brook no delay. It is not difficult to demonstrate that happiness, general well-being within oneself and between friends and within society, is a greater good than immediate pleasure. So it could be argued that the search for happiness in the sexual sphere leads to an ethic of restraint. Restraint is not an easy thing to achieve, but we could at least commend it in argument and help our young people to understand that the mature, happy person has to learn to practise it. The difficulty facing young people today is that they reach sexual maturity long before they have achieved wisdom in their relationships. If sex were simply a natural, value-free activity without consequences, then a straightforward hedonism might be the most appropriate and attractive response to the pressures of our sexuality; but there is little doubt from the experience of humanity that the pursuit of pleasure for its own sake, without reference to other values, is ultimately productive of pain and works against the getting of happiness.

A happiness ethic could lead to sexual restraint. If restraint were not possible, it would at least lead to an ethic of prudence and the careful use of contraception to avoid the unhappiness that disease and unwanted pregnancies bring. Discussion of these things would be on the basis of commending an ethic of restraint for the sake of happiness, rather than authoritatively asserting its efficacy. Part of the nature of such an ethic would be the way in which it was commended, so that the participants could own it for themselves and offer it the obedience of their hearts and wills. The approach would be pragmatic. Experience seems to teach that human beings in general will respond positively to such an approach, because they possess an innate moral intelligence, though it needs to be kindled and made reflective. It is undoubtedly the case, however, that children will continue to experiment with sex, and this will certainly be so if the subject is not addressed with appropriate honesty and helpfulness. Our approach to the subject should be based not on the sinfulness of sex, but on the laudable desire not to harm our neighbours and thereby increase their and our own happiness.

The moral calculus alters when it comes to discussing sexual relations between unmarried adults. Here the wise will apply many of the same criteria that we have followed in this chapter. No one can calculate all the consequences of any act, and ethics, especially sexual ethics, is not an exact science. Most people will recognize that a con-sensual sexual act between unmarried adults is one that depends upon the intention and commitment of the participants. Surveys show that most people in our society disapprove of unfaithfulness, though they strongly support not only the right of adults to enter sexual relation-ships but also the appropriateness of doing so in established partnerships. When all the modifications on behaviour have been applied that we have discussed in this chapter; when the sexual relationship is freely entered and appropriately expressed; when the consequences, intended and unintended, are responsibly accepted; what is there to condemn or forbid in the relationship, except on the basis of a tradi-tional understanding of sex that no longer commends itself? The Church entered itself as a referee in the field of sexual relations late in the game and its record is ambiguous, to put it charitably. It is right to want to protect the lives of the vulnerable from exploitation, but it ought to remove itself from the field as arbiter of the conduct of responsible adults. Adult Christians, like all wise people, will want to inform their consciences and guard themselves against self-deception, but they must be left to themselves to live their own lives and not become the object of the Church's official or unofficial disapproval. We will turn in the next chapter to a discussion of Christian marriage, but it is worth noting here how insulted cohabiting adults feel when they are treated like errant children or moral lepers by clergy they approach about marriage. It would be better if clergy spent more time helping people understand and cope with the difficulties of marriage rather than denouncing them for behaviour that is no one's business but their own.

The Christian Church has adapted itself to worse things than the present variety of sexual arrangements in society. It has approved slavery, practised racism and stoked the fires of a type of anti-Semitism that led to the worst crime of this century in the Holocaust. The practice of slavery is not exactly condoned in the New Testament, but nor is it condemned. Unfortunately, that cannot be said for anti-Semitism. There are paradoxes and ironies here, of course, but there is little doubt that the tone of the crucifixion narratives in the New Testament, moving and life-changing though they can be, are patient of an anti-Semitic reading. The famous controversies between Jesus and the Pharisees, filtered and interpreted by the authors of the Gospels as they undoubtedly were, led to anger at the Jews, as the Church moved away from its original roots in Judaism. The Gospel of John, in particular, clearly reflects a period when there was conflict between the small Christian sect within Judaism and the Jewish leaders. The motive of the evangelists might have been the desire to commend themselves to Gentile audiences. Whatever the motivation, and however ironic it is that the followers of a Jewish visionary created an enduring and structured hatred of his own people, the fact remains that the record of Christianity is blotted with some of the foulest crimes of history. This alone should induce moral modesty in its leaders. There is something offensive in an institution with so many crimes on its record setting itself up as an arbiter of people's love lives. It is the role of moral dictator that has to be eschewed: not only because it is grossly inappropriate in a body whose moral record is so compromised; but also because the authoritarian approach does not work in areas as sensitive and intricate as sexuality.

This does not mean that the Church should abdicate the area of ethical debate; but it does mean that it should engage in the debate on the same terms as anyone else who has a desire to help in the formation of a healthy society. That means abandoning some of its claims to special wisdom or authoritative knowledge in the complex field of human relations. Like all people of good will, it will want to assist in creating or maintaining social arrangements that will protect children and their parents from abuse, lovelessness and rejection. It has something to offer in this field from its own moral tradition and from centuries of pastoral experience and the wisdom that results. If it wants to help, as opposed to assuming the role of ideological protagonist, it will put forth its suggestions for discussion and testing, without the usual accompaniments of moralistic pontification. There has been a sexual revolution in Western society in the last half century. Much has been lost, but much has been gained. If there is less discipline, there is also less hypocrisy; if there is less long-term commitment, there is a deeper understanding of the reciprocal nature of good relationships. The social historians of the future will provide a more objective account of our society than we can be expected to provide. What we can recognize is that we are in a process of change, and change is no stranger to the human story. There have been shifts before and the Church has learned to adjust to them. Its dilemma is the ancient one of separating the essential elements of Christ's message from its incidental social accompaniments. It is, and must always remain, profoundly interested in the quality and intention that informs human sexual arrangements; it can afford to sit more lightly to the detail of the arrangements themselves. Without necessarily approving everything that happens in a particular phase of human social history, it should accompany the men and women who are inescapably caught in it and continue to offer them forgiveness and understanding.

CHAPTER EIGHT

Staying Together

We have already observed that marriage is in crisis today. In North America there is a one-in-two chance and in Europe a one-in-three chance that any marriage will end in divorce. Many women decide to have children, but choose neither to marry nor to cohabit permanently with their fathers. Many couples choose to cohabit and live in a committed relationship without recourse to a marriage either in church or before a State official. Much of the debate here is essentially semantic: what constitutes a marriage? The theological answer to that question is the pledge of the couple to each other and the sexual consummation of the union. We have already seen that the formalizing of this taking of each other by a couple is a late development in the Bible and in Christian history but, as is often the way in these matters, the custom of the aristocracy or the practice of the Church assumed a normative role. At first this was probably more a matter of fashion or imitation; inevitably, it became compulsory and both Church and State assumed a role that, while being useful and possibly advisable, was an usurpation of the freedom of men and women, within acceptable limits, to arrange how they wish to live. We have already noticed Karl Barth's observation that the Church did not have a theology of marriage, only a theology of the marriage service. Even this was a late arrival.

As marriage increasingly assumed a social and economic role in society and was used as a method of cementing alliances and claiming inheritances, it became important to develop proper legal safeguards against its misuse. Both Church and State became interested in the elements that created or effected a valid marriage. Although these were easily stated, they were also easily contested. To this day, the Roman Catholic Church, because it does not believe a valid marriage can be dissolved on earth, has recourse to a process of annulment for couples who wish to marry again after divorcing a previous partner. It sets out to prove that, in any given case, no marriage took place, even though the couple may have lived together for many years and given birth to children. The areas for investigation in this process of annulment are the elements that constitute a valid marriage. Clearly, there has to be no inhibition or obstacle to the marriage in the form of another spouse who is still alive. There has to be a proper intention to marry for life and observe the marriage vows. Each partner to the marriage must be in a fit state to take the promises with a clear understanding. For instance, if one of the partners has been drugged, hypnotized or otherwise suborned to the act, it is not a marriage entered clearly and advisedly. The final element in this list that constitutes a valid contract of marriage is sexual consummation, a recognition that the act of taking that originally constituted the relationship is still a key element in its legal establishment. I cannot claim to understand the intricacies of the Roman Catholic annulment system but, presumably, before issuing the document that releases the couple from the marriage, they seek to satisfy themselves that there was a defective intention at the time of the wedding, an unwillingness or incapacity to go fully into the relationship defined as marriage.

This type of exegesis of marriage may be desirable, and we shall soon explore the wisdom and usefulness of marriage understood in this way, but it is clearly a development of an original practice and not the original practice itself. Because State and Church perceived that marriage was an important element in the stability of society, they increasingly involved themselves in its organization and consequent responsibilities. For a long time they made it almost impossible for all but the powerful or very rich to get out of a marriage, no matter how abusive or destructive it was. The fascinating thing about our own day is that an increasing number of men and women are reverting to an earlier integrity. They do not see why society should involve itself in their relationships, as long as they are fulfilling their responsibilities and are not breaking the law. There have always been people who have refused to conform to the norms of society in this way, choosing to live by their own standards of worth and integrity rather than follow current practices. In our time this attitude has become common. We are experiencing a paradigm shift in the way we manage our intimate relationships. We now have a variety of arrangements, most of which can work successfully, none of which is immune to the difficulties all relationships confront. As we have already noted, a paradigm is a constellation of beliefs, values and techniques which are shared by the members of a particular community. Changes in these systems occur from time to time and, as with any shift in human arrangements, much is lost while much is gained. The discarding of old practices and the adoption of new ones is always accompanied by pain. New and important values are discovered, but there is always sadness and shock at the discarding of old traditions. We may regret the loss of stability the traditional arrangements provided, but we have to acknowledge that these changes occur in human social development.

The question that is being addressed in this book concerns the role of the Church during periods of social change. Because it is an ancient institution, committed not only to its own well-being, but to the well-being of society as a whole, it tends to operate conservatively and resist change. Many people value it for precisely that role. They see it as one of the institutions that help to protect us from chaos and disorder. This is why history is filled with Christian leaders who gave their support to the customs and social arrangements in their society and anointed them in the name of God. It would not be difficult to show how often the Church, in its various guises, has invested itself totally in the defence of an order that was being validly challenged from within. It has opposed the valid claims of science. It has anathematized democracy, particularly in its socialist form. It has opposed the emancipation of women. Indeed, the present Pope has announced that the question of ordaining women to the Catholic priesthood is forever closed. It should not surprise us, therefore, to see the Church clinging defensively to the shards of a disintegrating paradigm in the field of human relationships.

The question is, Why should it? The way we organize ourselves is not eternal, incontrovertibly decreed by God. We developed it because it suited us and we can modify or abandon it if it suits us. It is an enormous waste of energy to claim that any particular way of organizing society is uniquely decreed by God. A radical reading of the New Testament would supply us with several reasons for opposing various versions of the political order that have been defended in the name of Christianity; but there is little there concerning the organization of sexual relations that we can easily transpose into our own time. The wise solution would be to try to accompany and support people as they struggle to manage their relationships in a difficult time. We might even help them in their exploration of alternative styles of life, while encouraging them, as they do so, to try to love their neighbours as themselves. This does not mean that we have to give up having opinions on how best to organize society, but it does mean that we must give up the role of judge and assume the role of advocate. If we can make a good case for the values we uphold, they will secure the assent of many people who will not listen to our condemnations.

What we must try to avoid is the politicizing of ethics. Though it is never edifying, we are used to politicians playing to the opinions of their own constituents. At political rallies and party conferences they win applause by appealing to the prejudices of their listeners. This courting of the electorate by politicians is one of the necessary evils of democracy, and only the best and boldest politicians avoid it. It is not, however, the best way to establish truth, especially new truth. Christian leaders can easily fall into the political mode of speaking and end up treating Christianity as an ideology. Many Christians seem to think that is what it is, in any case. They confuse the fact of its unavoidable social role, its institutional reality, with its essential nature. They want the body that bears through history the dangerous memory of Jesus, who opposed the principalities and powers of his own day, to represent the very forces he challenged. So the man who identified himself with the outcasts and sinners, the people on the edge, the ones of whom society disapproved, is taken over by the forces of reaction who define themselves by their hatred of the very ones who heard his message most gladly.

In making any kind of defence of the right of people to choose how they want to live, provided they avoid damaging others, we expose ourselves to the charge of moral relativism. It is a charge that should not make us too anxious. Many of our moral and political institutions are related to their context and history, and few of them have any claim to absolute value. Claiming absolute value for our point of view is not the same thing as establishing it. Organizing human relationships is far from being an exact science with only one way of achieving it. Structures that work in one context, and that have established their legitimacy by the consent of the people, will not necessarily work in another, very different context. An interesting illustration of this is provided by the way members of the British Asian community, with children brought up in Britain, sometimes run into difficulties with their own families, as well as the law, when they forcibly try to apply the system of arranged marriages to women who refuse to adapt to it. This is not to say that moral judgements are always inappropriate, though the situation will always modify the judgement. Specifically moral claims will always be attended to, if evidence is offered in their support. In the moral as in the political sphere, absolute conclusions are rarely, if ever, arrived at, but decisions have to be made, because choices confront us. The choices will not infrequently be between competing versions of the good, rather than straight contests between right and wrong. A case for marriage can be made today, but we must admit that our definition must not be made too absolute. Women and men who choose to live together in an exclusive relationship and beget children are married in all but name, and the name is the least important part of the arrangement. Where the law has not caught up with these new arrangements it ought to do so, in order to protect the rights of all concerned, especially the children. The Church, if it is wise as well as compassionate, will affirm these arrangements and not look upon them as intrinsically inferior to legally or religiously enacted unions. But what is the case for marriage as traditionally understood?

Any union of a woman and a man inevitably takes on a wider significance than their own relationship. Their choosing of one another will, in most cases, bring them into close association with each other's families and a whole network of friends and relations. If they break up, they damage that network as well as themselves. It is obvious, therefore, that marriage, however broadly we define it, is an inescapably social act. Publicly celebrated marriages recognize and affirm this fact. Any institution as old as marriage has behind it a lot of accumulated wisdom. As well as expressing the social or corporate dimension, a publicly enacted marriage adds weight and significance to the choice that is being made. When two people come together to establish a family, they are doing something that is both far-reaching and uncertain. The choice of each other is the most momentous they are ever likely to make and it is one that should not be entered 'lightly or unadvisedly', as the Prayer Book puts it. The public enactment of marriage reinforces this sense of importance and helps to concentrate the mind of the couple on the profound seriousness of what they are doing.

The public context of marriage is an important element in its meaning, but the essence of the act lies in the promises the couple make. This aspect of marriage has a positive and a negative pole. It is in the nature of love to pledge itself. Even the seducer knows this. Love seeks to declare or disclose itself to the beloved. This disclosure and pledging of love is the usual prelude to the sexual act. When it is dishonestly given, and the dishonesty is discovered, it causes pain and a sense of violation in the person wronged. Marriage publicly undertaken dramatizes the pledging nature of human love. In marriage, love dares to speak its name.

The pledge also has a fortifying effect. It is difficult for us to live up to our aspirations, to achieve our good aims. This brings us to the negative pole, the realistic side of the marriage promise. We make these pledges to one another, not only to celebrate and affirm our love, but because we know that, formed as we are, being faithful to our loves is not always easy. The promise fortifies the will and is a recognition that love needs to be defended. The marriage vow recognizes what G. K. Chesterton called 'the law of the second wind'. In any relationship there are tight corners and steep hills, places where we are tempted to abandon the enterprise, because it has become too taxing or because some other prospect tempts us. The vow comes to our aid at these moments. We hold on because we have pledged ourselves; and if we hold on long enough we get our second wind. If we give up too soon, we will never experience the grace and exhilaration that can revisit and restore the most jaded of unions.

It is here that Christian marriage can be seen as a religious state and not just as a human arrangement, however sensitively understood. Most religious systems make use of vows and promises. As with marriage, these religious commitments have a negative and a positive pole. The intention is positive: to enter a particular relationship, whether with a community or with another person. There is often a sense of having been chosen as well as of choosing. For all the reasons we have explored, we know that being faithful to these vowed states is far from easy. That is why we make the promises: they fortify us, arm us against our own weakness in the years ahead, but we have to achieve balance here. It is possible to make these vows without a full understanding of their consequences for the years ahead; and it is possible to be too legalistic in interpreting their status. They are human realities and are, therefore, open to abuse and failure. They also speak about certain spiritual truths in human experience. They point to the fortifying effect of the vow, and they remind us that we should try to live honourably for our own sake and for the sake of others. We may think that an utilitarian approach to these profound matters is too mechanical and lacks profundity. A moment of calculation, however, may modify that opinion. A community in which people sit lightly to their promises will be an unstable community, lacking in trust, and unlikely to be happy. Our promises help to bind society together and create the security that enables us to trust one another. This is why Christian marriage, a state of religious commitment freely entered, is a strengthening element in human community.

There is also something severe and daunting about it. Jonathan Gathorne-Hardy certainly thought so. In *Marriage, Love, Sex and Divorce* he wrote:

> The fact that marriages last till death despite their pain-inflicting-structure can only *be* explained if they are seen as something not to do with welfare. Marriage is to do with salvation, it is a way of life, a religion. It is a place of discovery, where someone rubs, grates against themselves and their partner; where they bump together in love and rejection, and so learn to know themselves, the world, good and evil, the heights and depths. It is a fairly tough picture.
>
> It is also a profound one, whose truth raises echoes. Some marriages we all know become clear. Behind the deep angers or bleak despairs which only close, locked-in relationships can produce, you are also, sometimes, aware that you are finding out, living out, parts of yourself, often parts, forces, which are deep and painful. There is, besides, something cleansing in the grim, granite monogamy till death – standing out against the softening tides of present-day morality.[1]

Part of the difficulty for the Church today is that it only seems to have one document in the file marked 'human sexuality' – life-long monogamous marriage. Even if we believe that this is the best option available, it must also be obvious to anyone who thinks about the matter, that it is not universally achievable, so we must try to avoid making the best the enemy of the good. Where a brutal and unsympathetic marriage has broken down and the woman has divorced her husband (in Britain the majority of divorces are initiated by women), a number of good consequences can follow. We might argue that the best thing would have been a happy and life-long union. If that is not achievable, however, there are a number of consequent possibilities that should not be too lightly dismissed. The woman fleeing from an oppressive or brutal spouse might discover her own worth, identity and ability to cope and prosper on her own. That is a good outcome which is surely worth celebrating. The man whose wife has permanently left him might find enduring love with another partner and know how fortunate he has been. That is a good that is also worth celebrating. Most ministers of religion will be able to come up with numerous examples like these.

Are there good alternatives to marriage itself? The very pro-fundity of the marriage vows might be intimidating to a couple who are afraid to commit themselves to a relationship that is so final. Yet they might want to live together, hoping that their relationship will be enduring and mutually fulfilling. Is there any practical reason why the Church cannot assist in strengthening these relationships by devising liturgies of support and commitment that do not pledge faithfulness till death, but do commit the couple to fidelity as long as the relationship endures? If we were more versatile in our response to the complexities of modern relationships we might enhance the meaning and status of marriage by reserving it, in its fullest understanding, for those who really intended its meaning and entered it for life, come what may. This kind of pastoral versatility would assist people to stay together by supporting them at the level they had achieved, rather than, by offering them only the best and most difficult model, leading them into vows they are neither fully able to understand nor capable of fulfilling. At its best, the Church has practised this kind of pastoral versatility. It is sometimes, and misleadingly, called casuistry, the application of general rules to particular situations. Wise pastors have always known that each human situation is unique and, ideally, try to tailor the theory of perfection to the actual context in which people find themselves. This seems to have been one of the main insights of Jesus, though it was, significantly, one that generated deadly hostility from the fundamentalists of his day. He recognized that all constructs of law and religion were created to encourage human flourishing and not confine it. The Sabbath was made for humanity, not the other way round. The same is true of marriage and the other institutions we have created. The challenge for the Church is to conform its practice to its theory. Christian leaders are afraid that if they do this they will lower standards and encourage moral laziness. They seem to be confusing aspiration with compulsion. Moral perfection is not enforceable, but it can be commended in a way that makes it profoundly influential. In the Christian moral tradition, however, perfection has often had a paralysing effect on human goodness and spontaneity. We know that children who are offered conditional love by their parents grow up feeling they are on permanent probation, and caution becomes their determining characteristic. They see their duty as keeping out of trouble rather than risking something new and good. They are more afraid of failure than hopeful of success. This can create frightened and cruel personalities who grow up to hate and sometimes to persecute the reckless and creative people whose lives may be disordered but who are pursuing a dream rather than keeping out of trouble. As always, it comes back to our doctrine of God or ultimate reality: if we think of ourselves as offenders on permanent probation, supervised by an angry judge, then we will live carefully and watch the rules; our plan in life will be to get through it without being sent to detention. We will be very interested in what is banned and what is permitted, because obeying the rules is the way to safety. But if God is already on our side and loves us unconditionally, then we will be able to tolerate greater confusion and uncertainty in our lives. We will have the security to risk and experiment, even to get things wrong, because we know that we are already loved and do not have to earn what has already been given. In each case, the patterns of perfection may be the same, but the approach to them will be radically different. Unfortunately, the Church acts more like the head prefect in an authoritarian school than the poet of God's great love. This is certainly the case when we come to same-sex relationships.

The debate over homosexuality constantly threatens to tear the Church apart. We could argue that the issue has already divided Christianity in the epistemological sense: there are passionate disagreements on the subject. Later in this chapter we will look at some of the opinions that are expressed in the Christian community. What is predicted, however, is the institutional division of the Church over the issue – schism, the tearing apart of the Church's unity into competing bodies of opinion who are no longer able to live with the clash and pain of disagreement and opt, instead, to create new groupings of the like-minded. In sociological terms, schismatics choose to move from the creative discord of the Church into the stultifying concord of the sect. This kind of thing has happened many times in the history of Christianity, and it is just conceivable that it could happen over homosexuality. Before looking at the problem itself in some depth, therefore, I would like to offer a few reflections on managing the politics of the situation that faces us.

We have already alluded to the well-known distinction in the sociology of religion between sects and churches. Sects are essentially groups of the like-minded who define themselves more by what they exclude than by what they include. There is a history of division and sub-division in sectarian Christianity that offers further support to the definition. Sectarians are unable to live with people who do not share their opinions. As their convictions become more refined and defined, the sect, perforce, becomes smaller and purer. We find the same phenomenon in politics. A Church, on the other hand, defines itself essentially by its catholicity, its ability to contain differences within a larger unity. The Anglican Communion, in particular, has laid great emphasis upon the virtue of comprehensiveness; but this is a characteristic that marks most churches of any depth.

Living with contrary opinions, especially on sensitive and threatening matters, is acutely uncomfortable, which is why the sectarian impulse is so strong in human nature, but the fact remains that most human conflict is between opposing goods rather than between right and wrong. It takes a great deal of institutional wisdom and much personal magnanimity to live with these tensions. The main impulse is to try to resolve them by the victory of one side over the other. If that does not work, the next resort is separation, the schismatic impulse. Sometimes the disagreements are intractable and irresolvable, almost as much the products of nature as of human culture. When this is the case, the best that can be achieved is an agreement to differ, to live with the tension. As with marriage, however, this state of tension can be fruitful and transforming, as one tendency rubs against the other.

In the Church at the moment there is a debate about how to deal with the fact of homosexuality. All the responses we noted are present. Some want to triumph over their opponents and win their case; others want to separate from the tendency they abominate and purge themselves of its influence. The truest wisdom at the moment probably lies, not in resolving the conflict, but in learning to live with it. My own opinion will be made abundantly clear in what follows. However, I am not just a private person with opinions and a right to express them; I am a church leader who has to keep at least one eye on the management of change in the institution to which I belong and which I love, no matter how critically. We have already referred to the discomfort and uncertainty that attend any great shift in culture and opinion, and how carefully institutions have to be managed during these seismic upheavals. The most difficult and wisest course before the Church would be to agree to live with the unresolved nature of the debate on same-sex relationships for some time to come, allowing a variety of approaches and practices. The Church is not the only institution in society living with this issue. The military is in a similar predicament. There is a campaign in many countries to lift the ban on homosexuals serving in the forces. The ban has already been lifted, with no discernibly adverse effects, in France and the Netherlands (where the ban was removed 20 years ago), Norway, Denmark, Belgium, Spain and Germany. There is no ban in Switzerland, Australia or New Zealand. Israel, which arguably has the most effective military machine in the world, lifted its ban on gays in 1982. In 1996, Britain refused to lift the ban. In the US the issue has been fudged in a way that satisfies neither side but that may represent the best political compromise available in the present climate of opinion: they have adopted a 'don't ask, don't tell' policy when interviewing new recruits. This avoids unwarranted intrusions into the private lives of individuals, while leaving the official doctrine intact. If the truth were told, a policy of this sort has been operating in the Church for years, where bishops and selection conferences do not intrude into the private lives of ordination candidates unless they are invited to do so. It is unsatisfactory to the neat-minded, but it has the advantage of preventing splits in institutions that take longer to change than individuals. No matter what they may say about the issue, Christian leaders know that they live in an institution that reflects society and its divisions on this as well as on other topics. They may aspire to a neat theoretical solution, some by lifting the ban (the result I would like to see), others by making it absolute. The first solution is desirable but unachievable at the moment, while the other proposal is neither desirable nor achievable. Would it not be far better, therefore, to deal with untidy realities than to collude with tidy fictions?

What facts can we discover before expressing opinions or advocating solutions in this area? Let us try to understand the homosexual or gay orientation, as it is in itself, before it has become a problem for those who do not share it. First of all, we have to note that, morally and politically, sexual orientation is rarely a matter of choice. It is difficult to imagine anyone from, say, a conservative Christian background, either in the US or in Britain, choosing to become a gay person and thereby opening themselves to incomprehension, hostility and persecution. The autobiographies of gay people are full of episodes of dread, denial, escape and appalled self-recognition, many of them written by people who have never had a sexual experience nor ever been recruited by the hordes of predatory homosexuals who are supposed to stalk our society.

The second fact fortifies the first. Gay people in our own lifetime in Nazi Germany have been the target of extermination programmes, and there are people on the fringes of the Christian Right in the USA who come close to advocating them today. The persecution of gay people is strongly rooted in Judaeo-Christian tradition and in many other cultures as well. It may even be a part of the human psyche. Boys tend to persecute their more effeminate or sensitive contemporaries, bullying them as 'sissies', long before they understand the complexities of human sexuality. Sometimes the persecutors of gay people are hiding from their own unconscious sexual anxieties; sometimes they are expressing the ancient human distrust of the new and different. It is, therefore, easy to understand the rather self-conscious gay subculture of our era, which so outrages a certain type of thoughtless conservative, as a rebellion against persecution and a protection against hostility. Many gays on both sides of the Atlantic have had to create safe enclaves in large urban areas where they can live comparatively unharassed lives.

Another fact worth opposing is the assertion that the gay lifestyle is intrinsically promiscuous. This is what one journalist called 'the view from the emergency room'. If we gathered our statistics about automobile use from hospital emergency rooms we would decide they were the greatest menace to society ever invented. Some people would argue that they are, of course, but it would be just as true to say they have liberated and enhanced human life and are as safe as their drivers. The same might be said of the consumers of alcohol: the most visible and vocal are the ones we see staggering round the streets. If we judged all drinkers and the benefits of alcohol on the basis of its obvious public abuse we would come to very negative conclusions. The members of any group who draw most attention to themselves are unlikely to be the most representative of that group. This is as likely to be true of gays as of any other group.

The final accusation worth denying is that gay people are a particular threat to children. The evidence points in precisely the opposite direction. A great deal of child molestation is heterosexual and most homosexual child molestation is done by someone within the family, not by predatory strangers, though it would be wrong to claim that this never happens. The logic of the abuse argument points to the abolition of the family, which is still the primary locus of most sexual and physical assaults against women and children. The fact is that the overwhelming majority of homosexuals disapprove of paedophilia, which is a tragic but quite specific condition.

If homosexuality is a given rather than a contrived state; and if it is present in a certain percentage of the population; and if it is a state that opens gay people to misunderstanding and persecution; how should Christians respond? As a matter of fact, they respond in a variety of ways. We will explore some of their responses in the rest of this chapter.

The Westminster Dictionary of Christian Ethics says that there are four responses in the Christian community to the phenomenon of homosexuality: punitive non-acceptance; non-punitive non-acceptance; partial acceptance; and total acceptance. Before returning to that classification it is worth looking at another way of stating it, provided by Elizabeth Stuart in her book *Just Good Friends*. She says that most of the literature on homosexuality of the last 50 years has been written by heterosexual men, who have treated it as a problem within the field of Christian ethics. Gay people have had to sit on the sidelines watching scholars debate the reality of their lives and experience. Using the metaphor of the football match, she says that when the fundamentalist Christian gets hold of the ball he 'kicks it into the goal marked "perversion deliberately chosen, explicitly condemned by God's word, get cured or get out of the Church".' When the ball goes to the conservative he dribbles it towards the goal marked 'not deliberately chosen, probably born that way, but activity still condemned by God's word – it is OK to be it, not OK to engage in genital acts.' The perplexed liberal Christian swings the ball up and down the field and finally stands in the middle and says that, while it is true that scripture and tradition condemn homosexual acts, they did not know as much about the subject as we do today; and it is also true to say that the Church has a duty to uphold the ideal of heterosexual marriage, because that is what scripture and tradition do, so homosexual relations have to be looked upon as falling short of the ideal but, after all, the poor dears can't help it. Finally comes the radical, who also claims that marriage is the ideal, but why can't gay people marry like everyone else?[2]

The most suggestive thing about Elizabeth Stuart's football metaphor is where she places herself and other gay Christians – on the sidelines, as spectators of a debate that is actually about their lives. I want to avoid anecdotal evidence in this book, but it is worth pointing out that I know a number of gay clergy who share Elizabeth Stuart's chagrin. One of them told me recently that if the issue of gay clergy ever came before the General Synod for debate he would pack in the ministry, because he was not an issue, an ethical problem, a source of anxiety to Church leaders who don't know how to handle people like him. He was a Christian priest, trying to be faithful to the example of Jesus and trying (with success) to be a good pastor to his people. Fortunately, many gay Christians today refuse to remain on the touchline. They insist on getting into the game on the football field. This is easier for lay Christians and professional theologians than for parish clergy, whose position opens them to pressure, intimidation and possible Church discipline. We shall return to Elizabeth Stuart's own contribution to the debate in a moment. Meanwhile, let us return to the match that is being played on her metaphorical football pitch.

Hers is a more colourful typology, but there is considerable overlap between Stuart's classification and the one provided by *The Westminster Dictionary* which we have already quoted. What she calls Fundamentalists, and the dictionary calls Punitive Non-Acceptors, are people who claim to take the Bible literally on this and other matters. Since the Old Testament not only condemns same-sex acts but calls for their punishment, they are punitive in their rejection of homosexuality, and often call for the criminalizing of same-sex acts, even between consenting adults. This point of view is loudly expressed in sections of the Christian Right, both in the USA and in Britain. The text that is quoted to support this harsh position is from Leviticus 20:13: 'If a man lies with a male as with a woman, both of them have committed an abomination; they shall be put to death; their blood is upon them.' At issue is the moral or legal status of texts like this. How we use them will depend on our theory of scripture, but it is worth noting that even Fundamentalists are selective in their use of scripture. This part of Leviticus is what commentators call the Holiness Code. It lumps together a number of things and gives them equal status as abominations. It tells us that a man must not lie with a man, but it also tells us never to eat meat with the blood in it nor to cut off the hair from our temples or shave the edge of our beards. This is why Orthodox Jews, who try to observe this code in its entirety, allow the hair from their temples to hang down below the large Homburg hats they wear. The Holiness Code is a fascinating document filled with wise things as well as strange, and to our ears, exotic ordinances. Most people will take some of it and leave the rest, according to their own needs and the method of interpretation they use in handling ancient material of this sort. However, there is an increasing body of opinion that chooses to take these texts literally. We examined this attitude to scripture in Chapter 3 and there is no need to return to it here, except to remind readers that Fundamentalism of this sort is a very recent growth in the Christian garden and it owes more to the human need for certainty, and our willingness to submit our rationality to systems that will provide it, than to the nature of scripture itself. Those who believe that the Bible is 'the inerrant word of God', therefore, are likely to call for the punishment as well as the condemnation of same-sex acts.

Elizabeth Stuart's next player is the Conservative, who probably matches quite well with our dictionary's Non-punitive Non-acceptor. People who adopt or find themselves accepting this position on religious grounds accord scripture high evidentiary value, though they are more selective and less extreme in the claims they make for it than Fundamentalists. They know it is a historic reality and its history has to be taken seriously, but it is still normative for them. Since reverence for the Bible as a whole is for them an extremely high value, they find it impossible to get round texts like the one from Leviticus. Even more powerful for them is Romans 1:26–27:

> For this reason God gave them up to degrading passions. Their women exchanged natural intercourse for unnatural, and in the same way also the men, giving up natural intercourse with women, were consumed with passion for one another. Men committed shameless acts with men and received in their own persons the due penalty for their error.

Conservative Christians may be personally very compassionate towards gay people. They may lack the hatred and anger that characterizes the Fundamentalists who talk on the subject. Nevertheless, their religious position makes it impossible for them to explain away texts like Paul's. They do not wish to punish such acts, however. They see them as sins rather than crimes. They are often quoted as saying they love the sinner but hate the sin, and there is no reason to disbelieve them, though they sometimes show their love in ways the said sinners find puzzling. This is a very dominant position in the Church, especially in Evangelical circles, who are increasingly influential in Church politics on both sides of the Atlantic. It is an attitude that is also widespread in secular opinion in the older age-group, where same-sex relationships are likely to be dismissed summarily as 'unnatural'.

The player whom Stuart calls the Liberal comes close to the dictionary's definition of the Partial Acceptor. Liberal Christians have a symmetrically balanced double loyalty. They are loyal to the Christian tradition, which includes the Bible, but they are also loyal to Reason and the truths of new knowledge and human discovery. One writer claims that Christian Liberals are able to hold two tunes in their heads at the same time. They are frequently caricatured for their intellectual contortions, but that is because they are struggling to hold together two ways of receiving truth. Since truth-seeking is an intrinsically paradoxical activity, confident Liberals are not ashamed of their complexities. They want to be compassionate and understanding towards gay people; they want to listen to the new insights into human nature provided by modern knowledge; and they want to remain faithful to the heart of the Christian tradition and bring as many Christians as they can along with them. Holding all these elements together is not always easy, and Christian Liberals often fall into the trap of inconsistency. For instance, a report issued by the bishops of the Church of England some years ago on the subject of human sexuality was in many ways a classically Liberal document. It was trying to look in two directions at once: back towards the Christian tradition and forward towards the claims of the gay Christian community. The report went as far as to say that same-sex acts were fine for lay people but not for clergy. The bishops were criticized on all sides for this apparent hypocrisy, but there was a strong political logic in their position, and we owe it the duty of some sympathy. It is, however, essentially an interim position, a useful holding operation while the debate rages. Human beings always have to make these temporary adjustments during the long campaigns that characterize contested social change. In the history of the ordination of women to the priesthood, for example, there was a period when women were admitted to the order of deacons but not to the priesthood. This incremental approach was criticized by protagonists on both sides of the debate, but there was institutional wisdom in it as well as an inevitable degree of unsustainable hypocrisy. It helped people of a conservative temperament adjust to the presence of women in the sanctuary and habituated society in general to the sight of women in dog collars. Since acceptance of change is difficult for most people, we usually find ways of making it gradually, though wise leaders will understand and guide the process and not allow themselves simply to be the captives of it. The interim position adopted by the bishops of the Church of England is understandable in the circumstances, and magnanimous students of social evolution will recognize its tactical importance. It is, however, only a stage in the final acceptance of gay people into our structures and systems on the same terms as everyone else. We cannot say when that final state will be achieved, but it will not happen easily and will require much patience and goodwill on the part of reformers, as well as steady determination. We have already noted that the state of tension and anxiety in the Church on this subject is potentially explosive, so the balancing act achieved by the Church of England bishops has an obvious political logic to it, though it will be an impossible position to sustain indefinitely.

Elizabeth Stuart's fourth player is the Radical. Radicals roughly equate with the group described by *The Westminster Dictionary* as Total Acceptors. They argue that sex is no longer, if it ever really was, a procreative activity. Its main purpose is unitive, the bringing together of two adults into a relationship of faithful, sexual intimacy. They ask why this high doctrine of sexual monogamy cannot be applied to gay people. Jeffrey John, a priest in the Diocese of Southwark, has written a booklet, cogently and eloquently stating the case for this position. In *Permanent, Faithful, Stable* he pleads for the Christian community to help gay people achieve these stable, bonded relationships by blessing rather than condemning them. It seems to me that failure to see the wisdom of this approach is almost perverse and is another instance of Christians allowing the best to be the enemy of the good. For centuries Christian marriage was itself held to be far from the best: that accolade was reserved for celibacy. Even though it was grudgingly permitted, it was recognized that it was better to marry than to burn, so those who were not capable of the best, the life of permanent celibacy, were conceded the inferior state of marriage, presumably because it was better than rampaging fornication. One of the great battles of the Reformation was fought over the right of the clergy to marriage. Reformation theology still thought of sex as a disease, for which the discipline of marital fidelity was the partial remedy. Celibacy was thought, with a lot of evidence to support the claim, to be largely unattainable by men and marriage was a concession to their weakness. There is still a certain logic in this robust and unsentimental realism, but it ought to be applied evenly to the human condition. The ethical realism of the Christian tradition must apply to all human conditions. For those who cannot sustain or do not have the gift for a life of celibacy, the moral calculus points in the direction of a faithful, stable and permanent relationship. Christians who place a high value on chastity and fidelity ought to be putting their weight behind this approach. Even if they believe that gay sexual relationships are in some sense disordered, surely there is gain in helping to make them more ordered. Most of our moral choices are approximations to goodness and truth. Why is it only in this area that one class of people is expected to arrive at a moral perfection that none of us expects to achieve in other areas?

If we do argue for permanent unions for gay people, we must immediately admit that both Church and State will have to find mechanisms to acknowledge these relationships religiously and legally. At the moment permanent lesbian and gay relationships do not exist in law in Britain and in most states in the US, though the picture is different in parts of Europe. Gay partners are not recognized as next of kin in medical emergencies. If one partner dies the survivor has none of the rights that a widow or widower would have in a heterosexual marriage in making funeral arrangements or dealing with the deceased partner's property. It is for this reason that many advocates in the gay and lesbian movement are arguing for legislative action. Most lesbians and gay men want some sort of legalized same-sex partnership, though not necessarily modelled on marriage. There are three options: marriage, registered partnerships and rights for cohabitees. The final option could be usefully applied to heterosexual cohabitees. All three could be legislated and couples could choose the one they want. The main alternative to marriage is a registered partnership, an innovation specially designed for same-sex couples. It is a form of civil marriage in all but name, and one or two states in the US are exploring it as a possibility. In Europe, Holland has recently extended its civil marriage legislation to same-sex couples. Denmark, Norway, Sweden and Greenland have taken the same route. The same type of legislation may soon become law in Spain.

The other alternative to gay marriage would be to strengthen the legal rights of cohabitees to include recognition as next of kin, joint guardianship of any children and entitlement to spousal benefits, such as coverage by health-care plans and property and tenancy succession rights at a partner's death. The advantage of this approach is that it would offer the protection of the law to all cohabiting couples and would go a long way towards acknowledging the diversity and integrity of the different types of relationship that exist in modern society.

All of the attitudes to same-sex relationships outlined in this chapter exist in the Christian Church. As a matter of simple fact, therefore, it is just not possible to say there is *a* Christian position on the subject. What we have in the Church is a debate that will rage for years. This should not surprise us. Christianity is concerned to discover the truth in all things and truth is a slippery commodity. As we have already noted, it took those parts of the Christian community that now ordain women years to reach a decision, and it probably could not have happened any sooner. It is not possible to microwave human social and ethical development. Women entered the ordination debate late in the day, but their intervention was decisive. By the same token, we should be listening to gay Christians on the subject of homosexuality and refuse, any longer, to confine them to the touchlines of the debate.

In *Just Good Friends* Elizabeth Stuart begins to sketch the outline of a new sexual ethic based on the experience of gay and lesbian people. The new ethic is modelled, not on the exclusivity of marriage, but on the dynamic inclusivity of friendship. We might say, therefore, that a fifth player has appeared on the field who is likely to have a disturbing effect on the tactics of the others. Those who are exploring this position say that the value of limiting sex to permanent, bonded relationships, whether heterosexual marriage or gay partnerships, is not congruent with their experience or even their reading of the Christian tradition. They believe that friendship offers a better model, certainly for gay and lesbian people, and possibly even for the wider human community. It certainly seems to be the case that more and more young people organize their sexual relationships round the experience of friendship and not exclusively around marriage. This may not preclude them from getting married at a later date, but we know from the statistics that most people who marry today have been living together in a friendship that certainly involved more than sex but definitely included it. Elizabeth Stuart does not argue against gay or heterosexual marriage, but against the claim that these relationships alone validate sexual relations between people. She believes that we must listen not only to the past, to the tradition, but to the lived and living experience of people today in and outside the Christian community.

Throughout this book we have noted that periods of social change are always extremely painful, but are an inescapable aspect of human history. We will continue to disagree with each other over these and other issues and slowly inch our way to some sort of working consensus. Theological and legal validation usually follow social change; they hardly ever precede it. The validation of change will follow in the area of human sexuality in both Church and State. It is up to us to live through the maelstrom with charity, without denying ourselves the right to contend strongly for the truth as we see it. It is some consolation to remember that the Christian community, because of its passion for truth, is no stranger to conflict.

During the debate in the Anglican Communion on the ordination of women, two important principles emerged that helped us to handle the pain of disagreement and manage the pace of change. It was recognized that it took time for a new idea or practice to be received in any given community, so the doctrine of reception was developed to describe the process of incorporating change in the Church. It was also noted that the process of reception varied according to the cultural context, so the doctrine of contextuality was developed to describe the way the local situation could modify the process of reception. These ideas apply with equal force in the debate on same-sex relations: the process of reception will take time and it will vary according to context. In the case of the debate on homosexuality, however, a third limiting factor ought to be acknowledged: the permanent minority status of gay people. The fact that gay people will always be a minority in the human community places them permanently in a precarious position. They are always likely to be on the edge, prone to persecution and misunderstanding. This may be why so many gay people, in spite of the attacks of Christians, are so drawn to Jesus and his invitation to the heavy laden to come to him and find rest for their souls. It is humbling that so many of them choose to remain in the Church, in spite of its ambivalent attitude to them. It would be fitting if the Church acknowledged its debt to them, sought forgiveness from them, stopped arguing about them, started listening to them and left time to heal the wounds it has inflicted upon them. Homosexuals are classic people of the edge, perpetual minorities, permanently marginalized by the majority in the Church and in society. This is why many of them are drawn to Jesus, the man on the edge; and there can be little doubt that he would be drawn to them.

PART III

Making Sense of Community

CHAPTER NINE

Playing Jazz with God

I

art of the difficulty the Church faces in persuading people of an inquiring mind that there is a place for them within it arises because of the apparent fixity of our symbolical systems. For instance, we suggest solidity and immovability by our buildings, the most obvious witness to our presence in an increasingly indifferent society. People travel past churches in our cities every day of their lives, but they represent an increasingly alien type of consciousness to them. They suggest only the past; they are historical relics like castles and horse-drawn carriages. They are part of the heritage, part of the way we were but no longer are. That is precisely why some people like them, of course, and want to preserve them as they are or as they remember them from their own schooldays. They speak of the past, not of any kind of present reality. They are nostalgic havens from incessant change; they represent the best of what we have been or imagined ourselves to be. Like the films made by the British film industry, they allow us to wallow in nostalgia, to relive the past, but hardly ever to confront the realities of the present. We do the past well in Britain, probably because we are uncertain about the best way to deal with the future. Christianity is part of that past and can provide a dangerous haven for reactionary minds. What is missing is any sense that God is ahead of us and can be encountered in the future as well as remembered from the past. Increasingly, however, we are learning to see the Christian life as a journey, a spiritual exploration. The journey is a more appropriate symbol of the Christian life than a building rooted to the spot. People travel at different speeds. Some of them like a lot of company, some of them prefer to travel alone and, fascinating though the journey is, no one mistakes it for the city they are seeking. Saint Columbanus expressed it perfectly in a prayer: 'O Life, a road to life art thou, not Life. And there is no man makes his dwelling on the road, but walks there: and those who fare along the road have their dwelling in the Fatherland.'

If the static nature of our buildings is a sign to many people of the irrelevance of many of our ideas to their modern consciousness, fortified by public debates between modern scientists and Christian Fundamentalists over the nature and history of the universe, the way we denounce the way many people have chosen to live alienates them completely, because it is interpreted as an attack on their own personal integrity. People are usually quite tolerant of belief systems they do not share, but they do not welcome the kind of moral condemnation that often accompanies them. Moral rejection, being thrust to the edges because of the way we live or the unchosen circumstances of our life, is probably more painful than the kind of theological marginalization we have looked at. The types of people who feel morally edged out by the Church are significant. I don't know any arms traders, people who benefit from creating instruments of destruction, such as the anti-personnel land-mines that mutilate innocent people in the endless wars that are fought in the Third World, but if there are any in the Christian Church they probably do not feel too uncomfortable. They may occasionally have to sit under a sermon that tells the truth about the arms trade or they may hear of attempts at synods of the Church to condemn the trade and their country's reliance upon it. This may create momentary discomfort or anger, but there are plenty of ecclesiastical safe havens where even these minor discomforts will never be encountered. What they are unlikely to experience is the sense that their trade, or the profits they derive from it, systemically excludes them from a whole-hearted welcome in the Christian Church. It is very different, however, for the young gay man who, after years of secret guilt and self-hatred, is finding acceptance, a sense of belonging somewhere for the first time, in the gay community. He may even have encountered gay clergy in the safety of the homosexual subculture, yet he knows that his very existence is a source of embarrassment to the Christian community, in most of its official forms, and in some of them his existence provokes an ugly hatred. He is also aware of the dangers that lurk in the activities of tabloid journalists, whose newspapers profit from exposing the sexual activities of prominent citizens and who are particularly keen on throwing the spotlight on Christians. Many of these newspapers support crusades against lesbian and gay people and add to the anxieties felt by Christian leaders as they debate their status in the Church. We have already noticed how hesitant and agonizing that debate is. The young man will have heard of many cases where a life has been deeply damaged or destroyed because of the potentially poisonous mix of sexuality and Christianity. He will have read of priests who were removed from ministry because of some kind of sexual mishap. People will tell him about the young monk who committed suicide hours after being confronted by a journalist about a sexual incident with a stranger. Our young gay man will have plenty of reasons for feeling that Christianity is dangerous territory for him. If his anxieties need any reinforcing, they will get it from newspaper reports of debates in the Church about homosexuality and pronouncements by bishops on the sinfulness of same-sex relations. He will be puzzled by the knowledge he has derived from the gay community that there are many homosexual clergy in the churches, including bishops; his sources suggest to him that there may be more, proportionately, in the churches than in the general population; yet he is aware that there is a bitter dispute in the churches over the ordination of gay people. He will have read tabloid headlines excoriating 'poofs in the pulpit', but the irony will not have escaped him that many of the most sympathetic and helpful priests he has met are having to lead double lives because of the prevailing climate of opinion in the churches.

All of this may sadden and confuse our hypothetical young man. He may want to resume membership of the Church, without imprisoning himself in attitudes that condemned him to years of misery. It is not unlikely that, like most people, he has spiritual needs and suffers from a certain amount of confusion about how best to satisfy them. While he is glad that he has at last told the truth to himself and those nearest to him about his own nature, he also admits that he would welcome guidance in discovering a workable moral vision that would assist him in achieving self-discipline, without making impossible demands. He feels a strong call to follow the way of Jesus Christ and believes, instinctively, that he would be welcomed and strengthened by the man who was called the friend of sinners. There are descriptions of relationships in the Bible that move him deeply and call out to places in his own nature. The story of David and Jonathan celebrates the possibility of intimate male friendship. The obviously special relationship that Jesus had with the one called 'the beloved disciple', who lay on his breast at the Last Supper, according to the Gospel of John, touches him and draws him closer to Jesus. Official Christianity, however, is another thing entirely. He can stay on, clinging to the edges, at the price of secrecy and hypocrisy, or he can go sorrowfully away, resigned to the knowledge that there is no place in the Church he can occupy with integrity and honour. The anguish of this situation is played out again and again in every generation, as the mystery and complexity of human sexuality expresses itself in the lives of men and women in ways they did not choose.

Men and women who find themselves pushed to the edge by their sexuality must make a valiant effort not to internalize the hatred and shame that is projected on to them by Christians, while receiving from the Church and its moral tradition what strength they can. Like all Christians, they must try to avoid the kind of self-deception that we are all prone to. They will try to recognize the ancient wisdom of the purity of heart that desires the good of its neighbours and seeks to do them no harm. Christians on the moral edge will be honest about their own condition and its dangers and limitations. They will also try to find the courage to recognize that it is human, not divine, to make sweeping moral generalizations and categorize people without reference to their own history. God sees individuals, not categories or conditions. The Church, as an obviously human institution, has rules and the rules can change. They must never be allowed to dictate the soul's relationship with God: that is entirely personal and must not be usurped by the Church. The Church may say, from time to time, with due modesty, what rules it wants to live by in its own life. It must avoid exclusive claims that it is speaking for God, and it should always be open to the possibility of change. Indeed, an intimate knowledge of its own history should remind it that it has often opposed changes it has later sanctioned, giving rise to the accusation that in certain forms of Christianity everything is forbidden till it is made compulsory. The parables of Jesus would suggest that many surprises await confident and moralistic believers about who goes into the Kingdom first and who brings up the rear.

Our young gay man is not the only person who is likely to feel unwelcome in some versions of contemporary Christianity. There are other Christian irregulars who get pushed to the edge, such as the divorced, single parents and unmarried people who have chosen to live together. We have already looked at some of these situations and how the Church might respond to them. It is important for the people themselves to understand that the Church, even in its negative and moralistic modes, is trying, however clumsily, to help them discover the good for their own lives. We have noticed how often the Church has turned the best into the enemy of the good. It is usually its own ideals that lie behind the Church's ungraciousness towards those who have chosen, or find themselves inhabiting, a different reality. Even though the ideal may not always be achievable, even if we have questions about the nature of the ideal itself, its existence does remind us of the importance of discipline and constancy in human relationships. We can be certain, however, that God is more interested in us and our development and happiness than in our success at conforming to an abstract ideal. Abstract ideals are important as aspirations; they are less important than the human beings they are meant to serve and encourage.

Christians who find themselves on the moral edge of Christianity, by reason of their marital or personal status, have to practise enormous magnanimity towards the Church. They are like adult children who have to live with the fact that the parents they love are unable to shift gears in their understanding of the very different pressures and circumstances of today. They will learn to listen to their parents, without too much exasperation, while refusing to concede the automatic superiority of their moral vision. Their own circumstances may be different; they are not necessarily worse than the ones their parents faced. Just as important is the avoidance of counter-superiority, the subtle arrogance that takes pleasure in denouncing the arrogance of others. The liberating thing about Christianity, when it tries to follow the example of Jesus Christ and refuses to ally itself with structures of power, whether moral or political, is that it is a celebration of God's grace poured upon the righteous and the unrighteous, the ones who think their lives are sorted out and the ones who are still in a mess. It was for this reason that the poor and the sinners and the people on the edges of society heard Jesus gladly. They knew they were too weak and disordered to qualify for a heaven reserved for the perfect. The irony was that they were the ones who went in first, according to Jesus, trusting only in the mercy of God.

There has been a struggle in Christianity from the very beginning about its true nature. Was it a religion of law or a religion of grace? Was it a way of human salvation, a new version of the many systems that offered men and women a method that would make them right with God, or was it *gospel*, a new understanding that proclaimed that God was already on their side? As we have already seen, the understanding of the nature of God as Grace or Gift is central to the great parables in Luke's Gospel, but it was made theologically explicit by St Paul. As a result of his meditation upon the meaning of Jesus and his message, Paul developed the principle of justification through *faith*. It is not our own work that *justifies* us or makes us right with God, but God's grace and love towards us. This means that faith, like life, is a gift, and so is salvation, another of those awkward Christian words that have been so mauled and misunderstood. We do not, indeed cannot, achieve these things by our own efforts. They are given to us freely. Theologians, in discussing this important principle, have usually confined it to morality or ethics: nothing we can *do* wins us God's favour; faith recognizes that we already have it. It is a principle that is so revolutionary that it has been largely ignored in practice, though celebrated in theory, in the Christian Church. As a principle, it undermines all human control over God and makes all religious systems provisional and relative. This leads to a deconstructing of religious systems that most of us, especially if we have powerful interests in them, do not like, so we pay lip service to the principle, while making sure that people know that access to God, and the relationship with God we call salvation, is controlled and guaranteed by a whole range of human works: right behaviour, to begin with; then there is right believing; and there is also the right way of organizing the right system. All of these human devices try to protect God from the consequences of actually following the principle of justification by faith. One of the few theologians of our own era who penetrated to the radical nature of this principle was Paul Tillich.

In *The Protestant Era*, Tillich points out that the principle of justification through faith applies not only to the religious-ethical dimension, but to the religious-intellectual as well: 'Not only he who is in sin but also he who is in doubt is justified through faith.' He says that doubt about God does not separate us from God. 'There is faith in every serious doubt, namely, the faith in the truth as such, even if the only truth we can express is our lack of truth.' He goes on to tell us that if this state is experienced in depth and 'as an ultimate concern', God is present. He continues, 'So the paradox got hold of me that he who seriously denies God, affirms him. There is no place *beside* the divine, there is no possible atheism, there is no wall between the religious and the non religious. The holy embraces both itself and the secular.' He tells us that these ideas gave him a feeling of strong relief. Real religion, whether expressed in secular or narrowly religious terms, is about being 'unconditionally concerned'. This is why it is important to understand that no one is outside the divine life, no matter what God's self-appointed protectors may claim, so people who think of themselves as being on the edge of the Church must not thereby feel that they are distanced from God. Tillich goes on:

> You cannot reach God by the work of right thinking or by a sacrifice of the intellect or by a submission to strange authorities, such as the doctrines of the church and the Bible. You cannot, and you are not even asked to try it. Neither works of piety nor works of morality nor works of the intellect establish unity with God. They follow from this unity, but they do not make it. They even prevent it if you try to reach it through them. But just as you are justified as a *sinner* (though unjust, you are just), so in the status of *doubt* you are in the status of truth. And if all this comes together and you are desperate about the meaning of life, the seriousness of your despair is the expression of the meaning in which you still are living. This unconditional seriousness is the expression of the presence of the divine in the experience of utter separation from it.[1]

This means that people who are, as they might put it to themselves, on the edge of the community of faith, already are where they are meant to be. In spite of some of the things that might be said about them by the people who believe they are God's insiders, they are not to be deterred. Even if the Church is reluctant to widen its self-understanding to make them feel they are already inside, they are not to confuse the Church, however it is expressed, with the reality of God, even though their experience of God is through the divine truth of doubt, rather than through the corresponding mystery of assurance. They are, in honesty, where they are, and that is where they encounter the mystery we call divine. To be in this place calls for great magnanimity towards the Church, especially in its exclusive modes.

The Church itself seems to find this kind of magnanimity difficult to achieve at the moment, because there is a struggle going on for its very soul. During periods of intense change, when the acquisition of new knowledge accelerates, there is a temptation for institutions to hold on to their traditions long after they have lost their effectiveness. Faced with new questions, the perennial human temptation is to offer yesterday's answers. We have already seen that Thomas Kühn, the historian of science, describes these periods of change as *paradigm shifts*. The shift from one world-view to another is always painful and is resisted by those who are too deeply invested in the previous paradigm or are too fearful to accept the inevitability of the new. We see these struggles for the soul of institutions right across the human community, in politics, philosophy and the arts, as well as in religion; but there is a particularly complex struggle going on in Christianity at the moment, which is probably seen at its most dramatic in the United States of America, where a strident and irrational fundamentalism has emerged with a strongly repressive social and political agenda. The phenomenon is not confined to the USA. It has spread dramatically in Britain, where there is a burgeoning alliance between right-wing politicians and conservative Christians. We find a similar struggle going on in the Islamic world, where the pains and challenges of modernity are causing fundamentalists to re-establish essentially medieval models of society, especially where the status of women is concerned.

The main question behind this book is: Is there a single and inflexible template onto which untidy humanity must be pressed, a script that must be followed with unvarying accuracy if dissonance and disaster are not to engulf us? That is certainly the claim that is made by fundamentalists of all persuasions. They disagree among themselves as to what the divine blueprint is, but they are alike in the exclusive claims they make on behalf of the one they espouse. Invariably, they cannot endure the untidy freedoms that most human beings cherish, so they develop programmes and moral systems that will confine and control them, becoming increasingly restrictive as they confront the fractured reality of most people's lives. The argument of this book is that this lust for absolute systems and the ideologies that underpin them is itself a kind of faithlessness, an inability to live with the provisionality that characterizes human existence, and a refusal to adapt to it with grace and courage. We have all experienced speakers who arrive at a gathering with a fixed and predetermined script which they plough through to the bitter end, with no sense of its inappropriateness to the people in front of them and no ability to depart from it and engage with them in a living encounter. Sometimes this is caused by deafness to the response and needs of other people; sometimes it is caused by fear of having our inadequacies exposed by stepping out from behind the prepared script. If we can find the courage to abandon the text when necessary and improvise in response to the audience and its dialogue with us, we soon learn that we are making a new kind of music with people rather than forcing them to listen to the few tunes we have in our repertoire. This is the genius of jazz, and it requires not only courage in the performer but considerable musicianship as well. This kind of improvisation is pure music making, and in the history of the art it must have come before notation and written composition, just as story-telling came before writing and oral tradition came before the production of texts. Unfortunately, we have allowed these later developments, though good in themselves, to assume a moral primacy over our original genius for improvisation, so that we now insist on scripts and systems for every situation that confronts us, instead of relying, at least some of the time, on our innate sense of rhythm and timing.

This fear of departing from the text is in marked contrast to God's method in creation, which seems to be characterized by a genius for adaptation and improvisation. The picture of God which science gives us is more like a jazz player than the engineer of the Newtonian universe, with its fixed, mechanical laws and determinate purposes. Jesus, likewise, was more interested in responding creatively to human need than in sticking to the traditional script that put law before humankind. This ability to improvise and adapt has always characterized Christian history, though there has always been a tendency for the architects of particular adaptations to claim exclusive and permanent status for their particular creations. We have seen throughout this book how change has characterized the moral claims of Christianity, but the issue goes far deeper than that. In his monumental book *Christianity*,[2] the second volume of his study of the religious situation of our time, Hans Küng discusses five different types of Christianity. Using the paradigm typology of Thomas Kühn that we have already alluded to, he studies five great shifts in Christian understanding that have characterized our history. A swift review of these five Christianities will provide us with a useful method for summarizing our argument so far.

The first version of Christianity Küng discusses is what he calls the Early Christian Apocalyptic Paradigm. As the description suggests, the first Christians lived in daily expectation of the imminent return of Jesus Christ. The apocalyptic element in religion is a particularly difficult one for modern consciousness to understand, though it is still present in the current mix of religious attitudes. The word 'apocalyptic' itself refers to a future unveiling or disclosing of God's power in history that will overcome evil and establish a new reign of justice. From Paul's letters in the New Testament it is clear that he and his readers lived in expectation of the return of Jesus to establish a new kind of human reality on earth. It is this expectation that gives to some of Paul's writing its strong sense of the provisionality of history and its institutions. Why get embroiled in an age that was soon to pass away? This is why Paul's moral teachings have been described as 'an interim ethic' that was designed to steady people as they waited for the end. There are groups in contemporary Christianity that still live with this sense of expectation of the second coming and it can certainly have a concentrating effect on human consciousness, but most of us use this material, when we deal with it at all, by demythologizing it and applying it to the shortness of our lives and the certainty of death. What we cannot do is enter the consciousness of those early Christians who had become persuaded that Jesus would soon return on clouds of glory to establish a new kind of Kingdom on earth. We use their language in our hymns and liturgies, but we give it an entirely different set of meanings that are appropriate to our own day. There has, in short, been a profound shift in Christian meaning and understanding between their day and ours.

Küng's second version of Christianity is what he calls the Early Church Hellenistic Paradigm, going from the end of the first century of the Christian era to the beginning of the seventh. During this period the language and categories of Christian theology were established, as the Church wrestled with the meaning of Jesus and the nature of God, using the current philosophical vocabulary of the day. There are more continuities between Christianity today and this early expression of it than there are between us and the apocalyptic version, but there have been enormous shifts in consciousness in the intervening centuries that make it almost impossible for modern minds to use the philosophical categories that were adapted so ingeniously by the theologians of the fourth and fifth centuries to explain the mystery of God. Their genius and enthusiasm should give us the courage to do in our day what they did in theirs and find a way of talking about God that is consonant with our understanding of reality and our obedience to the truth. Küng does not suggest that this paradigm is obsolete, of course. Indeed, one of his themes is the continuity of these historic expressions of Christianity into our own day, though always at the cost of a certain inappropriateness and intellectual discomfort. Apart from Apocalyptic Christianity, which is now only a strand in various versions of Protestant Fundamentalism, each of the other paradigms continues today as a sort of Christian ideology. In the case of the Early Church Hellenistic version, continuity today is expressed through Orthodox Traditionalism, which is marked both by considerable theological subtlety and a certain cultural immobility.

If Küng's second version of Christianity is a paradigm of theology and the importance of finding an appropriate way of talking about God, his third expression is a paradigm of order and authority. He calls it the Mediaeval Roman Catholic Paradigm and it describes the emergence and continuing drama of the great Roman Church of the West, with its absolute claims and genius for imposing them through organization and the dedication of a celibate priestly elite. Küng's analysis of the church of which he is still a loyal if critical member shows, above all, the way in which it is the result of a historical process in which human and political realities had as powerful an influence as spiritual or biblical ones. Just as the theological orthodoxy of the second paradigm was the result of a marriage between Christianity and Greek philosophy, so the power of the third paradigm lay in a union between the Church and the political genius of Rome. The absolute nature of the claims made by Roman Catholic authoritarianism are impossible to sustain intellectually in a culture that recognizes the provisional and revisable nature of all human systems, but their very arrogance should give us the confidence to find structures that are appropriate to our time.

The fourth version of Christianity which Küng describes is what he calls the Reformation Protestant Paradigm. The Reformation has been exhaustively analysed, not least by Küng in this volume, but it is worth making the point that it, like every expression of Christianity, owes as much to the pressures of time and its politics as it does to the influence of the spirit of God or the example of Jesus. Reformation Christianity has been endlessly fissiparous and, in most of its traditional expressions, is the most tired and dated of the historic forms of the Church. But its abiding contribution to human spiritual history lies in the status it accorded to the Bible, whose translation into the vernacular and subsequent publication in the new printing presses were major factors in its success. The liberation of the Bible into the lives of ordinary Christians was not without its costs, however, and it introduced the virus of alleged scriptural inerrancy into the human story for the first time, with consequences that are still felt today in the phenomenon of Protestant Fundamentalism, which is having a powerful and damaging effect on several of the traditionally moderate churches of the Reformation.

The fifth type of Christianity Küng analyses is what he calls the Enlightenment Modern Paradigm. He traces it from its source in the scientific and philosophical revolution of the Enlightenment up to contemporary versions of what he calls Liberal Modernism, which is characterized by a desire to listen both to the historic Christian tradition as well as to movements of the day and the discoveries of new knowledge. Strictly speaking, Liberal Modernism is a tendency that is present throughout the Christian spectrum, including the Roman Catholic Church. It is not so much an organized system or movement as an ethos or set of commitments to certain principles, such as openness to new truth, no matter how uncomfortable, and the application of the scientific critical approach to ancient texts and institutions. Philosophically, it is the polar opposite of the various types of fundamentalism that characterize the uneasy condition of humanity in our time. Interestingly, Küng traces it as one of the formative influences on Vatican II that began an exciting period of reformation in the Roman Catholic Church, though its progress has stalled for the time being. Küng believes that a sixth version or paradigm of Christianity is emerging in our day that will be characterized by the search for human unity, expressed in a new ecumenism that will transcend our national and religious divisions, because it will understand both their importance and their provisionality. Emerging paradigms can be resisted or encouraged, of course. One of the purposes of this book has been to welcome the new reality and to help Christians encounter God through it, by responding to the circumstances of our time rather than running from them.

2

If this review of Küng's magisterial study of two thousand years of Christian history shows us that change and adaptation have been characteristic of the Church from the beginning, the same is certainly true of the human experience as a whole in societies that

DANCING ON THE EDGE

have not been isolated from the possibilities and pains of development. We have already seen how the human community has adapted to various versions of family structure and different expressions of sexuality. It is misleading to claim that any of these particular adaptations or improvisations have been uniquely virtuous or peculiarly suited to human well-being. All of them have been subject to the pressures of ordinary human inadequacy and the fractured reality of actual lives, and they have been formed, at least partially, in response to social and economic forces. Inevitably, as these forces shifted direction the social patterns they had formed changed their shape. This is something that the new familial fundamentalism refuses to acknowledge. It cleaves to the single paradigm or template theory of human relationships, claiming that there is only one correct way of organizing ourselves and our sexual and familial relationships. This is an essentially abstract approach to reality that simply refuses to acknowledge the historical or political nature of human experience. Its static perfectionism is the enemy not only of ordinary human happiness but of the genius of Jesus, which was passionate in its advocacy of the primacy of human need over all system and law.

A good example of the positive effect of social change upon actual human lives is provided by Margaret Forster's memoir *Hidden Lives*. It is a reflection on the changes in women's lives across three generations of a working-class family in Carlisle. The book is both moving and angering as it chronicles the stultifying effect of social and economic pressures on poor women in our society until very recently. Margaret Forster ends her book with these words:

> All the women whose lives and times I have touched upon would have been able to fulfil themselves in an entirely different and much more gratifying way if they could have benefited from the radical changes in the last half century from which I have benefited. Let no one say nothing has changed, that women have it as bad as ever.
>
> They do not. My personal curiosity may not have been satisfied but my larger curiosity, as to whether life has indeed improved for women like my immediate ancestors, is. And I am glad, glad not to have been born a working-class girl in 1869 or 1901. Everything, for a woman, is better now, even if it is still not as good as it could be. To forget or deny that is an insult to the women who have gone before.[3]

We have noticed throughout this book that change is painful and disorienting to most people, but that it is particularly resisted by those who derive some sort of privilege or power from the status quo. Sometimes this is an obvious and blatant refusal to share power and its benefits with some excluded group, such as Blacks in Apartheid South Africa or women in most human groupings up to and including the present day. Those engaged in the rearguard action are rarely candid in their reasons for refusing to share power or lift restrictions from the subordinated group. As we have seen, they offer elaborate theoretical justifications for the maintenance of existing evils or the refusal to remove arbitrary restraints upon the freedom of others. This is particularly the case in the area of sexual relationships. Ignoring J. S. Mill's wise advice that only harm to others justifies restraint of freedom, fundamentalists are never content with finding appropriate mechanisms for protecting people from harm, but must go on to deny people freedoms of which they personally disapprove. The history of the persecution of gay people is a particularly ugly example of this phenomenon, but other examples are easy to find. The plight of single-parent families offers us a good opportunity for the kind of social adaptation and improvisation we have been discussing. As with any particular expression of the provisional and fractured reality of actual lives, single-parent families can add to the pressures on community as well as making vital contributions to it. If we follow the evolutionary or improvisational principle advocated in this book, we will pour in support to these units of society by providing, for example, adequate child-care programmes that would enable the parents in question to get back into work and break out of their isolation and loneliness. This approach is not only more humane and compassionate, it is likely to be more effective in building up community and countering the atomization of society than any of the moralistic ideologies that dominate the scene at the moment.

Political institutions offer us even more blatant examples of the way in which the powerful construct reality to suit themselves. Absolutisms and oligopolies have always justified themselves with reference to high-sounding theories of government and the natural order that were cloaks for straightforward robbery. Saint Augustine illustrates this by telling the story of the pirate who, having been seized by Alexander the Great and asked what he meant by taking possession of the sea, replied: 'What do you mean by seizing the whole earth? Because I do it with a petty ship I am called a robber, but you, who do it with a great fleet, are called an Emperor.' The emergence of democratic societies has ameliorated rather than cured these profound imbalances in the way power is experienced. Democratic societies that are based on a system of political representation tend, in effect, to be governed by elected oligopolies who represent the interests of their particular constituencies rather than the good of society as a whole, especially its needier members.

Most people do not realize how discriminatory and partisan their attitudes and behaviour can be. This is why we have legal instruments for dealing with racial and sexual harassment, to name only two areas where power relations get distorted. It is in the nature of power to create preferential interest groups that take control and manage others for the benefit of themselves, however carefully they hide from the fact. The powerful, those with their hands on the levers of political and economic control, create great force fields around themselves that suck power from others and make them conform to their theory of reality. An obvious example of this is the existence of the vast and unjust imbalance in world trade, whereby the developed world systematically sub-ordinates the developing world to its own economic self-interest. Most developed institutions end up serving the interests of the powerful and create unjust dualisms in which those on the inside pay little attention to the interests of those on the outside. Sometimes the powerful reality is an idea, a political or economic theory. We have seen many examples in this century of the tyranny of ideas and their ability to create misery for millions of people. In our own day, many of the ills that characterize our society have their origin in a theory of the intrinsic wisdom of the economic market that is ruthlessly applied with little regard to its impact on human lives. We have persuaded ourselves that the negative effects of this policy on the ability of people to find work or housing are like fixed laws of nature, realities we must accept rather than challenge. The marketization of our culture has become an idol whose worship undoubtedly benefits some, just as it certainly reduces others to misery and estrangement.

There was a time when a consensus arose that a culture that permanently excluded a large part of the population from the good things of life could no longer be tolerated, that a system that enriched some and consequentially kept others in poverty had to be changed. Largely in response to pressure from reformers, a social evolution took place, so that by the end of the Second World War most democratic societies had committed themselves to a doctrine of solidarity with the poor and needy that gave them access for the first time to many of the benefits the wealthy had always enjoyed. The Welfare State has been criticized and, like any human institution, it has produced its own distortions, difficulties and vested interests, but it was and remains a noble ideal. Society assumed responsibility for its poor and its sick. Enormous social distinctions remained, of course, but there was an underlying conviction that we were part of the same community and it was unacceptable that some members were grossly deprived while others lived in luxury.

The phenomenon of homelessness, for instance, was seen not as an inevitable accompaniment of a market-driven social organization, but as an obvious injustice. That was one of the points of departure of the Welfare State. There were to be no disposable people, no tragic victims of an unalterable social system, because it was recognized that we could alter what we ourselves had created for the better good of the community. The Welfare State had its own inflationary dynamic built into it, but it was a splendidly explicit realization of the Christian Humanist claim that in society we are all members one of another.

We are now seeing a process of reversal of this way of organizing community and a return to an earlier paradigm, whereby the needy become not the responsibility of society as a whole, but the objects of the altruistic impulses of the individual. There has been a distinct philosophical move back to the charitizing of provision in our society, to private care, to an atomic theory of community that leaves support of the weak to the disorganized responses of the individual conscience. There is considerable evidence that society is becoming increasingly stratified and that we are returning to many of the social contrasts that used to characterize previous ways of organizing the human community. We are now in what commentators call the 30/30/40 Society: there is a bottom 30 per cent, who are the unemployed and economically inactive who exist on the margins of society and have little investment in its purpose or commitment to its well-being; another 30 per cent who, while in work, are in forms of employment that are structurally insecure; and there are only 40 per cent who can count themselves as holding tenured jobs which allow them to regard their income prospects with any certainty. Geoff Mulgan points out that until fairly recently it was possible to believe that the expansion of the economy might soon lead to such a rise in productivity that leisure time would increase and unemployment would become unimaginable. He writes:

> With the acceleration of globalization since the early 1970s this dream evaporated. While the less skilled found them- selves unemployed, the highly skilled were under more intense pressure to work longer hours. While a third of working-age men are now estimated to be out of work or underemployed worldwide, the elite of brokers, professionals and officials work around the clock, partly because complex, knowledge-based jobs are harder to divide up: five people working thirty hours a week is less efficient than three people working fifty hours a week. A century ago overwork was a sign of poverty. Today it is a sign of wealth and prestige.[4]

Another paradox of the market culture is that its very success breeds discontent and unhappiness. Mulgan says that these anxieties are more clearly expressed in fiction than in any other kind of writing:

> The characteristic dystopias of our time involve myopia, systems collapse, and the neglect of nature, whether their direct source is environmental disaster, the perverse effects of media on behaviour, the proneness of financial systems and computer systems to sudden crisis, or the vul- nerability of the population to unknown viruses. Many of the most compelling fictions portray a future where the market system has gone awry. Global corporations based on information and genetic technologies act beyond the reach of governments that have shrunk to impotence in societies racked by deep-seated social divisions and pervasive fatalism, and an economy where the lines between business and organised crime have evaporated.[5]

He is convinced that the market system, uncorrected by other val- ues and mechanisms, is not an adequate way of governing an increasingly complex world. An added paradox is that at a time when the global economy is making the lives of ordinary people more precarious and unpredictable, we are seeing a dismantling of the programmes that were developed to shelter the most vulnerable from the adverse effects of the market system and we seem to be reverting to a discredited method of supporting them. According to the old Two Nations theory of society, it was the duty of affluent and charitable citizens of the nation of plenty to go on soup runs and mercy flights into the nation of want. Given that kind of social dualism, people of goodwill will certainly want to engage in these activities, but they must never lose sight of the fact that the system itself is wrong and that care for the needy is better undertaken by the community as a whole organized through professional structures than left to the consciences and caprices of individuals. Many people in the churches spend their lives picking up the pieces broken by society, but we must never lose sight of the fact that the system itself is flawed and we have to go on challenging it. We have reached a strange time in history when we are reinventing destitution and at the same time are creating a new breed of over-worked millionaires. The global market economy is an enormous agent for change and wealth creation, but thinkers are beginning to acknowledge and address its excesses and the casualties it creates. The correction of its abuses will not be easy, but we can begin by acknowledging the central claim of this book, which is that all human systems and theories, secular as well as sacred, were made by us and can be altered or abandoned by us. We do not have to accept any system if we do not like its consequences. There is no reality, divine or human, that can force us to play from a fixed text long after it has ceased to benefit humanity. History is littered with abandoned scripts that were once held to have been dictated by God to justify slavery, genocide, the exploitation of women and the oppression of the poor. In every case the theoretical justification for these evils was shown to have been created by the powerful in order to cling to their privileges. By a number of memorable parables and prophetic acts Jesus exposed this kind of hypocrisy for what it truly was. Those who try to follow him today have to copy his example of speaking truth to power. Sometimes that word has to be spoken by the Church; sometimes it has to be spoken to the Church.

CHAPTER TEN

Surviving the Church

Throughout this book we have been making a case for the doctrine of the provisionality and revisability of all human systems and structures, including religious ones. Even a superficial knowledge of human history shows how often we have changed our minds about matters once thought to be fixed, certain and above criticism. We have seen this process at work in the history of ideas and in the development of human relations. It applies equally to the structures and institutions we have created in our journey through history. There seems to be an unconquerable tendency in us to claim too much for our institutions, to see them, not as human inventions that are reformable and revisable, but as permanent expressions of unalterable truth. Each evolutionary step along the human journey is fought over and debated as though the previous resting place were a permanent habitation. The most obvious example of this phenomenon is provided by the history of the democratic suffrage, the right to vote in government elections. Along each step of the way towards democracy reformers had to contend with traditionalists who passionately believed that the next extension of the suffrage would bring catastrophe, was profoundly unnatural and was clearly contrary to the will of God. The last battle fought in the prolonged war for democracy was over the extension of the suffrage to women. It was a hard and bitter fight, in which the suffragettes were vilified and persecuted. During the debate in the Anglican Communion over the ordination of women to the priesthood and episcopate, I read some of the literature produced during the battle for votes for women. The arguments used to oppose the ordination of women in our era were depressingly like the arguments marshalled against giving them the vote earlier in the century.

Human history is filled with similar examples. We organize ourselves for some purpose, in a way that suits the conditions of the day, and the arrangement works well enough. Then time moves on, the conditions change and we try to adapt to the new situation, only to confront our ancient inertia and the claim that change is impossible. This kind of conservatism is a universal human characteristic, so there may be some wisdom in it. There is probably an unconscious recognition that change has to be managed carefully if our institutions are to survive while they learn to adapt to new circumstances. There is always a legitimate debate between reform and revolution, between gradual or sudden change, but the argument is usually about managing, not resisting change, because change is a constant of the human condition. Unfortunately, the debate is frequently hijacked by reactionaries who are deeply invested, either emotionally or financially, in the status quo. It was here that Karl Marx contributed his greatest insight into the nature of institutions and the people who defend them. Paul Tillich paraphrased the Marxist insight in this way: 'Every theory which is not based on the will to transform reality is an "ideology", that is an attempt to preserve existing evils by a theoretical construction which justifies them.'[1]

Thinkers have spent much time and more ink on the theoretical construction of justifications of great evil. We have seen throughout this book that the Christian Church is not exempt from the tendency. Sometimes, as with its defence of slavery, racism and the grotesque contrasts of economic inequality, it has justified what Tillich called 'existing evils', usually on the grounds of divine mandate for their existence. A lot of its time has also been spent on justifying practices and institutions that are not so much evil as obsolete. It is here that it turns Christianity into an ideology, in Marxist terms. The rhetoric it uses, often very effectively, is all about the Church being above and beyond the vagaries of history. It is in history to transcend history, to offer men and women, trapped in time and change, the consolations of eternity. This is a specious but dishonest claim. It tries to identify God with, and limit God to, the instruments or occasions that were the means of revelation. The uncomfortable thing about radical faith, however, is that it knows that God must not be identified with the instruments that were the means of the divine encounter: to do so is to fall into the trap of idolatry. As we have seen, this is what fundamentalists of all persuasions do. They are unable to live with the paradox that the means through which we encounter the divine are not themselves divine and must, therefore, never be worshipped, though they may be reverenced and respected. We have already examined the tendency to foreshorten the mystery of revelation to the words of scripture so that the

Bible becomes literally the Word of God, rather than one of the means by which God's word comes to us. This is called Biblical Fundamentalism and we examined it in Chapter 3.

Equally dangerous is Morphological Fundamentalism, the identification of God with the structures and systems used by the Church to organize its life and promote its purposes. The sociologist Weber talked about 'the routinisation of charisma', by which he meant that any revelatory movement, originally focused on a visionary figure of genius, must organize itself if the primal vision is to be carried through history. Inevitably, however, much is lost in the process, for a fairly obvious reason. Human institutions, whether visionary or commercial, exist to achieve certain purposes. To achieve the ends, means have to be devised, processes developed. The institution still exists to achieve its purpose, but it is now something else as well: it is a process, a mechanism. It needs functionaries who will understand the mechanisms that have been developed to achieve the end. The processes can, themselves, be fascinating and absorbing; and their service attracts a certain type of person. What sociologists call 'bureaucratization' is the turning of the process itself from a means into an end: we become trapped or fascinated or simply embroiled by it, so that it becomes the purpose, the reason we are in the business. We become process people, rather than people with a purpose who require a process to effect it. The institution itself begins to fascinate us and command our loyalty; we become company people, morphological fundamentalists, people for whom the process has become the whole game. This kind of inversion of value happens everywhere, especially in the Church.

A radical view of human nature should lead us to the understanding that there can be no perfect structures, no absolutes in the sphere of human relations. This means that we should not invest ourselves neurotically in defence of structures that no longer serve us well. Defensiveness of this sort is difficult to avoid because we are insecure creatures, but we should try to observe ourselves at it. However, systems failures, like personal failures, should neither surprise nor depress us. Nor should we let them paralyse or disable us. They will only disable us if we make unsustainable claims on their behalf. The Christian tendency to theologize everything, including the way we organize ourselves, is one of our biggest dangers, seen most glaringly during the debate over the ordination of women. Gender differences were seen not as facts we might learn to adapt and adjust to the changing circumstances of our lives, but as eternal realities that fixed men and women forever in social and relational roles. This is a theological version of what Marx called an ideology. Christian thinkers are still engaged in preserving unjust structures by theoretical arguments that justify them, but the theology is usually a cloak to cover a straightforward refusal to share power. We have seen this phenomenon again and again in Christian history. The shorthand term for it is Original Sin. Tillich described it as the demonic element in human life, the tendency to create spiritual structures and arguments that justify evil. The seductiveness of the demonic is that it cloaks evil in the garments of righteousness. In the case of the continued subordination of women in Christianity, the evil is dressed in theological arguments about authority and tradition, but the inner motive, which is often unrecognized by the people who hold it, is the preservation of an injustice, either because its true nature is unrecognized or because it profits, in some way, those who embrace it.

An instructive parallel is provided by the race theories of National Socialism: in order to justify the persecution and extermination of the Jews, the Nazis persuaded themselves, by the construction of an elaborate race theory, that they were intrinsically inferior, scarcely human. The question to ask is, what came first? Did the theory come first and after that the persecution, or was the desire to persecute the motive that prompted the theory? The subordination of women in Christian history was a fact in search of a theory to justify it and theology, as ever, was eager to oblige. The same is true of other relationships where authority is exercised unequally. The history of the ordained ministry provides us with another instructive example. The thing that all exclusionary and divisive mechanisms have in common is a protective psychology that fears difference and disorder. Studies have shown us that what psychologists call the authoritarian personality[2] is desperately afraid of making mistakes, getting things wrong, earning disapproval, either parental or divine. It has to protect itself against accusation by rigid rules and precedents. Its main motive in life is avoidance of failure rather than pursuit of success. It creates unyielding structures and practices that are followed with almost superstitious exactness. Departure from these norms induces anxiety, and it is this insecurity that is the engine of persecution and hatred. Behind it all lies an idea of life as a test promoted by an exacting and unloving power. We dare not put a foot wrong; we must not bend the rules; we cannot be too careful. Fear is the great motivator. This is the

DANCING ON THE EDGE

kind of captivity from which Jesus Christ came to redeem us and the instrument that releases us is the forgiveness of sins.

We have already seen that any exposition of the doctrine of Original Sin and its effect on human realities has immediately to be balanced by the doctrine of the Forgiveness of Sins. This is a doctrine that has to be understood radically and universally, not simply applied to the area of personal ethics. The experience of forgiveness leads us to a radical understanding of the doctrine of Grace. We are saved, not by getting it right, but by the love that redeems us while we are getting it wrong. This experience of grace applies to much more than our personal failings, though that is the area to which we tend to confine it. Grace applies everywhere. It applies to structures, to ideas, relations and organizations. These all need constant forgiveness. Our efforts are constantly met by the grace of God filling what we lack, forgiving what we have done badly or left undone. Forgiveness of sins is a politically and personally liberating doctrine. We no longer have to make false claims, to live defensively, only honestly. It is all right not to have got it right; indeed, it is expected, it is understood. There is an unavoidable, developmental integrity in life. The whole point of it is our growth, the possibility of getting better at things, largely through trial and error. If we think we have to be perfect from the very start, then we trap ourselves in despair or in false claims, and end up pretending to a perfection we cannot possess.

Life is an experiment in human maturing, leading us from defensiveness to mature freedom. God expects us to be trying things out, getting things wrong, finding out who we are; and it is all taken care of, it is part of the covenant between us and God as made known in Christ. This knowledge should give us the kind of security in God's love that liberates us from defensiveness and perfectionism. We do not have to pretend, either about ourselves or the groups to which we belong.

It is also liberating to acknowledge that all our systems, moral, theological, ecclesiastical, political, are created for *our* sake not God's. We need them because of the flaws in our nature, because we need to learn to co-operate, because we are social creatures who need structure and order in our lives. It is a dangerous step to claim divine warrant, in any but the most general sense, for any of our systems. As we reminded ourselves in Chapter 3, the text to remember is the words of Jesus about the Sabbath, when he told us that it existed for us and not us for it. The test is always pragmatic: do our institutions, our moral systems, our ecclesiastical structures, make our lives more abundant; do they increase our maturity, our joy; do they enhance or diminish human flourishing? Are we open to the possibility of the transformation of reality or are we trapped in an ideology that leads us to defend obvious evils and injustices, even though we tell ourselves that our anxious opposition is in the name of the same God who warned us not to worship idols? It is important to acknowledge the relativity of all human systems, precisely because there is an opposite tendency in our nature that prompts us to sacralize them, to make provisional systems absolute and associate them exclusively with God. The recognition that all human systems are provisional, are made by us and can, therefore, be unmade by us, is enormously liberating and is an aspect of the freedom that Christ came to bring; it is a redemption from the power of idols. It also frees us to search for systems that are more appropriate to our day. All of this means that we will not invest too heavily, either theologically or morally, in our systems. We are redeemed, not by them, but by the God who is already on our side. The question Christians should ask themselves is, *Since we are already redeemed and forgiven, how should we live, how should we express that saving fact in our systems and relations?*

If we accept that the fact of original sin vitiates and distorts all human relations; if we accept that God's response to that systemic flaw in our nature and its institutions is forgiveness; and if we acknowledge that all our systems are provisional, how can we answer the question: *How did historic Christianity end up organizing itself the way it does and can anything be done about it?* Let us answer that question by stating a thesis that we shall spend most of this chapter trying to interpret: *The Christian system is the expression, often unacknowledged, of an obsolete, though still powerful structuralist paradigm.*

We have already seen that a paradigm is a pattern or model of reality, often unexpounded or unadmitted, that we adhere to and take for granted as though it were an eternal reality. The word 'structure', which we used to qualify the word 'paradigm', suggests a building, something fixed and static, something solid, something absolutely *there*. Let us look at an example of a particular structuralist paradigm that used to govern much Christian theology and organization and is still, though often unconsciously, extremely influential. According to this way of thinking, God is conceived as the originating First Cause that got everything going. This great engine of divine energy built a universe that is itself a kind of machine, a mechanism. It is solid, structured, articulated and ordered. In particular, it is ordered into laws and systems of precedence, with humanity, just lower than the angels, who are next to God, set over the created order. Heaven itself reflects this same paradigm of order. It is, for instance, exemplified in the angelic orders. Angels are bodiless intelligences in a hierarchical order between humanity and God, the creator of both. Tradition holds that the order of precedence is seraphim, cherubim, thrones, dominations, virtues, powers, principalities, archangels, angels. Angels guard us, archangels instruct us, virtues look after our spiritual welfare, powers drive away Satan, principalities direct our lives aright, dominations strengthen us against temptation, thrones help us to persevere, cherubim give us wisdom, seraphim fill us with heavenly love. The human order reflects this angelic hierarchy, descending from the monarch at the apex, through level after level, down to the peasant who only has his dog to order around. However implausible this great paradigm of order and gradation may seem to us today, it governed the Church's and society's understanding of themselves until very recently. It is still there in the background, sitting in the attic like a dominating grandparent whose anger and confusion play havoc with our attempt to live our own lives.

For most of the Christian era this paradigm of order and hierarchy was interiorized by Christians. Like the best plausibility structures, it was treated as a given; it was part of the fixed order of things, the very nature of reality; it was not something we had ourselves created and could, therefore, amend or adapt. Rebelling against it, wanting to change it was thought to be not only vain but sinful and unnatural; it was like complaining about the need to breathe. This great institutional paradigm had certain dominating characteristics through which it was expressed and incarnated. It was a system of order and authority, privilege and obedience; it was, above all, a minutely detailed system of inequality. Every institution reflected these characteristics, including churches, schools, factories and families. It was the way things were done. The system was as timeless as the mountains, as unalterable as the tides and the rhythms of the seasons. Though it has lost much of its plausibility today, it still hangs over us like a slowly receding mist and its influence is powerful; it affects our self-understanding and modifies our attempts to create new and more appropriate patterns that will help us in both Church and society.

The Church that most clearly reflects this paradigm of order and distinction is the great Roman Catholic Church, described by one of its own theologians as the last surviving absolute monarchy. For centuries it has preserved itself against the changes that have characterized most other human institutions. Two things have contributed to this successful resistance to the pressures of change. It has preserved itself against challenge by a theoretical claim that justifies its structure as having been divinely established. In this it is not unique, of course; most systems of Church government claim to have been established by God in some sense, if only because they claim to be closer to the models found in the New Testament, however tendentiously interpreted. What is just as obvious is that models of Church government inevitably and unavoidably reflect the patterns found in secular culture. The Papacy clearly reflects the style and nomenclature of the emperors of Rome. However, this theoretical defence of the Roman system as a spiritual ideology cannot, on its own, account for its continuance. The power in the system lies in the dedication of an elite, celibate caste of spiritual rulers, whose self-sacrificing way of life and comparative poverty, when they are at their spiritual best, protect them against absorption into the surrounding culture. In the debate that is going on in the Catholic Church over the celibacy of the clergy, the Pope clearly recognizes that a married clergy would rapidly accommodate the ministry to the surrounding culture and would probably be the beginning of the end of the closed Roman system. By standing against both the ordination of women and the marriage of the clergy, he is almost certainly guaranteeing a continuing period of turbulence in the Church. The paradox is that, were he to go on resisting a married clergy, but permit the ordination of celibate women, he could probably maintain the authoritarian ethos of the Roman system for much longer. Inevitably, the presence of women priests and bishops in the Roman Church would alter its ethos, but the cultural change would probably be more rapid were the Pope to allow clergy to marry.

The central point at issue in all these disputes is the nature of rule and authority. We know that models of government in Church and State have varied down the ages and that the Church has often copied patterns from the civil authority. It copied the authoritarian models that were prevalent during its own formative period and it has, in various ways, evolved alongside the State. For instance, the Anglican Communion, which used to be governed by spiritual officers called bishops (from the Greek word for 'overseer'), is now governed by synods, a form of representative assembly that includes bishops but is no longer exclusively controlled by them. This is obviously an inevitable kind of evolution in democratic cultures, and there is nothing particularly surprising about it, though it can increase the tendency towards fascination with the process as opposed to the purpose of the Church, and has already bred a new species of ecclesiastical politicians. The difficulty arises because of the Church's passion for offering ideological or theological reasons for everything it does. If we have taught for centuries that a particular way of doing things was not just sensible or appropriate to the situation, but was decreed quite specifically by God, then we run into serious trouble when it no longer serves us well or when it is challenged by Christians who have learnt from their experience in secular organizations that there are clearly better ways of doing things. In spite of the claims made by institutional theologians, it cannot be demonstrated that Jesus intended to found the body we now call the Christian Church. It can be argued that the Church is the extension or continuation of his message and memory; it can even be argued that its development has been guided by the Holy Spirit; what cannot be claimed is that Jesus set up the system, however rudimentary, that evolved into the full complexity of historic Christianity. The New Testament is quoted in support of the many succeeding systems of Church government, and there is usually something to be said in favour of most of them. What has to be opposed is the tendency to make any of them fixed, final and incapable of yielding to the challenge to evolve systems that are more appropriate to the day. We have already seen how this tendency is fighting a rearguard action against bringing women into the ordained ministry. The ordained ministry itself, female or male, can become an expression of this kind of rigidity. It is this version of morphological fundamentalism we must now challenge.

In order to disenthrall ourselves from the paradigm of rule and order in the ecclesiastical sphere as well as the secular, we must listen to the great critique that has been levelled against it, particularly in our own time. The critique comes from three different angles. The first we have already touched upon in our mention of the Marxist insight that power always seeks to legitimize itself with a justifying theory. This is a simple but revolutionary insight. Once we interrogate the pretensions and assumptions of power and challenge its place in the nature of things, our consciousness begins to change. Amazement begins to grow until we reach the moment when we recognize that for centuries we colluded with a system that infantilized us. This should neither surprise nor embitter us. We have seen too often how human beings collude with their own oppression and say amen to the doctrine of their own inferiority. It is all an illusion, an intricate management exercise, whereby power sustains its place on the pinnacle of the temple.

The second angle of criticism comes from Jesus himself, when we hear him freshly and radically. Jesus has always been co-opted by people in power to sanctify and anoint their own privileges. This should not surprise us, either. Alasdair MacIntyre coined a new epigram to express this melancholy reality: 'All power tends to co-opt and absolute power co-opts absolutely.'[3] It is amazing, however, that we have allowed Jesus to be co-opted by the powerful, especially when we confront the reality of his own testimony in the New Testament. The main force of his witness was against systems of exclusionary divinity and exclusionary humanity. The way Marcus Borg puts this is to describe the opposition between the politics of purity, a religious system based on excluding people from God, either ritualistically or morally; and the politics of compassion, a perspective from which God is seen as one who longs to draw humanity into the divine life in love and mercy and is intent on breaking down every wall of separation. So dominant is the hierarchical paradigm, the system of exclusion and infinite gradation, that it has even modified the way we read the flaming words of the New Testament.

There the words still sit, however, primed to blow up all exclusionary systems and every hierarchy of power. The two greatest texts that do this are Mark 10:35–45 and Philippians 2:5–11. In Mark 10 we hear the sons of Zebedee seeking a place in the new exclusionary kingdom they expect Jesus to set up, so that they can rule over others. The other apostles are furious when they hear about this demarche, not because they believe that the brothers have misunderstood the nature of Christ's kingdom, but because they got their bids in first. The encounter provided Jesus with the occasion for the great saying:

So Jesus called them and said to them, 'You know that among the Gentiles those whom they recognize as their rulers lord it over them, and their great ones are tyrants over them. But it is not so among you; but whoever wishes to become great among you must be your servant, and whoever wishes to be first among you must be slave of all. For the Son of Man came not to be served but to serve, and to give his life a ransom for many.

(Mark 10:42–45)

More mysterious but just as revolutionary is the passage found in Philippians 2, where we read that Christ Jesus, 'who, though he was in the form of God, did not count equality with God a thing to be grasped, but emptied himself, taking the form of a servant, being born in the likeness of men.' This is the great *kenotic* text, *kenosis* referring to the self-emptying of God in Christ. Christians have assumed too easily that it refers to a single event in salvation history, the Incarnation, when God came among us for a season. What if the doctrine is infinitely more radical than that? What if it expresses the eternal nature of God? What if it tells us that it is God's nature to go forth eternally from God's self; not to hoard the divine life or enjoy it for its own sake, but to express it in creation as well as in the eternal mutuality of the Trinity? What if *kenosis*, the divine self-emptying, is not seen as an event in history but as an eternal reality that expresses the very nature of God? Were this to be true, then we are left with the extraordinary paradox of a God of 'unpower' who is yet the source and origin of all power. However we deal with these paradoxes, they do demonstrate that Jesus, the man from God, the man who discloses the nature of God, sets himself against the paradigm of power as dominance and gradation, and becomes its victim.

The third angle from which we can begin to offer a critique of the paradigm of power and rule is from the new insights of modern cosmology at which we have already glanced. According to the new physics, the universe has three characteristics: it is dynamic, not static; expanding, not limited; evolutionary, not hierarchical. It is a vast experimental process and modern cosmology is able to take us back to the microsecond just after the birth of the creation 15 billion years ago. Everything in the universe, all the matter that now composes billions of stars and galaxies, was an incredibly dense mass, so small it could pass through the eye of a needle. From that point it expanded very rapidly and at only three minutes from zero most of the main elements of the universe were formed. We have already noticed that the expansion in the first ten seconds was so rapid and violent that astronomers coined the phrase the Big Bang to describe it. Fifteen billion years later the universe, which is still expanding, achieved consciousness in us and started asking questions about itself. Before these discoveries we had a picture of the universe as a great machine, solid, material, predictable. Now we are getting used to descriptions of the process as being like brilliantly improvised music. However we picture it to ourselves, we have to acknowledge that we live in a universe that is still being created and in which realities are being tested and discarded, tried and adapted. The new cosmology suggests a God of continuous creativity who is constantly at work.

This dynamic picture of God as being still engaged in the process of creation fits the modern understanding of the Trinity as a community of eternal mutuality and self-giving. This is put with particular vividness by Elizabeth Templeton in her book, *The Strangeness Of God*:

> The strangeness of God, if the Trinitarian character of that reality is taken seriously, is that the last thing God can be is an individual. Far from being the cosmic projection of our microscopic existence as individuals, God is one for whom atomic self-sufficiency is an impossibility, since what identifies him is the uncoerced communion of being in which father, son and spirit are only in the mutual giving and receiving which sustains each. It is no option for God to be father without son and spirit.[4]

This means that God's very nature is intrinsically collaborative and expresses an eternal mutuality of self-giving. From that communion of eternal self-offering comes forth the universe and the Church, which are themselves expressions of that community of mutuality and sacrificial love. This understanding of the universe and the God who is creating it is the very opposite of, is in profound contradiction to, the great pyramid theory of order and status upon which so much of our history has been built. This is where we must take our stand today. This dynamic, trinitarian, experimental paradigm should inform our understanding of Christ, of morality, of the nature of theology and the being of the Church. Unfortunately, many of our structures still reflect the discarded paradigm. Indeed, there are more than remnants of this power metaphysic reflected in the life of the Church and the ordering of its ministry, as we have already seen. Ministry as an icon, as a public expression of the hidden paradigm, still reflects too many elements of the hierarchical model.

We are learning some modesty in the Church today about the exaggerated claims we have made about ourselves and our role in society. Our models of ministry, in particular, are increasingly influenced by wise management practice in industry and commerce. Ministry today is increasingly modified by collegial models of episcopacy, where bishops are part of the structure not rulers of it, by mutuality in ministry at the parish and national level, and by the emergence of synodical structures that have brought elements of representative government into the Church. The public theatre of ministry, however, especially in churches that maintain the traditional model, has not caught up with the emerging paradigm: with its mitres and distinction in role, title and mode of address, it still expresses the discarded paradigm.

A good analogy is provided by the British monarchy and class system. These still exercise enormous power in Britain, though they are obvious anachronisms that hinder us from discovering more appropriate structures for our day. It is not too wide of the mark to see the traditional understanding of ministry and its public expression as analogous to the troubled role of the Royal Family in Britain. We retain a lot of the theatre of ministry and monarchy, partly because we enjoy it and partly because we are not sure what might replace it and whether it would be any better. What is clear, however, is that the underlying metaphysic on which it once sat solidly has been eroded. It is crumbling before our eyes. If we argue to retain anything from the traditional systems today, in Church or society, our arguments are all pragmatic; we no longer offer a theological defence. We may have a taste for the theatre of authority, but in actual practice we want it to be answerable to the common good and reflect current human development and self-understanding. These social and ecclesiastical transitions are inevitable. People of a conservative, not to say nostalgic, temperament may regret the fact, but the fact remains that institutions like species must adapt if they would endure. Our dilemma today is that we have retained too many of the mechanisms that were designed to protect the mystique of monarchy and ministry long after the mystery has departed from them. It would be more honest to work out what purpose a demystified monarchy and a demythologized ministry might usefully serve than put our energy vainly into trying to remystify or remythologize them.

As far as the fact of the ordained ministry is concerned, some things ought to be acknowledged immediately. The first is that the ministry does not create the Church; it was created by the Church. Bernard Shaw said that all professions were conspiracies against the laity. Inevitably, the ordained ministry has usurped many functions that do not belong exclusively to it. This is not just true of ordination, the service in which we set people apart for particular tasks. It is a fact that the theatre of ordination has long since eclipsed the theatre of baptism, the service that incorporates people into the Church. Maybe the theatre of the respective sacraments would not matter if it did not also reflect the realities of structural power. The ordained ministry evolved to help the Church be the Church; now it often seems to prevent as much as it enables. We have communities of the baptized, churches in New Testament terms, that are deprived of full sacramental life. In Roman Catholicism this is because of a shortage of priests; in Anglicanism a shortage of money has led to a shortage of priests or to an inappropriate way of deploying them. The professionalizing of the priesthood, making it a financial burden on the laity; or the transformation of ministry into a special caste, as in Roman Catholicism; both end by depriving the Church, the baptized, of the rights they were given at baptism. This is an ecclesiastical version of the kind of usurpation of function we see throughout human history. *But it shall not be so among you.*

If the historic model of ministry is not delivering the bread, we must find others that will. Increasingly, this is happening along the lines expounded by Roland Allan, who believed that each community of Christians should be able to generate ministry appropriate to its own needs, and the last criterion that should be considered is the financial one. It is already beginning to happen. The Church uses a variety of ministerial arrangements, including priests who work without stipend and trained lay ministers. One of the most intriguing developments is the use of lay ministers in the Roman Catholic Church to compensate for the shortage of priests. In some parts of the world, many Roman Catholic congregations are effectively and effectually pastored by lay people, many of them women. These developments should be welcomed by the professional clergy

DANCING ON THE EDGE

and should not be seen as inferior mechanisms, substitutes for the real thing. There is no permanent real thing except the life of the Church itself, which, like any intelligent organism, will adapt to changing circumstances because it knows that it bears a reality through time that is expressed historically but must never be limited by history.

One of the many paradoxes in the present situation in Church and State is that the Church holds on to patterns and practices it learned from society long after society itself has discarded them. One of the lessons that has been well learned in modern management theory is that institutional leadership, whatever its form, exists to promote the purposes of the institution that creates it: leadership exists for a purpose. Old models of institutional life assumed that autocratic methods of governance were natural and were, therefore, the only ones available. Modern insights teach us that autocratic models are not only unpleasant, they are inefficient. Management theory today emphasizes models of co-operation and collaboration, because they are the best way of getting things done. Only institutions that have turned leadership into an ideology resist these new insights. Wise leaders in any enterprise learn to distinguish process from purpose and constantly adapt the means towards the end, not vice versa. Wise leaders also have a high level of self-knowledge and the inner security the examined life brings, so they do not insulate themselves against challenge by psychological or theological mechanisms. Ordained ministry has to be reinterpreted along these lines today. The ordained should be the animators of the Christian community, the people who help the community achieve its ends. Their role in the Church is not one of privilege or power, though, wisely used, it will be of considerable influence. Increasingly, those ordained to particular tasks in the Christian community will be sought for their intrinsic gifts rather than their professional training or acquired abilities. Foremost in them will be a level of personal security that will enable them to operate without being too entangled in their own personal needs and anxieties. The need to control others and every situation they find themselves in is the mark of the insecure, authoritarian personality. Such people are unable to handle criticism, confusion and doubt, so they constantly project their own personal drama onto the community. Inner security is an original endowment of the self that is rarely acquired by an adult who does not already possess it. There is some evidence that people with a need to control others and live in a protected environment are frequently attracted to the ordained ministry, probably because it has earned a reputation for providing outlets for these needs. The paradox is that the secure and relaxed personality is put off the ministry for the same reasons. This may be an argument for reversing the present methods of selection. At the moment our selection processes are based on a mystical experience called vocation or the call. The Church then proceeds to validate or reject this call, with traumatic effects on those who are rejected. As we move into a different kind of Church culture we will probably have to develop a new understanding of vocation that starts from within the community and moves to the individual, so that people will no longer offer themselves but will, instead, be chosen.

Another primary characteristic we must look for in the ordained is personal accessibility and approachability, which are also intrinsic characteristics. Related to these is the ability to be open to new experiences and unlearn the old. Charles Peguy, the French Catholic mystic and pamphleteer, told us to 'go and learn how to unlearn.' It is a wise maxim to live by, especially today. One of the marks of contemporary society is its fluidity and uncertainty, especially in the area of work. We are told by economists and management theorists that there are few jobs for life. Now the talk is of portfolio-workers, people who perform a variety of tasks for society, some paid, some on a voluntary basis. The old, static industries are giving way to new patterns of employment and new attitudes to leisure. The Church is bringing up the rear in understanding and applying these changes. But she has much to contribute to modern society in a period of convulsive change. At her best, she has defined people by who they are and not by what they do. She has helped to deepen the lives of men and women down the ages by putting them in touch with the life of God and the work of the spirit in the human community. When she ceases to be preoccupied with her own life and the survival of the institutions she has created to further it, she may yet resume her role as one of the great spiritual teachers and guides of humankind.

CHAPTER ELEVEN

Dancing on the Edge

*I*f there is to be a place in the Church for people on the edge, people who do not conform to the official Christian profile, what is their discipleship to be like? The word 'disciple' implies the process of learning, of being apprenticed to one who is further on in the spiritual life. What is suggested is development and growth, the steady practice of appropriate disciplines. Most of the world's spiritualities practise discipleship, the slow training of the learner in the mysteries, traditions and mystical technologies of the chosen path. Christianity was first called the Way, and it has within itself spiritual and ascetical resources available to those who wish to apprentice themselves to its traditions. What would the path of discipleship look like for a modern Christian?

The first thing to establish is that truth will be a fundamental value for this type of Christian. Being human, our grasp on truth will always be limited, partial and subject to change and revision, but our commitment to it, as we are able to receive it, must be without reservation. This is why the debate between creationists and evolutionists is so tragically beside the point. Creationists mistake the nature of spiritual truth and fail to recognize its highly symbolical character. It is spiritually unimportant which version of the chronology of creation we espouse, whether it is seven days six thousand years ago, according to the now discredited chronology of Archbishop Ussher, or the unimaginably vast stretches of time postulated by modern science. Creationists rob scripture of its potent symbolical and mythological importance by insisting that it provides us with infallible historical information. They end up concentrating on the mechanics of revelation, the form rather than the content of the story, and render themselves incapable of interpreting its meaning in ways appropriate to our day. They turn Christianity into a particular type of scientific ideology, one human theory among many, and remove its ability to transcend the human condition and become universally contemporary.

Another version of this kind of dangerous nostalgia for the alleged simplicities of a bygone era is provided by various current versions of right-wing Roman Catholicism. These want to revert to a pre-Vatican II type of sensibility in which the Church withdraws itself from the icy currents of modernity, and artificially submits to a previous paradigm of authoritarian piety that keeps lay people, and especially women, firmly under the thumb of the hierarchy. Systems that require people to hand over their critical faculties and uncomfortable freedoms to religious or political dictators are potently attractive to certain kinds of people all of the time and to many others some of the time, especially during periods of accelerating and disorienting change. These extreme authoritarian versions of religion, and we find them in all traditions, are ideologies rather than faiths. They are examples of the way we cling to particular historic expressions of belief that might have been appropriate in a previous era, but can only be maintained today for the wrong reasons. Authoritarian versions of religion are more like each other, and other authoritarian systems, than they are like the gracious freedom proclaimed by Jesus Christ. Truth is an important value for Christians, because it rescues us from the temptation to make permanent idols of spiritual and intellectual technologies that are no longer of use to us. If we persist in carrying them with us they become dangerous and unnecessary burdens. A story from the Buddhist tradition captures the dilemma perfectly:

> A man walking along a high road sees a great river, its near bank dangerous and frightening, its far bank safe. He collects sticks and foliage, makes a raft, paddles across the river, and reaches the other shore. Now suppose that, after he reaches the other shore, he takes the raft and puts it on his head and walks with it on his head wherever he goes. Would he be using the raft in an appropriate way? No; a reasonable man will realise that the raft has been very useful to him in crossing the river safely on to the other shore, but that once he has arrived, it is proper to leave the raft behind and walk on without it. This is using the raft appropriately.

Truth-seeking requires a necessary asceticism; it calls upon us to give up what we are tempted to cling to for the wrong reasons. Mary Magdalene clung to her memory of Jesus in the Resurrection garden and had to be told to let go, not to cling, or she would render herself unable to receive the new gift the spirit wished to give her. In John's Gospel, Jesus described himself as 'the way, the truth and the life'. The way of Christ is the way of truth. Following truth means that we must allow ourselves to be stripped of traditions and teachings that helped us over many a river, if we want to continue on our journey. Jesus warned us that by holding on to things we would run the risk of losing our very souls. This is a notoriously difficult truth to live by, because it may even call upon us to give up our understanding of God if it comes between us and truth. We have to make a radical identification of God with truth, so that truth becomes God for us, the absolute value by which we try to live. This is the reality behind the unnerving spiritual violence that seems to be a part of all the mystical traditions. It is why Meister Eckhart said he prayed to God to rid him of God, and it is why followers of another way are told that if they meet the Buddha in the road they are to kill him. We are to rid ourselves of idols, the human constructs that are useful to us only as long as we recognize their provisionality, the consoling projections of our own needs that trap us in dishonesty unless we unmask them and acknowledge that they are our own creation. This is why we need not be afraid if we fall into atheism in our pursuit of truth. Most atheisms are the result of a relentless look at reality, and believers should welcome the commitment to truth that lies behind them. If there is what we mean by God then the experience of atheism and unbelief must be a part of it, may even be understood as a necessary purging of false ideas and uses of God. Only the self-conscious and enduring choosing of absolute evil can separate us from God, never the choosing of truth.

This is why making ourselves disciples of truth also involves the discipline of contemplation. We have to look steadily and without fear at the new reality that confronts us, knowing that it could be a gift from the God who is already ahead of us. The stages we go through in opening ourselves to new truth are the classic stages of spiritual evolution. There is the moment of conversion when we allow the new idea or way of seeing reality into our minds for the first time. The reception of the new truth may be exhilarating or it may be followed by despair, because it calls us to leave behind much that has been precious to us. In the Christian mystical tradition there is a terrible experience of spiritual desolation called the dark night of the soul, when the disciple is deprived of all consolation and clings almost without motive to prayer that has lost its meaning. There is an equivalent experience that we might call the dark night of the intellect, when the soul clings joy-lessly to an inescapable truth that comes as a wound. At these times we have to find the courage to say yes to the truth, blindly following the paradox that Christ is truth before he is Christ, and in following truth we will fall, at last, into his arms.

The modern Christian, living on the edge, will still try to fol-low the ancient disciplines of the tradition, though the meanings they are given will be more tentative and experimental. Central to the way is the experience of rebirth: 'unless a man is born again, he cannot see the kingdom of God.' The Christian tradition is rich in metaphors and sacraments, spiritual mechanisms, that communicate directly to our hearts. Baptism, with its symbolism of going down into the waters of death to rise again to new life, is a potent metaphor for the endless process of turning towards truth and good-ness that characterizes the life of the disciple. Christians have tradi-tionally taught that baptism is administered once for all, but the modern practice of frequently affirming the promises once made at baptism is a constant reminder that we are initiated into a process, a way, not accorded a fixed status. We are baptized into the life of reflection and increase in self-knowledge, sometimes described as confession of sin. This part of the tradition calls us to personal hon-esty, the truth that is in the inward parts. It reminds us that, as Plato said, the unexamined life is not worth living. This does not mean the kind of guilty soul scratching that compulsively berates itself, usually for unimportant faults. It is, rather, a call to see ourselves, increasingly, as we are and not as we imagine or hope ourselves to be; it is a commitment to understand the springs and motives of our own conduct and opinions. The discipline of self-knowledge is not followed because it is a forensic or penal requirement; it is for the sake of reality and the joy that confronting it brings. The Christian tradition offers several mechanisms to assist us in this part of the journey. There is what is called sacramental confession of sin to a minister or spiritual friend. This is designed to remove the crippling burdens of guilt that most people carry around with them, like the man who refused to leave the raft on the river bank. Related to confession of sin, but different from it, is the discipline of what is called spiritual direction. At its healthiest, little direction goes on in this relationship. But much is shared, and encouragement and chal-lenge, sometimes one more than the other, are given, with a conse-quent growth in self-knowledge. There are an increasing number of people in the Christian tradition who are able to offer this kind of help to fellow travellers.

There has to be an inescapably public or political aspect to the life of the modern Christian. This will express itself in two ways. The first is what is described as works of mercy or good deeds, the kindly ministry to the needs of others. Disciplined followers of the way will practise mercy both methodically and spontaneously. The giving of alms, the sharing of our own good fortune with the less fortunate, will be organized through charitable giving, the covenanting of a certain portion of our income to organizations that exist to help alleviate the needs of others. The only trouble with this essential practice is that it can distance us from the real face of need and formalize mercy and good works into transactions between our bank account and the offices of the charities we support. That is why we must allow ourselves to respond unmethodically, spontaneously, to immediate need as it confronts us. We can be kind to strangers, we can commit acts of extravagant and immediate generosity to the poor, worthy or unworthy, who confront us. Indeed, uncalculating acts of extravagant generosity are probably the closest we get to entering the mystery of the divine nature. But the main opportunities for mercy that come to us are usually not surprises: they are provided by the people we live and work with and encounter in our normal lives. It is often easier to commit ourselves to kindness to strangers than to those who confront us daily where we live, and thereby allow ourselves, in the words of the old Scottish proverb, 'To be a saint in the causeway, but a devil at hame.' The most basic and profitable advice from all traditions tells us simply to perform the duty that lies at hand with grace and attentiveness. The Abbe de Caussade called this 'the sacrament of the present moment'; practised assiduously, it will provide us with all we need for the sanctification of our lives.

Alongside these private acts of mercy and commitment there has to be another response that is best described as political. There is an inescapably systemic or structural side to human need: the poor require more than our alms; the systems that cause their poverty have to be challenged and changed. We have already noticed how we have created economic structures in the world today that are based on the permanent exclusion of many people from the benefits of the free-market system. In order for some to do very well, many others have to do very badly. The market theory acknowledges that disparity but claims that it is an inescapable part of the logic of capitalism, a logic that has the status of a natural law. We have already noticed how people with power always devise theories to justify their retention of it, even when it is at the expense of others. We saw this in the churches when men devised elaborate theological justifications for excluding women from the ordained ministry. For this reason, the modern Christian is inescapably committed to justice as well as mercy, to confrontation as well as kindness. We confront not only individuals who require our succour, but systems that have to be challenged and overthrown. Political action is an unavoidable concomitant of Christian faith, and it will often pit us against those of our own household in the Church who have learnt to collude with systems that oppress others. We will find ourselves fighting on two fronts, therefore, as we challenge injustice in Church as well as in society.

Christians travel in company. The community provides us with support and the opportunity to practise the great Christian virtue of charity or selfless love. If baptism is the symbol of the individual's constant need for personal renewal and submission to the purging fire of truth, the sacrament of the Eucharist, the service of thanksgiving over the bread and wine, is the symbol of the life of the Christian community. The Christian sacraments are actions that communicate more profoundly than words. The Eucharist is the great symbol that represents our need for spiritual nourishment. It has been practised in the Church since the beginning of the Christian movement and puts us in touch with the tradition in a way that nothing else does. While there is an inevitable temptation for individual Christians to see it as an expression of personal devotion, it is, in essence, a corporate act, something that the whole congregation does. Christian worship is rooted in the ancient wisdom of human solidarity and the sense that it is something that we do as a people. One of the purposes of worship or corporate prayer is the hallowing of time: all systems of discipleship require a regularity of practice that habituates us to some sort of spiritual rhythm in our lives; and experience teaches us that support and strength can be found in performing these exercises with others. We call them offices or works of devotion, services that express a corporate rather than a personal approach to God. Most Christian traditions have systems of devotion that encourage people in the practice of public prayer with others. Even the experience of corporate silence is different to the experience of personal silence. Too many claims have been made for the importance of 'going to church', and too often the experience when we get there is spiritually stultifying rather than encouraging, but the universality of the practice in all faiths and traditions points to its continuing validity as a way of not only strengthening private faith, but of engaging with others in a way that can transcend our preoccupation with ourselves.

The Eucharist is not private prayer, but private prayer is an important part of the Christian way. Prayer is an enormous reality, and its methods and practices are as wide as human need. There was once a tendency in the Church to confine prayer to certain kinds of vocal formulae. That is no longer the case. There has been an enormous widening in the understanding and practice of prayer in the Christian community in recent years, and there are almost as many methods as there are types of human personality. In fact, there are religious communities that more or less customize methods of prayer for particular types of people by applying what are called psychometric techniques that define personality profiles and suggest prayer systems appropriate to them. In prayer we open ourselves to an encounter with the possibility of the divine; we dispose ourselves to be guided and challenged by the spirit. Others, never ourselves, may see the fruits of compassion that result. We all learn to pray as we can and not as we cannot, but there is one aspect of the practice of private prayer that is universally valid and profitable, the practice of silence and centring the self. This is an intensely physical experience in which, by learning to still the body and hold ourselves in silence, we acquire peace in our own hearts. All the wise spiritualities teach the importance of the practice of stillness as an antidote to the violence of hurry and activity in our lives. Like all the best advice it is simple and can be started immediately, where and as we are. It is another aspect of the truth that taught us that we already have everything we need in front of us for the following of the way and that we need not submit ourselves to elaborate and exotic disciplines for the sanctification of our lives. Duties and opportunities for mercy lie at hand and we can practise stillness wherever we find ourselves.

Compassion ought to be the last as well as the first word in the Christian vocabulary. It is the loving-kindness of God that is made known to us through Jesus Christ. The goal of formation of the Christian character, the object of the spiritual disciplines of the Church, is the emergence of a type of compassion that is not inconsistent with righteous anger. It will place the Christian on the edge where the outcast and sinner live. As we have already seen, it calls the Christian to the disciplines of advocacy on behalf of the rejected, and solidarity with them in their place on the margins. This discipleship of the edges is likely to lead to conflict with powerful institutions, spiritual as well as social and political. It will involve collisions with the Church as well as with the State, when they organize themselves against the weak. None of that should surprise or dismay us. Christians on the edge try to follow Jesus and he invariably leads them into danger.

But this should not be the last word, this sense of trouble ahead, of conflict and the need for courage. All of that will still be required of us as the cruel versions of Christianity become increasingly vocal and organized in their persecution of those of whom they disapprove. The very last word should be about joy and exhilaration, about dancing on the edge. Fear is the great enemy of humankind, fear of change, fear of the other. It is fear that turns us into persecutors and bigots, because it forces us to turn to false certainties and to turn against those whose freedom challenges our anxieties. The way of faith and particularly the way of faith in Jesus of Nazareth is the complete opposite of this kind of neurotic defensiveness. It calls us to a life that is more like taking part in a rolling jazz session than trying to march in step on the barrack square. Making that kind of music requires the discipline of keeping in touch with what is happening among our companions and with the music itself. Above all, it calls for a kind of commitment or faith that lets us go with the music right to the edge, and over it if necessary, because we follow one who told us not to be afraid, since he was already away ahead of us.

Notes

PART I: MAKING SENSE OF GOD

1 *Making Sense of God*

1. William Griffin, *C. S. Lewis: The Authentic Voice* (Lion, 1986), p. 266.
2. David Peat, *Blackfoot Physics* (Fourth Estate, 1994), p. 39.
3. Ibid., p. 42.
4. John Polkinghorne, *Reason and Reality: The Relationship Between Science and Reality* (SPCK, 1991), pp. 80–81.
5. Fulk Greville, Lord Brooke (1554–1628), *Chorus Sacerdotum.*
6. Evelyn Underhill quoted in Dorothy Phillips (ed.), *The Choice Is Always Ours* (HarperCollins, 1989), pp. 78–9.
7. From Patricia Hampl (ed.), *Burning Bright: An Anthology of Sacred Poetry* (Ballantine Books, 1995).
8. Abraham Heschel, quoted in Allan Ecclestone, *Gather the Fragments* (Cairns Publications, 1993), p. 93.
9. John Polkinghorne, *One World: The Interactions of Science and Theology* (SPCK, 1986), p. 40.
10. Ibid., pp. 45–6.
11. John Polkinghorne, *Science and Creation* (SPCK, 1990), p. 75.
12. John Polkinghorne, *Reason and Reality*, op. cit., p. 76.
13. David Wilkinson, *God, The Big Bang and Stephen Hawking* (Monarch, 1993), p. 72.
14. Ibid.
15. C. S. Lewis, quoted in Sheldon Vanauken, *A Severe Mercy* (Hodder & Stoughton, 1997), p. 92.

2 Can God Have a Son?

1. Pascal, *Pensees*.
2. David Peat, *Blackfoot Physics* (Fourth Estate, 1994), p. 227.
3. Arthur Peacocke, *Explorations in Science and Theology* (Templeton London Lectures, RSA, 1993), p. 15.
4. Conway Powers, *Guide to a Disturbed Planet*.

3 Is God a Fundamentalist?

1. William Shakespeare, *The Sonnets*.
2. C. S. Lewis, *The Weight of Glory* (SPCK, 1954), p. 8.
3. H. M. Kuitert, *I Have My Doubts* (SCM, 1993), p. 281.
4. Ibid., p. 282.
5. Ibid., p. 283.
6. Ibid., p. 284.

4 Why Does God Allow Suffering?

1. Primo Levi, *If This Is A Man* (Vintage, 1996), p. 109.
2. Richard Dawkins, *River out of Eden* (Weidenfeld & Nicolson, 1995), p. 95.
3. Arthur Peacocke, *Explorations in Science and Theology* (Templeton London Lectures, RSA, 1993), p. 9.
4. R. C. Lewontin, *The Doctrine of DNA: Biology as Ideology* (Penguin, 1991), p. 10.
5. Peacocke, op. cit., p. 12.
6. Ibid., p. 13.
7. Angela Tilby, *Soul* (SPCK, 1994), p. 194.
8. Peter Daino, *Mary, Mother of Sorrows, Mother of Defiance* (Orbis Books, 1994), p. 29.
9. Ibid., p. 4.

PART II: MAKING SENSE OF OURSELVES

5 Unhappy Bedfellows

1. R. S. Thomas, *No Truce with the Furies* (Bloodaxe Books, 1995), p. 30.
2. *Something to Celebrate* (Church House Publishing, 1996), p. 111.
3. Peter Brown, *The Body and Society* (Faber & Faber, 1990), p. 424.
4. Ibid., p. 399.
5. Quoted in Jock Dalrymple, *Jack Dominian: Lay Prophet?* (Geoffrey Chapman, 1995), p. 127.
6. Janet Walker in *The RSA Journal*, Vol. CXLIII, No. 5456 (January 1995), pp. 29ff.
7. Elizabeth Stuart, *Just Good Friends* (Mowbrays, 1995), p. 113.
8. Ibid., p. 113.
9. Walker, op. cit., pp. 29ff.
10. Ibid.
11. Stuart, op. cit., pp. 116ff.

6 Sex and Why It Bothers Us

1. *Paradise Lost*, Book IX, lines 1005–15.
2. Steve Jones, *The Language of the Genes* (Flamingo, 1993), pp. 106–7.
3. David Suzuki and Peter Knudtson, *Genethics* (Harvard, 1990), p. 7.
4. Ibid., p. 7.
5. Ibid., p. 12.
6. Ibid., p. 12.
7. Jones, op. cit., p. 97.
8. Ibid., p. 99.
9. Robert Wright, *The Moral Animal: The New Science of Evolutionary Revolution* (Vintage, 1995), p. 89.
10. Jones, op. cit., p. 108.
11. Wright, op. cit., p. 90.
12. Jones, op. cit., p. 109.
13. Robin Baker, *Sperm Wars* (Fourth Estate, 1996).
14. Mary Warnock, Green College Lecture (1996).
15. Wright, op. cit., p. 357.
16. Ibid., p. 357.
17. Ibid., p. 367.
18. Peter Abbs, *Personae and Other Selected Poems* (Skoob Books, 1995).

8 *Staying Together*

1. Jonathan Gathorne-Hardy, *Marriage, Love, Sex and Divorce* (Summit Books, 1981), p. 297.
2. Elizabeth Stuart, *Just Good Friends* (Mowbrays, 1995), pp. 1ff.

PART III: MAKING SENSE OF COMMUNITY

9 *Playing Jazz with God*

1. Paul Tillich, *The Protestant Era* (James Nisbet, 1995), p. xxix.
2. Hans Kung, *Christianity* (SCM, 1995).
3. Margaret Forster, *Hidden Lives* (Penguin, 1995), p. 3.
4. Geoff Mulgan, *Connexity* (Chatto and Windus, 1997), p. 92.
5. Ibid., p. 96.

10 *Surviving the Church*

1. Paul Tillich, *Systematic Theology*, Vol. 1 (James Nisbet, 1960), p. 85.
2. See especially Norman Nixon, *The Psychology of Military Incompetence* (Futura, 1988), 256ff.
3. Alasdair MacIntyre, *After Virtue* (Gerald Duckworth, 1981), p. 103.
4. Elizabeth Templeton, *The Strangeness Of God* (Arthur James, 1993), p. 23.